COUN

for Seemingly

IMPOSSIBLE
PROBLEMS

OTHER BOOKS BY THE EDITORS

By Dr. Lee N. June

The Black Family *(with Matthew Parker)*

Evangelism and Discipleship in African-American Churches *(with Matthew Parker)*

Men to Men *(with Matthew Parker)*

By Sabrina D. Black

Can Two Walk Together? Encouragement for Spiritually Unbalanced Marriages *(Moody Press)*

Prone to Wander *(with LaVern A. Harlin) (Church Initiative)*

By Dr. Willie Richardson

Reclaiming the Urban Family

Sharing Christ as You Go *(Christian Research and Development)*

COUNSELING

for Seemingly

IMPOSSIBLE PROBLEMS

A BIBLICAL PERSPECTIVE

formerly titled *Counseling in African-American Communities*

LEE N. JUNE, PHD & SABRINA D. BLACK, MA
EDITORS
DR. WILLIE RICHARDSON, CONSULTING EDITOR

ZONDERVAN®

ZONDERVAN.com/
AUTHORTRACKER
follow your favorite authors

Counseling for Seemingly Impossible Problems
Copyright © 2002 by Christian Research & Development
Formerly titled Counseling in African-American Communities

Requests for information should be addressed to:
Zondervan, Grand Rapids, Michigan 49530

Library of Congress Cataloging-in-Publication Data

Counseling for seemingly impossible problems /
    Lee N. June and Sabrina D. Black, editors ; Willie Richardson, consulting editor.
      p. cm.
    Includes bibliographical references.
    ISBN-10: 0-310-27843-0
    ISBN-10: 978-0-310-27843-6
    1. African Americans—Pastoral counseling of.   I. June, Lee N.
II. Black, Sabrina D.   III. Richardson, Willie, 1939–
BV4468.2.A34 .C68   2002
259'.089'96073—dc21

                                            2002004147

Names and details have sometimes been changed in stories and case studies.

Interior design by Beth Shagene

Printed in the United States of America

07 08 09 10 11 12 • 10 9 8 7 6 5 4 3 2 1

Contents

Part 3: Confronting Issues of Mental Health

Part 4: Confronting Other Critical Issues

Preface

For many years, I have been an advocate, along with others, for the Bible as a power and a force in solving problems in counseling. I believe that our Creator, the author of the Bible, perfectly understands human nature, sociology, and psychology. He has given us the Scriptures, which contain principles to live by to help us avoid problems, and has given us the solutions for solving problems. I am not against behavioral or medical science; we need these disciplines. But I believe the Bible, being holistic in its approach, goes much deeper in discovering the root of problems rather than simply treating symptoms.

Christian Research and Development has been training churches and individuals in biblical counseling for the last twenty years, and we have recently joined together in establishing the National Biblical Counselors Association. Our mission is to "advance the use of God's Word in counseling and mobilizing lay counselors for the body of Christ, partnering with professional and pastoral counselors."

The association is purposely made up of biblical counselors, therapists, social workers, physicians, psychologists, psychiatrists, pastors, and laypeople. What we all have in common is that we are Christians and believe in the power and the authority of the Bible.

Most of our practitioners are in urban centers, facing some of the most complex and challenging counselees and employing cutting-edge techniques. We work together and cooperate as a caregiving team. For example, there may be a pastor, a lay counselor, a social worker, and a physician working together to care for a person with Bipolar Disorder. The team is guided by the biblical principles that teach that people can be changed, restored, and healed or can learn to live productive and fruitful lives with an incurable disadvantage.

The contributors to this book are representatives of the national team of Christian caregivers. We have chosen some of the most difficult subjects to present in this book as an effort to advance the use of the Bible in problem solving and to demonstrate how professionals and lay caregivers can work together to generate a better quality of life for so many who are in need of help in our community.

— Dr. Willie Richardson, President
Christian Research and Development

Lee N. June and Sabrina D. Black

Introduction

The purpose of this book is to assist helping professionals who are Christians or who are sympathetic to the Christian faith and are seeking to employ the best of psychological, psychiatric, and medical principles while staying true to biblical precepts. It is also intended for persons who are facing the issues that are discussed and seeking ways to effectively deal with them.

The topics discussed in this book represent some of the most perplexing issues of our time and may be appropriately called "tough issues." In order to grapple with these issues, we have asked persons in the field who are confronting them and are effectively dealing with them on a regular basis to offer practical suggestions/advice/tips to the practitioner as well as the person suffering from the problem at issue.

The book is divided into four sections. Part 1 deals with addictions. As the world and society become more complex, old addictions remain and new ones come on the scene. Hence, we have chosen to present in this section the old prevailing issues of alcohol and drug addictions along with ones that have only recently gained national attention — gambling addiction, sexual addiction, and the Internet.

In Part 2, issues that we label "family" issues are discussed. Given the critical role the family has in the Bible as well as in society, we wanted to provide solutions to some of the tough issues that threaten to weaken this institution if not dealt with appropriately, such as domestic abuse, sexual abuse, incest, divorce, and blended families.

Part 3 confronts five areas that we have labeled "issues of mental health." While other issues in this volume may also be considered mental health issues in a strict sense, we use this term here in order to highlight the need for mental health and/or biblical counseling interventions. The five areas covered are depression and bipolar disorder, schizophrenia, attention deficit hyperactive disorder, suicide, and grief and loss. Grief and loss are discussed in two different chapters so that we could present a medical perspective as well as include a personal testimony of someone who has dealt with grief and loss.

Part 4 covers five areas that cannot be neatly categorized in our typology—hence, we have simply labeled them "other critical issues." Included here are conflicts, healthy and authentic faith, demonology, unemployment, and research. The topic of conflict is paramount because failure to deal with it effectively may affect a number of other areas. In a world where the number of religions is increasing exponentially, the question of a "healthy and authentic faith" must be raised. The topic of demonology would not be found in a typical book on counseling, but it is presented here because it is an issue of concern within the Christian community. We also carefully considered in which section to include it and decided that it belongs here because it does not neatly fall into any of the other areas covered.

Further in Part 4, whether a person has a job is critical to his or her dignity and self-worth. The final topic, research, is included in order to encourage practitioners to give attention to this area and to show how it can be fairly easily incorporated into one's daily work.

We wish to thank each of the authors for their willingness to contribute to this project. We appreciate what they are doing in their sphere of influence and believe that by their allowing their individual works to be placed in a combined volume, the overall positive effect on the kingdom of God will be multiplied. A special thanks to Dr. Willie Richardson, pastor of Christian Stronghold Baptist Church (Philadelphia, Pennsylvania) and president of Christian Research and Development, both for his pioneering work in a number of areas and for his foresight in encouraging that such a book be written.

This project is prepared under the auspices of the National Biblical Counselors Association. However, some of the views expressed may not represent those of NBCA. NBCA was established in 1999. Its purposes and activities are presented in the appendix. We thank NBCA for its overall sponsorship of this project. It was through the NBCA conferences that the vision for such a book was born.

Finally, we thank Ms. Anna Yokoyama and Ms. Ramona Tillman for their untiring clerical and general assistance with the project.

As editors we are honored to have had the privilege of pulling this volume together. We therefore present this book to the public with the hope, prayer, and expectation that it will be used of God to further edify the body of Christ.

Part 1

Confronting
Addictions

Sabrina D. Black

Chapter 1

Gambling Addiction

Sabrina D. Black is the founder and clinical director of Abundant Life Counseling Center, an outpatient mental health facility that emphasizes spiritual values. She is also director of the counseling ministry at Rosedale Park Baptist Church. She is a Limited Licensed Professional Counselor, Certified Addictions Counselor, and Certified Biblical Counselor with twelve years of experience in individual, family, and group counseling. She has degrees in psychology and counseling. She has expertise in the fields of gambling addiction, sexual addiction and sexual abuse, relational problems due to substance addiction, issues relating to clergy and ministry leaders, marital conflicts and communication, boundaries and spiritual growth, stress, anxiety, burnout, and anger management. She is an active member of the National Biblical Counselors Association, American Counseling Association, and the American Association of Christian Counselors.

In addition to doing mental heath counseling, Black serves as adjunct faculty at several universities, is an overseas missionary, and is making a local and global impact in the world. She is a national and international speaker for conferences, retreats, and workshops. Black lives in Detroit, Michigan, with her husband, Warren José Black. They have a son, Kenyae, and two grandchildren, Armonte and Zari.

The poster caught my attention: "You don't have to do drugs to get hooked by a dealer. Compulsive gambling can be every bit as destructive. It's not just cards either. It's the track; it's pull-tabs, the lottery, and every other kind of gambling. They can cost you your savings, your house, even your family. This is one addiction where the cops may not bust you, but the dealer might" (Minnesota Department of Human Services 1992).

In 1976 approximately 1.1 million people in the United States were probable compulsive gamblers. This figure represented less than 1 percent of the population. Yet the mental health community did not officially diagnose and take seriously this excessive problem until 1980. That was the year that measurable characteristics for diagnosing gambling addiction were presented in the *Diagnostic and Statistical Manual of Mental Disorders, 3d Edition* (DSM-III 1980). How many individual lives and families do you suppose had been devastated by then? Yet more than twenty years later, and though many people have been awakened to the addictive cycle involved with gambling, the church is still asleep. The church has been lulled into thinking it is "those people out there," not the members of our own congregations. Those in bondage (including Christians) will compromise their values and their biblical principles. They may even seek benevolence (money from the church) to pay their overdue bills as a bailout from financial devastation.

This chapter will provide education and awareness of this escalating problem. It will also include information to equip the church to make a proper assessment and referral or to do an intervention.

WHAT HARM CAN REALLY BE DONE?

Many believe that gambling is the economic salvation of a city. Others argue that it will lead to degradation. Some rationalize that having more jobs, an increased tax base, and money for schools and community groups makes gambling a great opportunity. However, when we look at gains versus losses wherever gambling is prevalent, we see that the odds are never in the favor of the community or the individuals living there. Consider those across the country who have lost much and still believe they can parlay their last dollar into a dream. Consider the impact on Mabel, Donna, or the friends and family of Jihad.

For the past nine weeks, except for the week that she was in the hospital for inflammatory arthritis, Mabel (not her real name) faithfully attended the Friday night bingo games. Most of the women in her auxiliary played. Since her husband's death two years ago, she was lonely and tired of being home alone. She looked forward to seeing her friends at their favorite table in the fellowship hall and playing her lucky board. Like the other ladies, Mabel was happy that they could help the church raise money for the new playground. She didn't even mind when she lost, because the money was going to a good cause. When the church offered free transportation to the casino on Saturdays, Mabel's group was the first to board the bus. She could now get back the money she lost playing bingo and win even more on the

9. Has jeopardized or lost a significant relationship, job, or educational or career opportunity because of gambling.
10. Relies on others to provide money to relieve a desperate financial situation caused by gambling. (DSM-IV 1994, p. 618)

There are still others whose level of functioning has been impaired, although they may not be labeled pathological.

Gambling has become the vice of choice for the masses. According to Rogers in *Seducing America: Is Gambling a Good Bet?* (1997), gambling expenditures each year exceed the amount of money spent on films, books, amusements, and music entertainment combined. He indicated that studies show the following statistics on gambling for U.S. citizens:

- 95% have gambled at some time in their lives
- 89% approve of casino gambling
- 82% have played the lottery
- 75% have played slot machines
- 74% have frequented casinos
- 50% have bet on horse or dog races
- 44% have used playing cards
- 34% play bingo
- 26% have bet on sports events

TYPES OF GAMBLERS

Many of those who gamble sit next to you at church on Sunday. You may say to yourself, "If they were gamblers, I would know about it." However, this is not necessarily so. Gambling is often referred to as the invisible addiction. People who have a gambling problem are not stumbling and falling down; they are not slurring their speech. One can't smell the results of gambling. There are, however, some key similarities and differences between gambling addiction and substance abuse. One difference that is important to understand is that unlike the alcoholic, the gambler is very functional until the bottom is hit. Not all gamblers bottom out; but when they do, intervention is absolutely necessary if they are to recover financially, spiritually, relationally, and emotionally.

According to Custer and Milt (1985), there are six different types of gamblers: professional, antisocial personality, casual social, serious social, relief-and-escape, and pathological/compulsive. These gamblers range from those who are very controlled and patiently wait for the best bet, to those who cannot stop (without intervention/treatment) no matter how hard they try. In *When Luck Runs Out* (1985), Custer and Milt provide brief descriptions similar to those listed below for each type of gambler:

Professional — Gambling is this person's primary source of income; he makes a living at gambling. He is usually very controlled and calculating about making the best bet.

Antisocial personality — The life career of this person is getting money by illegal means. Those who gamble try to fix gambling games. They usually have difficulty controlling their criminal tendency.

Casual social — Gambling is one of many forms of entertainment. The person gambles infrequently and would not miss it if he or she had to stop. This form of gambling rarely progresses to a problem or becomes pathological unless it is a response to trauma or a predisposing factor.

Serious social — The person gambles as a major source of entertainment, plays regularly at one or more types of gambling, and does so with great absorption and intensity. He or she can stop but would miss it. They rarely escalate to compulsive but are often associated with the "golf widow, football widow," etc.

Relief-and-escape — Gambling is a major activity in this person's life and is of equal importance with family and business, but the rest of this person's life goes on without its integrity being seriously impaired. This type rarely progresses to problem/pathological gambling unless there is trauma or predisposing factors.

Pathological/compulsive — This person meets the clinical criteria as defined by the DSM-IV (1994) under impulse control. Progressive patterns to their uncontrollable behavior compromise and disrupt major areas of functioning. Gambling is the only important thing in life, and this person ignores family and business and often turns to crime to support his/her habit. High rates of suicide attempts, dual diagnosis, and dual addiction are prevalent.

Within the six types of gamblers, there are also two subtypes. The classic pattern found to be common in the early years of treatment and recovery was the *action gambler*. Action gamblers were usually domineering, controlling, manipulative men with large egos. They saw themselves as friendly, sociable, gregarious, and generous. Their average IQ was over 120.

They were energetic, assertive, persuasive, and confident. In spite of all this, they usually had low self-esteem. Historically, they started gambling at an early age (often in their teens) by placing small bets on sporting events or playing cards with friends or relatives. They progressed through the phases of the disorder over a ten-to-thirty-year time span.

Action compulsive gamblers gamble primarily at *skill* games such as poker or other card games, craps or other dice games, horse and dog racing, and sports betting. These gamblers dominate both legal and illegal sports betting. They gamble to beat other individuals or the "house" and often believe they can develop a system to achieve this goal. During the desperation phase of the disease, action gamblers often begin to gamble for escape, medicating the pain they are feeling from the destruction created by their gambling with the narcotic-like effect of slot or, more likely, video poker machines (National Council on Problem Gambling 2000).

With more and more people receiving treatment, a new subtype was identified and became easily recognizable. The face of the gambler was changing. The label *escape artist* or *luck gambler* was attributed to the women with problem or pathological gambling problems. It was later found to have broader application to everyone who met some of the following criteria:

- Finds gambling becoming a problem later in life, frequently after 30 or as late as 80.
- Gambles at luck games, slot machines, video poker, bingo, lottery, other machines.
- Gambles for different reasons than action gamblers.
- Is numb, almost in a hypnotic-like state while gambling.
- Gambles to escape problems.
- Is free from physical or emotional pain while gambling.
- Is a nurturing, responsible person the majority of adult life.
- Has often been the victim of abuse.
- Does not like confrontation and is in desperate need of empowerment.
- Often becomes compulsive almost immediately once predisposing factors emerge.
- Sometimes has winning episodes after becoming compulsive, but at this point winning is simply a means of gambling longer. Money is like play money, Monopoly money.

WHO'S AT RISK?

Gambling is this country's newest great American pastime. And although everyone is at risk, prevalence studies show that there has been an increase in gambling by minorities, youth, seniors, and those of lower economic and educational status. Winning the lottery is now the number one American fantasy. High schools are scheduling mock casino nights. Slot machines are available in restaurants. Charities are graduating from bingo to Las Vegas Nights and Millionaire Parties. Grandparents are giving children lottery tickets for birthdays and Christmas. Retail outlets are selling toys that look like slot machines as well as a variety of playable card games used in gambling houses. The masses are playing with both real and play money.

America's youth are getting more of an education in the school hallways than most teachers, counselors, and parents would imagine or would like to admit. The new curriculum includes promotions that are not measured by ACT, SAT, and MEAP scores. It's no longer what you know but really how you play the game. Students are gambling on the new curriculum (poker, pool, lottery) to help them get a passing grade with their peers and those whom they admire.

People love winners. For youngsters who lack self-esteem, winning a bet provides an instant though temporary boost in confidence and esteem. Gambling makes them feel important and looked up to by others — part of the group and powerful — a remarkably heady experience for a youth and one they most assuredly would like to repeat. For many young people this imprint is the beginning of a downward spiral on an addictive journey.

Odds are, you know a teen that gambles. The typical profile is not what one would expect. These young people are usually competitive, intelligent, high-energy, articulate, impulsive, risk takers, achievement-oriented, good students (particularly at math), and clever at rationalizing and justifying behavior. They usually have part-time jobs, and they may have engaged in some other form of addictive behavior (drugs, alcohol, eating, shopping). In a phone interview in February 2000, Ed Looney, executive director of the Council of Compulsive Gambling of New Jersey, outlined the following characteristics of adolescent teen gamblers:

- Gamblers are usually male — 95 percent; female 5 percent.
- Games of choice among male adolescents include betting on sports games, cards, dice, lottery, horses, and casinos.
- Female adolescent gamblers tend to bet on lotteries, casinos, racetracks, bingo, and playing cards.

The following activities provide teens with betting opportunities that can lead to gambling problems: pool, Internet, video games, and sporting events (Black 2000).

Why do teens gamble? They gamble for many of the same reasons as adults. Often there is a history of gambling in the family, or the behavior is the result of influence from parents, teachers, or other role models. Sometimes it is due to problems at home — the teen is looking to escape from the cruel reality of misuse, abuse, or abandonment. Low self-esteem, boredom, peer pressure, and excitement seeking are possible causes. To win money, to gain attention from peers, or just to have fun are also cited as reasons why teenagers gamble.

Another motivation is the powerful influence of advertising. Although gambling addiction is not a new problem, this is the first generation to grow up in an environment where gambling is legal and promoted through every form of media. Adolescents are finally being informed through the school systems about the dangers inherent in smoking, alcohol, and drug consumption. Few, however, are being informed about the potentially addictive qualities in gambling.

PHASES OF GAMBLING

Compulsive and pathological problem gambling is a progressive behavior disorder that has three phases: winning, losing, and desperation. It is characterized by uncontrollable urges to gamble.

In the *winning phase*, gambling is fun, exciting, entertaining, and "rewarding," with occasional big wins. The gambler has unreasonable optimism, exhibits irrational thinking, and fantasizes about the big win. Unfortunately, what starts out as just fun can lead down a gloomy road.

Consider the case of Donna (not her real name). Donna came from a loving two-parent home. The family events on the weekends, however, focused on gambling and drinking. Rent parties and running numbers were a way of life for many in the neighborhood where she grew up. This did not seem like a problem. Donna learned basic math by counting cards. Her father would reward her with money when she was able to calculate probabilities. As she grew older, she looked for additional ways to make a little money using her talent with numbers. It was all fun and games until she realized that she had an appetite for the slot machine. Donna had a well-paying job and enjoyed the finer things in life such as traveling, lots of friends, and a great career with a large portfolio.

She started out playing the lottery casually as a young adult until it progressed to every day. According to Donna, she had a winning strategy. It seemed to be confirmed by the fact that she picked the lucky number at least three times a week. Getting paid was exhilarating; so was having the owner of the corner stores in the area know her by name. She had begun taking trips on the weekends to Vegas and Atlantic City twice a month before she noticed that she couldn't stop. The memory of that first big win on the slots kept her going — the sound of the tinkling coins, the flashing red lights, and the people cheering as she filled the buckets with money. That was the only "big win." However, she was convinced that if she did it once, she could do it again. She had to do it again — she had to play at least long enough to get her money back. After three years, Donna could feel the strain on her finances and her body; she would stay out late going to the casino and get up early and go to work the next day. It started affecting her job, as she called in more and more due to sickness, family matters, emergencies, or whatever story worked at the time.

To cut down on time, she started engaging in online Internet gambling. This way she could just feed her addiction from the confines of her home. Soon she maxed out her credit cards and burned all her resources. Finally, her relationships became more distant. She was not returning calls or going out with friends. This pattern became noticeable to her family and friends. She found herself making up stories, telling lies, and forgetting one lie to the next.

Donna is a born-again Christian. As Donna was in church one Sunday listening to the words of a song ("Prone to wander, Lord, I feel it, prone to leave the God I love. Here's my heart, Lord, take and seal it. Seal it for thy courts above"), her heart became heavier. She knew she was trapped in a cycle of behavior that she could not break on her own. Donna didn't know what to do but cry out for help before she fell completely into an abyss. As she walked out of the sanctuary, she passed a note to her pastor. It conveyed one word — HELP.

Over time, the gambler moves to the *losing phase*, where his or her bets are increasing although he or she is losing consistently. The person gambles to recoup losses (called "chasing the bet"). The gambler will sell personal possessions or borrow from others to stay "in action" in the game. There is such a preoccupation with gambling that the person will neglect or miss school, work, and other important activities.

The *desperation phase* comes just before hopelessness. The person resorts to any means necessary, including illegal activity, to cover bets.

Gamblers alienate themselves from family and friends and exhibit decreased self-esteem, depression, and panic. The desperation phase can even lead to suicide.

Consider the case of Jihad. Surrounded by about a hundred mourners, Jihad Moukalled was buried about 1 P.M., following a funeral service in Detroit. Two hours later, the gathering tripled as the bodies of his wife and three children were buried in a separate area of the same cemetery. The Moukalleds were found dead on a Tuesday morning by their maid, a discovery that set off waves of hysteria and disbelief among friends and relatives who heard the news.

On his final red-eye from Las Vegas, Jihad Moukalled had had much to consider. There were the mounting gambling losses, the $500,000 he'd skimmed from his printing business, the $60,000 in credit card debt. There was the $80,250 second mortgage on his home that had been refinanced three times since November 1997. There was the cash he'd borrowed from friends — money he could not repay. And there was his pregnant wife, Fatima, and their three young children, asleep early Tuesday in the family's Farmington Hills home. There was much to consider (see Zeman et al. 2000).

This is part of the text from the note Farmington Hills police say was left by Jihad Moukalled before he killed his pregnant wife, three children, and himself:

> It is over. I can no longer keep going. Over ten years ago I started gambling. I started gambling and it has been as if time stood still since. There is nothing more destructive to life than gambling. I wonder why there are government agencies to fight drugs and not gambling. A drug addict destroys his life, a gambler destroys his life and the lives of those he cares about and care about him. For everyone I owe money to I have nothing to say but ask for your forgiveness. Family and friends please forgive me. I never ever had a bad intent toward anyone. I think that I was gripped by the hope of "one more shot." I did not know how else to escape what I got myself into. All my friends have been helpful and generous so was my relatives but I was beyond salvage.

Like others before him, Jihad felt hopeless and helpless. Addictions impede human freedom and diminish the human spirit. The Latin root for addiction is *addicene,* "to give assent, to assign or surrender." In ancient times it was used to describe someone (usually an enemy) who was captured and kept in bondage or slavery. What a fitting description for an addict! What may begin as an attempt to avoid pain and experience well-being will over time become all-consuming, even idolatrous. The repeated association between pain relief/euphoria and the particular behavior pattern produces a rush that becomes psychologically entrenched. The remembrance of this rush will compel a person to give energy to things that are not his true desires. In the book *Addiction and Grace* (1988), Gerald May makes a profound statement as it relates to the believer: "Addiction may oppress our desire, erode our wills, confound our motivations, and contaminate our judgment, but its bondage is never absolute" (p. 18). Thus no matter how bad the situation is, there is always hope. We have the assurance that Jesus came to set the captives free, and that includes those who are in bondage to addiction.

TREATMENT AND INTERVENTION

The primary goals for helping those struggling with the compelling urges of gambling addiction are to help them overcome, to see them released from bondage, and to encourage them to live an abundant life in the fullness of what God has called them to be. In order to achieve this goal, the following twelve areas should be addressed in detail during counseling intervention:

1. Recognize and own the addiction.
2. Identify unmet psycho-spiritual needs.
3. Learn to identify feelings and process emotions.
4. Understand the addictive cycle and downward spiral of sin.
5. Grasp and respond to immediate and long-range consequences.
6. Face pain courageously and stop pretending or avoiding.
7. Identify triggers, improve critical thinking skills, and develop a strategy for coping with life.
8. Strengthen who one is in Christ through the practice of spiritual disciplines.
9. Develop accountability within the family and the fellowship of believers.
10. Embrace and exercise the ability to choose; accept responsibility for choices.
11. Resolve guilt and shame issues and move toward forgiveness.
12. Revise financial plans, develop a debt repayment schedule, and make restitution.

Because gambling is usually a hidden addiction until it reaches the point of desperation, many gamblers don't receive intervention until this phase. Like anything else that is not good for you, the time to do something about it is as soon as it is discovered. However, some people are blind to their own destructive patterns and need someone else to point out behavior that is questionable. Many gamblers see their activity as just harmless fun, another form of recreation. They don't consider the devastation that may lie ahead. The illusion of control is present until they try to stop. The casual social gambler, serious social gambler, and the relief-and-escape gambler can all stop by themselves but would miss the activity. However, the professional, antisocial personality, and problem/pathological/compulsive gambler will definitely need intervention.

There are several assessment tools that can be used in order to determine an individual's level of addiction. These tools include:

- DSM-IV Diagnostic Criteria
- South Oaks Gambling Screen
- GA Twenty Questions
- The Wager — 2 Questions
- Attitudes Belief Survey

Each of these tools is available on-line from the National Council on Problem Gambling or other gambling recovery sites (see list at the end of the chapter).

In addition to assessing the gambler's level of addiction, the counselor must gather data by completing a bio-psycho-social-spiritual inventory. This inventory gives the counselor an overview of the individual's level of functioning in each of these areas. It also provides a historical profile of the family and any generational sins, curses, or dysfunctions. The counselor will need to gather data on the client's history of gambling and the various forms of debt that have been incurred.

The counselor should ascertain how many of the warning signs the individual, co-workers, or family members have identified. Among them:

- Chronically late to appointments
- Unexplained absences or disappearances from work or family events
- Excessive use of sick days
- Recreational time centered around gambling activity
- Frequent requests to use phone
- Borrowing money from family members, friends, and co-workers
- Arguing with others about money owed to them

- Frequent requests for advances in salary
- Numerous company credit union loans
- Credit card or loan billings mailed to work
- Receiving phone calls or visits from bookie, creditors, or other strangers
- Money and other small items (jewelry, appliances, electronics) missing from home
- Decline of grooming habits, sleepiness, eyes bloodshot
- Appearing to be depressed or anxious
- Preoccupied, lack of concentration
- Constantly lying about everything
- Complaints about family or other personal problems

Treatment usually begins because someone who cares about the gambler wants to do an intervention or recommends him or her for counseling. Many people are reluctant to be a part of intervention. Some of them have believed one or more of five myths regarding the intervention process:

- The addicted person must want help before he can get it.
- The addicted person must hit rock bottom before he can get help.
- The addicted person will quit on his or her own eventually.
- The addicted person has a right to do it; no one should interfere.
- The addicted person might become worse if someone intervenes.

As the body of Christ, we cannot just watch our brothers and sisters on the road to destruction and not try to make a difference. Every soul lost is important to God. We should be about our Father's business: proclaiming the gospel, showing the way, and then advancing the kingdom. God has called us to be good stewards of our time, talent, and treasure. Those who gamble are exhibiting poor stewardship and violating Scripture. Galatians 6:1 states, "Brothers and sisters, if someone in your group does something wrong, you who are spiritual should go to that person and gently help make him right again. But be careful, because you might be tempted to sin, too" (NCV).

The role of the counselor is to walk alongside the gambler during this season of life and assist him or her in the recovery process. The counselor needs to be someone who actively participates in the session, not someone who just listens and takes notes. The counselor is most effective if he or she is directive, structured, and resourceful. The gambler will need intense accountability. The counselor needs to work in conjunction with the Holy

Spirit in the session, or he or she will become a part of the gambler's con game. The role of the Holy Spirit is to restore lives, give hope, indwell and empower the believer, and convict concerning sin.

THE BIBLE AND GAMBLING

Many still wonder: Is gambling sin? No justification for gambling can be found in the Bible. Gambling appeals to luck and chance, disregards the sovereignty of God, and promotes pagan superstitions. Gambling violates Christian stewardship of our relationship with others. Gambling undermines a biblical work ethic and human reason and skill. Covetousness, not godly contentment, is the chief end of gambling, which encourages greed, materialism, and the love of money. In most cases, gambling is associated with a host of social and personal vices, thus violating God's command to avoid every kind of evil (Evans 1995). Even if the gambler does not view the behaviors associated with his or her gambling as sin, there is no question about the bondage he or she is experiencing.

Biblical Intervention

"The spirit of the LORD is upon me; because He has anointed Me to preach the gospel to the poor; He has sent me to heal the brokenhearted, to proclaim liberty to the captives and recovery of sight to the blind, to set at liberty those who are oppressed" (Luke 4:18 NKJV). Jesus came to deliver us from bondage.

The world may say, "Once an addict, always an addict," but according to the Word of God there is hope, and healing is available. This is not an attempt to spiritualize what many consider an addiction to be: a sickness or disease. Addiction begins and ends with a choice. In the beginning, the person is choosing to anesthetize whatever pain or discomfort in life he or she may experience. When people choose to reach out to something other than God, this is the beginning of idolatry. At some point in the process — and it varies from one individual to the next — the person loses control of his choices, and the addictive substance — in this case gambling — is making the choices for him.

There is a saying among alcoholics: "The man takes a drink, the drink takes a drink, then the drink takes the man." Gambling addiction has a similar progression. However, there is a window of time where, although the urges and temptations are intense, the person can still escape. According to 1 Corinthians 10:13, "No temptation has overtaken you except such as is common to man; but God is faithful, who will not allow you to be tempted beyond that what you are able, but with the temptation will also make the way of escape, that you may be able to bear it" (NKJV). During the time that the person is tempted, he or she can choose to flee evil and avoid the downward spiral of sinful behavior.

Christians have the admonition in Romans 6:11–13 to "reckon yourselves to be dead indeed to sin, but alive to God in Christ Jesus our Lord. Therefore do not let sin reign in your mortal body, that you should obey it in its lusts. And do not present your members as instruments of unrighteousness to sin, but present yourselves to God as being alive from the dead, and your members as instruments of righteousness to God" (NKJV).

The gambler in recovery does not have to be a slave to sin. As they reckon themselves to be alive unto God through Jesus Christ, gamblers will develop a routine of spiritual disciplines that will help them to resist evil. These disciplines may include prayer, fasting, Bible study, Scripture memorization, and so forth. It is the power of God active and available in people's lives that helps them to break whatever bondage in which they find themselves entangled. In the absence of developing a personal, intimate relationship with the Lord, any changes that are made will only be temporary, and the person will continue to relapse into old dysfunctional and destructive behaviors.

Basic Steps Prior to Spiritual Intervention

Before undertaking any type of spiritual intervention or biblical counseling, intercessory prayer is necessary. Those who will be involved in the gambler's recovery process will need to be educated on what they are dealing with, and they will also need support. There are three basic steps to starting over for the person in recovery: (1) confession, (2) communication, and (3) commitment.

Confession. The unsaved individual needs to confess with his mouth the Lord Jesus Christ and believe in his heart that he died for humankind's sins and rose again, providing new life. The saved person needs to confess his faults to someone else: "If we confess our sins, he is faithful and just to forgive us our sins and to cleanse us from all unrighteousness" (John 1:9 KJV). Part of the healing that will take place includes connecting and establishing intimacy, as the person is vulnerable and transparent with someone else. This also promotes accountability because there is someone who is aware of the person's struggles and what he is professing to do about his recovery.

Communication. As the recovering person begins to share and talk with others, the greatest challenge will not be speaking the truth in love, it will simply be speaking the truth. Addiction is a lifestyle of deceit and deception. The gambler has established a pattern of exaggeration and minimization. His life is the classic fish story; every time you hear it, it is more a whale of a tale. The person may have lied to avoid conflict, consequences, or condemnation. Interacting with family, friends, and others may be difficult, based on the level of mistrust due to broken promises. Participation in a biblically based 12-step support group is a great opportunity to practice communication.

Commitment. The individual needs to consider it so and walk in deliverance. Even though it may seem difficult at first, he or she has to be determined to continue to move forward in recovery. When things are difficult, so many, like the children of Israel, want to return to Egypt (which represents bondage). The gambler needs to be committed in order to not be "entangled again with a yoke of bondage" (Galatians 5:1 KJV).

Relapse Prevention

Recovery from addiction is like walking up a down escalator. It is impossible to stand still. When you stop moving forward, you find yourself moving backwards. You do not have to do anything in particular to develop symptoms that lead to relapse. All you need to do is to fail to take recovery steps. The symptoms develop spontaneously in the absence of a strong recovery program. Once you abandon a recovery program, it is only a matter of time until the symptoms of past acute withdrawal appear. And if nothing is done to manage them, the gambler will experience a period of out-of-control behavior that we call the *relapse syndrome*. Relapse does not simply mean returning to the acting-out behavior. Those in relapse will begin to exhibit the behavior patterns and attitudes that they practiced when they were dysfunctional. The relapsed person is taking steps backward toward a powerless and unmanageable lifestyle (Booth 1997).

The gambler in recovery should be constantly moving forward (pursuing holiness and practicing godliness). He is pressing "toward the mark ... of the high calling" (Philippians 3:14 KJV). Through discipline (1 Corinthians 9:27) and keeping our bodies under control (Colossians 3:5), he will be better prepared to handle future temptations. Galatians 5:16 tells us that if we walk in the Spirit, we will not fulfill the lust of the flesh. It does not say that we will not be tempted, but we will not yield to temptation.

Even the process of recovery has triggers that can lead to temptation. Some of the temptations are trying to do too much too soon, the myth of the instant cure, exhaustion and apathy, major life changes, forgetting to be grateful to God, expecting too much from others, or letting up on the practice of spiritual disciplines. The gambler in recovery needs to be encouraged, empowered, and equipped to live an abundant life.

CONCLUSION: GAMBLING IS A BAD BET FROM A TO Z

Addiction, Abuse, Abandonment
Bankruptcies, Bondage, Bailouts
Crime, Corruption, Communicator declines
Dishonesty, Debt, Domestic violence
Entrapment, Enticing, Emotional breakdown
Families destroyed, Financial devastation
God removed from the throne, Guilt, Greed
Homes mortgaged, History of addictions
Idolatry, Infidelity, Irresponsibility
Judgment poor, Job loss, Jaded perspective
Kill life (suicide, homicide), hopes, and dreams
Lies, Loan sharks, Legal issues
Mood swings (euphoria, depression)
Nothing sacred, Nothing safe, Narcissistic
Oppression, Obsession
Personality changes, Problems in relationships
Quarrelsome, Quandary
Reality lost, Resentful
Self-absorbed, Suffering, Suicidal
Trust destroyed, Tribulations
Unaccounted for time and money
Victim, Vacillation, Violation, Violence
Worry, Withdrawn, Warfare
X marks the spot where a vibrant life used to be
Yoke of bondage, Yearnings overwhelming
Zero, Zombie, Zonked

(Sabrina D. Black © 2001)

The church needs to wake up and help to deliver those in the body of Christ who are living the nightmare of gambling addiction.

ANSWERS TO QUIZ

	Gambling	Gaming
1. Card games with friends	■	☐
2. Video poker	☐	■
3. Slot machines	☐	■
4. Super Bowl pools	■	☐
5. Bowling jackpots	☐	■
6. Sports betting with bookies	☐	■
7. Lottery	☐	■
8. Bingo	☐	■
9. Horse races	☐	■
10. Betting on golf	■	☐

REFERENCE RESOURCES

Berman, L., and M. Siegel. 1992. *Behind the 8-ball: A guide for families of gamblers.* New York: Fireside Press.

Black, S. 2000. Odds are you know a teen who gambles. *Christian Counseling Today* 8: 24–27, 73.

Booth, L. 1997. *Spirituality and recovery.* Long Beach, Calif.: SPC Limited.

Custer, R. L., and H. Milt. 1985. *When luck runs out.* New York: Facts on File.

Diagnostic and statistical manual of mental disorders, 3d edition. DSM-III. 1980. Washington, D.C.: American Psychiatric Association.

Diagnostic and statistical manual of mental disorders, 4th edition. DSM-IV. 1994. Washington, D.C.: American Psychiatric Association.

Evans, T. 1995. *Is gambling a good bet?* Chicago: Moody Press.

Heineman, M. 1992. *Losing your shirt.* Center City, Minn.: Hazelden.

_____. 1988. *When someone you love gambles.* Center City, Minn.: Hazelden.

Lesieur, H. 1990. *Understanding compulsive gambling.* Center City, Minn.: Hazelden.

Looney, E. 2000. Telephone interview. February.

May, G. 1988. *Addiction and grace.* San Francisco: Harper & Row.

Minnesota Department of Human Services. 1992. *A poster.* St. Paul: MDHS, Mental Health Division Gambling Treatment Program.

Moody, G. 1990. *Quit compulsive gambling: The action plan for gamblers and their families.* Chicago: Moody Press.

National Council on Problem Gambling. 2000. Washington, D.C.

Rogers, R. M. 1997. *Seducing America: Is gambling a good bet?* Grand Rapids: Baker.

Zeman, D., A. Klein, H. McDiarmid Jr., N. Warikoo, M. Helms. 2000. Big gambling debt results in a tragedy. *Detroit Free Press* (22 November).

ADDITIONAL RESOURCES

On-Line Help

North American Training Institute *www.nati.org/teens*

National Council on Problem Gambling *www.ncpgambling.org*

The Council on Compulsive Gambling of New Jersey *www.800gambler.org*

The Wager *www.thewager.org*

Gambling Hotline

National Council on Problem Gambling

24-hour confidential help-line

1-800-522-4700

Gamblers Anonymous *www.gamblersanonymous.org*

Live Dramatizations Related to Gambling

The Rainbow Drama Guild

Jettie Davis, Director

15780 Murray Hill

Detroit, MI 48227

Sabrina D. Black and LaVern A. Harlin

Chapter 2

Sexual Addiction and the Internet

Sabrina D. Black is the founder and clinical director of Abundant Life Counseling Center, an outpatient mental health facility that emphasizes spiritual values. She is also director of the counseling ministry at Rosedale Park Baptist Church. She is a Limited Licensed Professional Counselor, Certified Addictions Counselor, and Certified Biblical Counselor with twelve years of experience in individual, family, and group counseling. She has degrees in psychology and counseling. She has expertise in the fields of gambling addiction, sexual addiction and sexual abuse, relational problems due to substance addiction, issues relating to clergy and ministry leaders, marital conflicts and communication, boundaries and spiritual growth, stress, anxiety, burnout, and anger management. She is an active member of the National Biblical Counselors Association, American Counseling Association, and the American Association of Christian Counselors.

In addition to doing mental heath counseling, Black serves as adjunct faculty at several universities, is an overseas missionary, and is making a local and global impact in the world. She is a national and international speaker for conferences, retreats, and workshops. Black lives in Detroit, Michigan, with her husband, Warren José Black. They have a son (Kenyae) and two grandchildren (Armonte and Zari).

LaVern A. Harlin is a member of Rosedale Park Baptist Church, where she started counseling ministry in 1989. She received her Foundation of Biblical Counseling certification through Christian Research and Development. She serves and counsels in various areas, including sexual addictions, abuse victims, marital problems, depression, discipleship, and group therapy. She is currently attending Michigan Theological Seminary and completing a degree in counseling psychology. Her heartbeat is in the area of biblical Christian counseling and the discipleship of women. One of her life verses is Ephesians 4:12–13: "To prepare God's people for works of service, so that

the body of Christ may be built up until we all reach unity in the faith and in the knowledge of the son of God and become mature, attaining to the whole measure of the fullness of Christ."

Some of the most powerful addictions do not involve alcohol, other
drugs, or food but are equally destructive. This group of addictions,
in which the victim is caught in a tornado of repetitive, life-control-
ling behaviors, is called *process* or *behavior addictions*. The processes that
can become addictive include, among others, Internet usage, gambling,
work, compulsive worry, compulsive anger and rage, shopping, exercising,
and sex.

This chapter focuses on two forms of addiction that were once separate
but are now being linked: sex and the Internet. It will also provide information to help pastors, laypeople, and counselors recognize individuals
that are trapped and need to be set free from this bondage. These uncontrolled sexual behaviors have ensnared all ages in every walk of life.

Sexual temptation and addiction is as much a part of our community
and culture as baseball is our national pastime. African American churches,
as well as all churches, need to take a serious look at this problem because
it is prevalent in the world and is growing from the pulpit to the pews. If the
church is to be a voice in dealing with these process addictions, then we
need to become better equipped to recognize them in our congregations
and to handle the problems they bring. We need to obtain insight as well
as training in the area of counseling and theology to break the appetite and
bondage of these addictions.

Addiction is a state of compulsion, obsession, or preoccupation that
enslaves a person's will and desire. Addiction sidetracks and eclipses the
energy of an individual's deepest, truest desire for love and goodness.
Addiction causes one to devote oneself to something, someone, or some
activity or experience. We exchange Jehovah (the All-sufficient One) for the
gratification of our flesh. We want our needs met now. We indulge our bodies to a point where we cannot control their urges or resulting behavior.

Professionals who work in the field of sexual addiction assert that sexually compulsive behaviors have reached epidemic proportions (Carnes
1983, 1992, 1998; Lasser 1996; Shelly 1992; Weiss 1998). The National
Council on Sexual Addiction and Compulsivity (Amparano 1998) estimated that 6 to 8 percent of Americans are sex addicts, or between 16 and
21.5 million people. From the pulpit to the pew and from our house to the

White House, we have become "prone to wander." On any given Sunday, the person who you are sitting next to could be addicted to one or more substances or processes, including sex and the Internet.

To a person with a sexual addiction, sex is like alcohol to an alcoholic, or other drugs to a junkie. It is a fix that the sexually addicted person will do just about anything to get. Despite what is shown in the movies and hyped in the media, sexual addiction is not fun. It is a compulsive drive that brings short-term thrills and long-term miseries. To subdue the addiction can be the most important decision in a person's life next to accepting Jesus Christ as Savior and Lord.

Sexual addiction is more deceptive than most other addictions. It provides the illusion of pleasure. Before sexual addiction became known for what it is, those who practiced it called it "feeling good" or "getting off." The sexually addicted person becomes so blinded by his compulsion that he believes he is not sexually addicted. His usual rationalizations go something like: "I'm just having fun" or "Everyone does it" or "Why are you so uptight about sex?" However, certain behaviors conclusively establish that a person is sexually addicted.

WHAT IS SEXUAL ADDICTION?

The National Council on Sexual Addiction and Compulsivity (Amparano 1998) has defined sexual addiction as "a persistent and escalating pattern of sexual behavior acted out despite increasing negative consequences to self and others" (p. A1). The operational definition of sexual addiction is a "pathological relationship" with a mood-altering experience (Carnes 1983). Sex addicts are individuals who are out of control and have lost their ability to say no. Their sexual behavior has become a continual downward spiral. Sex is no longer a source of pleasure, but a reality of pain. The sex addict relies on sex for escape, comfort from pain, or relief from stress. The compulsivity is the primary need in the addict's life as opposed to enjoying satisfying relationships with family, friends, or co-workers. Research indicates that the dynamics common to other addictions like alcohol or drugs can extend to other obsessive behavior, such as sex and the Internet.

Most people see sexual behavior as a moral choice and the addiction as a moral failure. Sexual addiction eventually affects every part of the person's life, including self-respect, relationships with family and friends, finances, and career. For the sexually addicted person, sex is not the profoundly wonderful, God-given experience it is supposed to be. It is enslavement that eradicates one's will to make choices freely, which results in bondage.

Sexual addiction stems from an abuse of the natural sex drive that each person is born with. The abuse can start at any time in life. It then progresses until it becomes a compulsion with which the sexually addicted person cannot cope. The natural sex drive can be abused by force in childhood (i.e., incest, molestation, etc.) or by choice in adolescence and adulthood (i.e., promiscuity). For millions of people who are attempting to deaden their pain, sex is a drug. The pain can have many faces: loneliness, childhood abuse, low self-esteem, fear of failure, fear of success, pride — the list is endless.

People with sexual addictions are no longer considered just the "perverts" to joke about. They are some of the respectable people you know: corporate executives, doctors, lawyers, preachers, presidents, deacons, neighbors, family members — yes, even counselors. They are often the people you would least suspect. They could potentially be all of us, including you and people in your congregation.

Most people caught in the world of sexual addiction feel a deep, heavy loneliness. Their loneliness is caused by the sexual addiction, but in too many cases the person believes that the sexual addiction is the answer to loneliness. In more advanced cases, sexual addiction can lead to withdrawal from the world at large. There are thousands of sexually addicted people who have no relationships outside of their addictions.

Sexual addiction is actually an issue of intimacy. Those in bondage will need to acknowledge and deal with their feelings (good or bad) and then connect with others at an emotional level. Effectively overcoming a sexual addiction entails helping the sexually addicted person change his or her relationship perspective. In comparison, dealing with drugs or alcohol entails getting the addicted person to change their reality.

Based on the research and clinical experience of Carnes (1992), the forerunner in identifying and treating sexual addiction, ten signs indicate the presence of sexual addiction:

1. A pattern of out-of-control behavior
2. Severe consequences due to sexual behavior
3. Inability to stop despite adverse consequences
4. Persistent pursuit of self-destructive behavior
5. An ongoing desire or effort to limit sexual behavior
6. Sexual obsession and fantasy as a primary coping mechanism

7. Increasing amounts of scxual experience because the current level of activity is no longer sufficient
8. Severe mood changes around sexual activity
9. Inordinate amount of time spent in obtaining sex, being sexual, or recovering from sexual experience
10. Neglect of important social, occupational, or recreational activities because of sexual behavior (pp. 11–12)

No single checklist can describe a sex addict, but the following common characteristics are often identified:

- Exhibits a number of preferred sexual behaviors, arranged in a definite ritualized order, which are acted out in an obsessive scenario
- Experiences periods of escalation, de-escalation, and acuity
- Continues to act out despite serious consequences, including health risks
- Severe financial losses, injury, loss of family, and even death
- Delusional thought patterns, including rationalization, minimization, and projection

The Cycle of Sexual Addiction

Sexual addiction follows the same progressive nature of other addictions. Sexual addicts struggle to control their behaviors and experience despair over constant failure to do so. The addict is engaged in an addictive cycle on a continual basis. The cycle has four distinct and sequential components: preoccupation; ritualization; compulsive sexual behavior; and shame, despair, and guilt.

Preoccupation. The mind is completely engrossed with thoughts of sex. Because of the initial release experience, the mind has been psychologically entrenched to believe that sex is a feel-good substitute that will provide relief when one is feeling anxious, stressed, depressed, overwhelmed, unappreciated, angry, bored, and so forth. This constant mental state creates an obsessive search for sexual stimulation, no matter what that acting-out behavior may include. It is so consuming that (at its most intense) it will render the individual nonfunctional. He or she will eventually become impaired emotionally, mentally, occupationally, and financially. Sexual addiction is a life-dominating sin. If allowed to go unchecked, it has the ability to affect every area of the addict's life.

Ritualization. The special routines that lead up to the sexual behavior intensify the preoccupation, adding arousal and excitement. The person who has a sexual addiction starts planning when he wakes up in the morning what he is going to do that afternoon. She plans on Monday what she is going to do on Saturday and begins to prepare for the acting-out event. Visualizing the acting-out behavior intensifies the excitement. It's the buildup, the preoccupation, and the mindset that feeds their need, which is why their minds must constantly be renewed. Their perspective will need to change from how the world does things to believing and doing what God's Word says.

Compulsive sexual behavior. The actual act. Sexual compulsivity is the inability to control one's sexual behavior. This compulsive behavior is the cornerstone of the addiction. To be preoccupied and to ritualize are precursors to this stage. However, without the acting out, the addiction is not established because the behavior is still somewhat under control.

Shame, despair, and guilt. When sex addicts finish acting out their ritual, the gratification is followed by a disappointing empty void. There is an immediate rush, a gratification that lasts for a brief time. But when it is over, the person wonders, "Is that it? I've been planning this, waiting for this, looking forward to this. I get it, and it's over!" The addicted person is overwhelmed with guilt and shame. He or she is left at the point of despair — the feeling of utter hopelessness (and powerlessness about the behavior). To relieve the feelings of despair, the mind and the body will crave for more of what provides relief. The mood-altering activity plummets the addict back into preoccupation, and the cycle starts all over again.

Subsystems of the Addictive Cycle

Just as the addictive cycle is self-perpetuating, the larger addictive system kicks in, reinforcing itself. The four component subsystems are the belief system, cognitive dissonance, impaired thinking, and unmanageability (Carnes 1983, 1992).

Belief system. We equate the belief system of a sexual addict with Eve's belief system in the Garden of Eden. Eve believed a lie as though it was the truth, and so the enemy beguiled her. This is how the addict's belief system operates. Because of the lies they believe, their behavior is often in conflict with their thoughts, values, and principles. The very essence of who they are is compromised over and over again.

Cognitive dissonance. Psychologists might use the term *cognitive dissonance* to describe the battle inside a person who believes one way and acts another. For example, a woman will normally feel intense cognitive dissonance if she secretly carries on an affair with another man while pretending to be happily married to her husband. Society, her mother, and her friends say she should be happy in her marriage, but she is living out her sexual compulsion with various forms of outlets besides relationships. During the establishment phase of the addiction, the most important indication of faulty beliefs is when the addiction increases the addict's negative feelings about him- or herself. Being out of control comes to mean "I am a bad, unworthy person."

Impaired thinking. Flowing out of the faulty belief system is impaired thinking. Usually, impaired thinking involves a distortion of reality: "Is it live or is it Memorex?" Other types of impaired thinking include denial, rationalization, self-delusion, self-righteousness, or blaming others (consider the thinking pattern of Eve in the garden). Anxiety and alienation occur in the family. Relationships are neglected. The addict violates personal values such as honesty or fidelity. Procrastination and low productivity at work may compound the difficulties.

Unmanageability. The addict's life becomes unmanageable. In the beginning, the person has an addiction; but in the end, the addiction has them.

Levels of Sexual Addiction

Three primary levels have been used to define the range of behavior exhibited by people with sexual addiction problems.

Level one includes behavior that is perceived in our culture as acceptable. The reality is that widespread practice conveys a public tolerance for sexual activity. These practices include masturbation, multiple heterosexual and homosexual relationships, pornography, and prostitution.

Level two is specific sexual behavior that is generally regarded as nuisance behavior. These behaviors include being an exhibitionist, a voyeur, or a transvestite; engaging in bestiality; taking indecent liberties; and making indecent phone calls.

Level three includes sexual behavior that is dangerous, abusive, or life threatening (Carnes 1983). These behaviors include incest, child molestation, sexual abuse of vulnerable adults, and rape. Sexual addicts do not always start at level one or progress from one level to another. It depends on the individual's appetite. Other often-overlooked examples of out-of-control sexual behavior include having multiple affairs (fornication/adultery), dangerous sexual practices, anonymous sex, compulsive sexual episodes, and intense vicarious experiences.

A CASE STUDY

> Like a city whose walls are broken down is a man who lacks self-control.
> (Proverbs 25:28)

Richard had a reputation as the counselor for handling tough cases (especially those relating to sexual sins). His appearance and outward conduct epitomized Christian character, integrity, and respect. A man who had given himself up to the service of the Lord, his family, and his church, Richard was a man's man. The clinical director at the center where he worked had full confidence in him just as Moses had in Joshua. At times counseling cases would be given to Richard from the director because of the difficulty of the case and also for the director's safety and security. Richard was recently given a case that involved a young woman who was entrapped in a very tangled, sexually addictive lifestyle.

When he first received instruction on the case from the director, Richard was very humbled that he was given the opportunity to counsel the young Christian woman. He was also excited because he had previously been successful in helping others with what he thought was a similar problem. At the time, Richard didn't realize that the director had forwarded the case because of his own addictive background and sexual struggles. The director was wise in following the first step in counseling: he recognized his own vulnerabilities and established boundary markers against those things that would cause him to be tempted and fall back into sinful behavior.

As the young woman began to unravel her story of multiple partners, of opposite and same-sex encounters, her reality became Richard's fantasy. She had come to know the person of Jesus Christ through salvation, but her behavior was habitually addicted to sex. Her mind saw relationships as distorted encounters of sexual fantasies. As she unraveled the sordid details of her private life, she began to trust her counselor because of his knowledge of the Bible and his empathy and understanding of her shameful lifestyle.

Hour-long sessions turned into ninety minutes and sometimes almost two hours. She looked at it as a form of needing extra help because her life was so entangled that it was like a spider in a web. Little did she know that Richard was like a fly caught in the web of her addicted lifestyle. The counselor had become a vicarious participant. He needed another fix by way of longer sessions and more explicit details of her past. It reached a level where Richard started to fantasize about his client. He could smell her when she was not around, and he heard her voice when it was completely silent. Before long he was masturbating daily and visualizing her addictions by revisiting them in his mind.

Was this a form of unconscious entrapment or seeking subliminal seduction? From a Freudian perspective, the id was driving the ego, and there was a sexual fixation and transference from the counselor to the client. Regardless of how we formulate it, we must learn to recognize our vulnerabilities and have safeguards. Failing to recognize the appetite of these urges within him caused Richard to stumble.

How Do We Help the Counselor?

In the process of recovery and rebuilding, we must first caution ourselves as noted in the Scripture: "Brothers and sisters, if someone in your group does something wrong, you who are spiritual should go to that person and gently help make him right again. But be careful, because you might be tempted to sin, too" (Galatians 6:1 NCV). There is a natural tendency, unless you are fully grounded in the Word of God, to have some mental voyeurism taking place when you hear the sins of others. There are many counselors who experience vicarious pleasure as they listen to their clients share about sexual activities. You don't need to have every sordid detail of your client's sexual experience. Just to know that it was dysfunctional is sufficient.

Establish boundaries within your mind prior to counseling. Pray for the Holy Spirit to protect your mind against voyeurism and other potential hazards. If you have a personal history of sexual sin and experience sexual stimulation as your client shares, then you should consult with another counselor to address your concerns. God can guard your mind against the enemy's attack. Just as you will recommend to the person with the addiction the importance of renewing the mind, be firm in casting down your own vain imaginations and taking every thought captive.

Secondly,

> Therefore do not be partners with them. For you were once darkness, but now you are light in the Lord. Live as children of light (for the fruit of the light consists in all goodness, righteousness and truth) and find out what pleases the Lord. Have nothing to do with the fruitless deeds of darkness, but rather expose them. *For it is shameful even to mention what the disobedient do in secret....* Be very careful, then, how you live — not as unwise but as wise, making the most of every opportunity, because the days are evil. (Ephesians 5:7–12, 15–16)

Repeating too many details of sexual behavior may not be healthy for you or your client. Even without the details, discussions relating to sexual addiction may be explicit. If you're going to blush every time someone says *penis, vagina,* or even more graphic terms, consider taking cases that are not sexually related. Every man and woman should know his or her own limitations. Realize that you may be tempted and you will need to get help.

Finally, there is wisdom in having a team of counselors. Don't try to do this on your own. Some people may be in far over their heads. Refer to the recommended list of books at the end of this chapter. Listed also are Internet sites, organizations, and support groups for sexual addiction. There are many resources available in the field.

It would also be wise to get the proper training. Don't try to walk in unprepared and not covered in prayer when dealing with areas of addiction you don't know anything about. Be careful of issues of codependency and transference. There is a tendency for the counselee to develop a dependency on you, as if you have all the answers. And since you don't, you need to constantly direct them to God.

If a man or woman is going to function in a pastoral, leadership, or counseling role, character and integrity need to be consistent. Richard made several critical mistakes. As he began to give more of himself in the therapeutic process, he gave less of God. He became arrogant, thinking he could save this client from the depths of her addiction. He failed to invoke the presence of Jesus, who is the wonderful counselor. Jesus is able to deal effectively with all of our issues and to keep us from unrighteousness as he works through us. Richard's sexual sin became a revelation of an even deeper problem — his walk with God. Not only did he abuse the power of his position, but he also violated the biblical admonition to "watch yourself, or you almost may be tempted" (Galatians 6:1). Scripture clearly states that when we walk in the Spirit, we will not fulfill the lusts of the flesh (Galatians 5:16 KJV).

The "Dark" Side

We all have a dangerous side. Understanding the ramifications of the "dark" side is important in our work as counselors of clients with sexual addiction problems. If we want to be effective in our ministry of helping others overcome their addictive lifestyles, we need to acknowledge and overcome our own. Even though we may not be acting out, we still need to admit that we have a dark side. Paul described this concept in Romans 7:15–24, when he talked about the war waging within him. Clearly, there are times when the good that we would do, we don't do; and the very evil that we know not to do, we find ourselves doing. When we try to convince ourselves that we don't have a dark side, we not only do damage to ourselves but also to the people we're trying to help. Counselors, like everyone else, have a dark side that needs to be confessed. As counselors, we model for clients how to confess, confront, and control the wickedness of our hearts through the power of the Holy Spirit.

The addicted person fulfills and lives out a secret private world — a world we call the dark side of their desires. The dark side of desire is the struggle within that leads the addicted person to act out in ways that are contrary to the biblical standards set forth in the Word of God.

Confronting the Dark Side

We often talk about people with the spirit of Jezebel — a woman with a dark side (see 1 Kings 16:29 — 22:29). But did you ever consider the plight of people with the spirit of Ahab (her husband)? While speaking at a conference, someone was asked to define the spirit of Ahab. He didn't hesitate: "He's a punk." That was a pretty strong response. Not what we would have said, but we may have at least called him a "wimp." Depending on what neighborhood you grew up in, you may say he was a weakling or henpecked. We need to call it what it is. And some of us, even as counselors, have the spirit of Ahab. Our clients come in and clearly present sin, and we don't confront it, we don't challenge it. We coddle them and hold their hands. We tell them it's going to be okay, and we explain about the love of God. The things we say are true, but what about the wrath of God if they don't walk away from that behavior?

First Peter 4:2–7 says,

> As a result, he does not live the rest of his earthly life for evil human desires, but rather for the will of God. For you have spent enough time in the past doing what pagans choose to do — living in debauchery, lust, drunkenness, orgies, carousing and detestable idolatry. They think it strange that you do not plunge with them into the same flood of dissipation, and they heap abuse on you. But they will have to give an account to him who is ready to judge the living and the dead. For this is the reason the gospel was preached even to those who are now dead, so that they might be judged according to men in regard to the body, but live according to God in regard to the spirit. The end of all things is near. Therefore be clear minded and self-controlled so that you can pray.

How long do we allow people to stay in darkness? When we counsel our clients, it needs to be with a sense of urgency. They have been wherever they are far too long. We need to move them from that place. If the Lord comes today, he should be able to say, as it relates to our work with clients who have sexual addiction problems, "Well done, my good and faithful servant." Every time the client comes for counseling, we need to confront sin. There should be no spirit of Ahab in us. People come to see us for counsel because they believe we are in a position to help, because they know we are going to give them the Word of God.

Remind clients that God is not mocked. Those things that they are doing will eventually catch up with them, even though they may be doing those things in secret. The things that we do in secret will be exposed to the light. The Lord gives us opportunities for repentance. He gives us opportunities for change. He is longsuffering with us. He gives us a chance to do right and live holy. We need to do that quickly, not linger and wait. The Lord will judge; if you continue on a downward spiral, you can indeed expect judgment. For many, experiencing the consequences of their behavior is helpful in bringing about change. We need to stop telling people just about the love of God; we need to tell them about the wrath of God. They need to know what happens when you stay on that downward spiral, where it actually ends.

So confess and acknowledge that all have sinned and fallen short of the glory of God (Romans 3:23). "There is none righteous, no, not one" (v. 10 KJV). Nobody's righteous; all of us have fallen at some point. Our hearts are wicked, deceitful; and half of the time, we don't even know the wickedness of our own hearts. So we need to constantly go to God and say, "Lord, reveal to me what's in my heart, show me the changes I need to make. Even the smallest of things. . . . What is it, Lord, that you would have me do, that you would have me change?"

Then confront, using Romans 6:1, "What shall we say then? Shall we continue in sin that grace may abound?" (KJV). Absolutely not. God forbid that any one of us would continue in sin. God forbid that any one of your clients would continue in sin. You don't want them to yield the members of their bodies as slaves to unrighteousness; you don't want them to be slaves to sin any longer. The Lord has come to set them free. The counselor needs to challenge them to walk in that freedom. You don't want them to be entangled in the yoke of bondage. Whatever it is that God has set them free from, they need to run from it. Scripture says to flee evil. You can help people to be set free if you are set free yourself. Be mindful that it is the gratification of the flesh that compels you, the grace of God that constrains you, and growth in God that controls you.

Satan Meant It for Evil

Richard was not the first to abuse or misuse his position. In 1998 a leading noncommissioned army officer faced a court-martial about his sexual behavior toward subordinates. At that time, the Pentagon had already spent $1.2 billion on sexual harassment issues in fiscal 1997. Meantime, over the last two decades the Catholic Church has faced numerous problems arising from the sexual behavior of priests, including a $154 million settlement of a lawsuit in the Dallas diocese and, in early 2002, a wide outbreak of charges in various dioceses, especially Boston. Protestant, Jewish, and Islamic groups have experienced financial losses and turmoil over the sexual behavior of church leaders. For clergy, sexual scandals have been a nightmare and crisis in almost every religious tradition (Carnes 1998).

In 1998 President Clinton gave credibility to a disorder that has long been established. He wasn't the first prominent figure to exercise such indiscriminate behavior, but because the world was watching his confession on CNN, *World Report,* and every other talk show in town, people began to pay more attention. The public scandal of someone who proceeded to act out anyway, even with an incredible amount to lose if exposed, has opened the door of help to many.

THE INTERNET: AN EVER-PRESENT TEMPTATION

> For every well-known Christian television personality or author whose impropriety is widely publicized, there are any number of lesser-known pastors, Bible teachers, and para-church workers who quietly resign or are fired for sexual immorality. Most of us can name several. The myth that ministers are morally invulnerable dies slowly, however, even in the face of overwhelming evidence. But there never has been a mystical antibody that makes us immune to sexual sin. Even those of us who haven't fallen know how fierce is the struggle with temptation. (Alcorn 1998, p. 42)

Temptations are ever before us. Sex has skated right into our living areas and family rooms via computers and television. Imagine watching what is supposed to be family entertainment with your children and seeing a continual display of sexually inappropriate material. The last thing you would expect to see on a Sunday afternoon skating program would be men falling down and humping the ice as they slid across the floor, or women bumping and grinding as they ice dance to songs like the Rolling Stones' "I Can't Get No Satisfaction" and Peggy Lee's "Fever." Clearly, sex sells and has become commonplace in our society.

In contemporary culture, sex has become largely a matter of the imagination, although not much is left to imagine. In just a few short years pornography has exploded in popularity and has found its way into American homes via cable television and computers. In his article, "Sex and the Internet," Gary Webb (2001) states, "Never before has a society been exposed to so much graphic material and sexual interaction, all a few clicks away, 24 hours a day, available to adults and kids alike" (p. 88). The negative impact that sensually enticing material can have on an individual's sexuality has been ignored by many. We are at times subliminally seduced by sexual propaganda, and at other times we willingly overexpose ourselves without regard to repercussions, says Webb.

Today nearly every family motel chain offers on-demand "adult movies." Digital cable and satellite TV services offer hard-core porn on pay-per-view, not to mention the soft-core fare on the premium channels. And though the old-fashioned "adult entertainment" business seems to be in a renaissance — bolstered by hundreds of new stripper and lap-dancing clubs — the sexual medium of choice is the Internet, which offers pictures, videos, and live streaming Web-cams for every "taste." Pornography exposes the mind to lewd and lascivious visions that need to be removed so that the mind can be renewed (Veith 2001).

Everywhere we turn, we are exposed to sexual graphics or activities in some form or another. This has escalated in the media (print, television ads, etc.) and has risen to a new level on the Internet. According to Webb (2001), "At no time in American history has pornography been so widely accessible to the general public — in full-color, full-motion pictures of every kind of sexual act imaginable (Levels 1, 2, and 3). Instant porn is free of charge and delivered to your home, 24 hours a day, 365 days a year" (p. 90).

For sex addicts who have a modem and a mouse, there is no need to connect in real life. Sexual addiction has already been established as an intimacy disorder. The Internet feeds into this already solitary experience. Solitary — though not in the sense that the person is alone — they are disconnected emotionally in the relationship.

The Internet allows people to literally create and secretly test new personalities before trying them out in the real world. Reinventing oneself is a way to fulfill an unmet need. The loss of a social identity on-line allows one to reconstruct an ideal self in place of a poor self-concept. Those who suffer from low self-esteem, feelings of inadequacy, or frequent disapproval from others are at high risk for addiction to the Internet.

Broken marriages, lost jobs, failing school grades, forgetting to handle business and tend to personal hygiene, or something as simple as remembering to eat are just some of the consequences being reported in media articles as the experience of people who feel they have become addicted to the Internet.

A major phenomenon involving the Internet is the occurrence of on-line affairs. Would you be upset about your spouse having cybersex (spending three to six hours a night on the telephone or computer talking to somebody, flirting, using sexually suggestive language)? If the answer is yes, then they probably would have the same discomfort with your use of the Internet in the same manner. It's not the medium of communication that's relevant here; it's the effect that such a detour can have on your primary relationships.

There have been numerous cases in which people started out on the Internet for the purposes of engaging in casual conversation, but the conversation ended up being highly sexual in nature. In addition, because of the accelerated intimacy that they experience, people became more involved more rapidly than they had intended. People will often share information on-line that they would not ordinarily share in other relationships. In some cases people may be experiencing levels of intimacy and self-disclosure that is unparalleled in their real-life relationships! Needless to say, this can be highly problematic to marriages or relationships. The ease of conversation, combined with the sexual themes that often appear in Internet communication, offer serious competition to sometimes mundane real-life relationships. After all, how can everyday life compete with the intense uninhibited excitement of relationships on-line?

We try to numb our discomfort in a wide variety of ways, with the Internet being the latest. The great debate on whether the Internet can be an addiction is still waging. We believe that anything that consumes you has the potential to be addictive.

RECOVERY

Do we have to wait until our leaders are lost on-line or the next in line (to purchase an X-rated video) before we take action? Does sexual sin need to get to level three, four, and five before people finally become outraged about it? As the people of God, we should be appalled at levels one and two. When we see our brothers and sisters on this path of destruction, bells ought to ring, red flags ought to wave, and alarms should go off. There should be such a sense of urgency created in us that we would do whatever is necessary to help set them free.

So how do we help break the bondage and strongholds of our brothers and sisters? We go to where the problem exists: the mind. While sexual addiction generally manifests itself in our physical realm, it gets its beginning in the mental realm. The sex addict needs to renew his or her mind, which means the healing process of restructuring the way he or she thinks.

In God's Word we find hope, help, and healing for all victims of addiction. Romans 12:1–2 states, "I urge you, brothers [and sisters], in view of God's mercy, to offer your bodies as living sacrifices, holy and pleasing to God — this is your spiritual act of worship. Do not conform any longer to the pattern of this world, but be transformed by the renewing of your mind. Then you will be able to test and approve what God's will is — his good, pleasing and perfect will."

Our belief system and impaired thinking must be changed and renewed. We don't want to be unstable and double-minded (James 1:8). As a man thinks, so goes his action. Ephesians 4:22–24 holds the key to break the addictive system: "You were taught, with regard to your former way of life, to put off your old self, which is being corrupted by its deceitful desires; to be made new in the attitude of your minds; and to put on the new self, created to be like God in true righteousness and holiness."

Maintaining secrecy is part of the old belief system that needs to be put off. The greatest fear of a person who is in bondage to sex is that they will be found out. Ironically, the greatest way to experience relief is to be exposed. We are told in James "to confess your faults one to another . . . that ye may be healed" (James 5:16 KJV). The accuser of the brethren (your enemy, the devil) will always haunt you with the belief that you will be destroyed when the truth is discovered. Those with sexual addictions believe their willpower (which they do not realize has already been lost) will enable them to quit when they are good and ready. The false belief system says, "If I quit now, while nobody knows, I do not have to confess anything." When they are unable to succeed, they are plunged into an abyss of despair. And they have certainly learned *one* quick cure for despair — acting out sexually (converting emotional response to behavior with the absence of logic).

Imagine how difficult that must be! If their greatest fear is that they are going to be found out, then how do they seek help? This is clearly an oxymoron. A crossroads for sex addicts occurs when they wonder, "Is there someone out there who is safe, somewhere I can go to share my shame, guilt, despair, and sin?"

There can be several goals for treatment. The following items are not exhaustive but may serve as a starting point for setting a client's goals. Each of these will need to be tailored for your specific client:

- Surrender to God's process in accordance with the Word for being set free.
- Establish sobriety/abstinence from acting out behaviors.
- Follow a Scripture memory plan for renewing the mind.
- Break through denial in each area of life being affected by this life-dominating sin.
- Understand the nature of the addiction, including cycle, levels, bondage, and deliverance.
- Develop a support system, an accountability plan, and discipleship goals.
- Deal with issues of guilt and shame.
- Grieve losses and establish new life.
- Improve intimacy in family and other relationships.
- Establish appropriate boundaries for any and all former triggers.

Hebrews 12:1 says, "Let us lay aside every weight, and the sin which doth so easily beset us, and let us run with patience the race that is set before us" (KJV). When people are leaving an addictive lifestyle, there are numerous triggers and weights that they need to lay aside. For example, if pornography was a problem, the person may need to monitor all reading materials, especially those with pictures of partially dressed woman (e.g., *Sports Illustrated* swimsuit issue, Victoria's Secret catalogue, numerous women's magazines). Former sex addicts may also need to monitor their exposure to many television programs, movies, and videotapes. A person may decide to only watch programs that are for a general audience or those things that they would be willing to encourage Jesus, an innocent child, or their mother to view with them. "I will be careful to live a blameless life — will you come to me? I will walk in my house with blameless heart. I will set before my eyes no vile thing. The deeds of faithless men I hate; they will not cling to me" (Psalm 101:2–3).

CONCLUSION

Praise the LORD, O my soul, and forget not all his benefits — who for-
gives all your sins and heals all your diseases, who redeems your life from
the pit [destruction, KJV] and crowns you with love and compassion.
(Psalm 103:2–4)

It is important to communicate to those you counsel that no matter how
deep the despair or how devastating the downward spiral, God reaches
down into the depths and delivers. Living in extremes is associated not only
with addiction but with instability as well. Those coming out of sexual
addiction have a difficult time sharing their bondage because the cost seems
too great. People don't relate or try to understand the dilemma they are facing; they are just judgmental: How could you? Why would you? How dare
you? The moment you admit to the slightest indiscretion, you are bom-
barded with questions you still have yet to answer yourself.

Jesus' response to those caught in sin was to admonish them to go and
sin no more. His approach was so different from ours. There was no inqui-
sition, no lecture, no badgering, no clauses or conditions. An encounter
with Christ was life changing. After being in his presence, the person went
away empowered and equipped to confront whatever was in the path of his
recovery. The person was simply instructed to change and not look back.
The process of recovery for process addictions begins with you and your
client being in the presence of Jesus.

REFERENCE RESOURCES

Alcorn, R. C. 1998. Strategies to keep from falling. *Leadership Journal* (winter):
     42.
Amparano. J. 1998. Sex addicts get help. *Arizona Republic,* September 25: 11–12.
Anderson, N. T. 1998. *A way of escape: Freedom from sexual strongholds.*
     Multnomah, Ore.: Harvest House.
Arterburn, S., F. Stoeker, and M. Yorkey. 2000. *Every man's battle: Winning the
     war on sexual temptation one victory at a time.* Colorado Springs: Waterbook
     Press.
Carnes, P. 1983. *Out of the shadows: Understanding sexual addiction.* Minneapolis:
     Compcare Publishers.
_____. 1992. *Don't call it love: Recovery from sexual addiction.* New York: Bantam
     Doubleday Dell.
_____. 1998. Scandal and significance: The problem of being powerful and pow-
     erless. *Professional Counselor* 13: 6.

Dobson, E. G., and T. Dollar. 1995. Restoring a fallen colleague. *Leadership Journal* 92: 106–21.

Lasser, M. R. 1996. *Faithful and true: Sexual integrity in a fallen world.* Grand Rapids: Zondervan.

Moeller, B., ed. 1995. The sex life of America's Christians. *Leadership Journal* (summer): 30–31.

Shelly, E. G. 1992. *Sex and love: Addiction, treatment and recovery.* Westport, Conn.: Greenwood Publishing Group.

Travine, S. 1995. Compulsive sexual behaviors. *Psychiatric Clinics of North America* 18: 155–69.

Veith, G. E. 2001. The pornographic culture. *World Magazine* (April 7): 16.

Webb, G. 2001. Sex and the Internet: A special report. *Yahoo: Internet Life* 7, no. 1: 1–7.

Weiss, D. 1998. *The final freedom: Pioneering sexual addiction recovery.* Fort Worth: Discovery Press.

ADDITIONAL RESOURCES

Sex Addicts Anonymous (SAA)
P.O. Box 70949
Houston, TX 77270
(713) 869-4902
www.sexaa.org

Sexaholics Anonymous
P.O. Box 111910
Nashville, TN 37222-1910
(615) 331-6901
www.sa.org

Sexual Compulsives Anonymous (SCA)
Old Chelsea Station
P.O. Box 1585
New York, NY 10013-0935
1-800-977-HEAL
www.sca-recovery.org

Sex and Love Addicts Anonymous (SLAA)
P.O. Box 119, New Town Branch
Boston, MA 02258
(617) 332-1845
www.slaafws.org

Sexual Recovery Anonymous (SRA)
Planetarium Station, P.O. Box 73
New York, NY 10024
(212) 340-4650
or:
P.O. Box 72044
Burnaby, BC
V5H 4PQ Canada
(604) 290-9382
www.sexualrecovery.org

Codependents of Sexual Addiction (COSA)
P.O. Box 14537
Minneapolis, MN 55414
(763) 537-6904
www.primushost.com/~cosa/

Place of Refuge for Pastors/Church Leaders

Eagle's Nest Retreat Ministries
John Gowins
P.O. Box 437
Ouray, CO 81427
1-800-533-4049
Professional counseling and vacations, at minimal cost, to ministers and their families.

Focus on the Family — Pastoral Ministries Department
H. B. London Jr.
Roger Charman
8605 Explorer Drive
Colorado Springs, CO 80920
(719) 531-3347
Resources, referrals, and face-to-face consultation. Audiotape subscription series called "Pastors to Pastor," regional gatherings, tapes, and booklets, and a weekly fax letter called "The Pastor's Weekly Briefing."

Annette V. Hampton

Chapter 3

Dealing with Addictions through the Twelve Steps with Godly Principles

Annette V. Hampton is a certified biblical counselor with twenty-five years' experience in counseling and has facilitated and co-facilitated numerous therapy and growth groups. She has been Assistant Dean of Students at Bethel College in North Newton, Kansas, and the Director of Student Life at Messiah College. Currently she is the Director of Educational Opportunity Center at the University of Pennsylvania in Philadelphia. She holds a bachelor of arts degree in education from Messiah College and a master of science degree in student personal administration and counseling from Shippensburg University. Annette also has a master of social work degree from the University of Pennsylvania and has taken several doctoral classes.

Hampton is the director of the counseling center at Christian Stronghold Baptist Church in Philadelphia, where she has been a member for the past thirty-six years. She is a biblical counselor instructor, lecturer, and national speaker. She and her husband, Byron, are the parents of three children.

Freedom is a precious commodity that can only be fully appreciated and experienced by those who have been delivered from self-hatred, self-centeredness, self-denial, and self-destruction. Freedom comes in knowing what your responsibilities are in the Lord and in fulfilling his will for your life. Addictions are a bondage that may oppress your mind, body, and emotions and eclipse your ability to imagine a life apart from their grips. Twelve Steps with Godly Principles focuses on the addictive person's dependence and reliance on God through the Holy Spirit not only to deliver them from their addiction but to help them to discover the false thinking (the root of the problem) that provides the fuel for remaining in addictive patterns.

No one in his or her right mind would wish a lifestyle of addiction on their enemy, let alone on themselves. However, according to the National Household Survey on Drug Abuse, in 1999 an estimated 3.6 million Americans (1.6 percent of the total population age 12 and older) were dependent on illicit drugs. An estimated 8.2 million Americans were dependent on alcohol (3.7 percent). Of these, 1.5 million people were dependent on both. Overall, an estimated 10.3 million people were dependent on either alcohol or illicit drugs (4.7 percent).

There are various reasons why people get into drugs. Some are introduced to drugs through social interactions, others by simply experimenting, still others in trying to nullify some pain in their lives. Consequently, many people find themselves trapped. However, there is a solution to the addiction web. The solution is in successfully completing a 12-step spiritual journey, with God as our guide and his Word as our sustainer. God is a God of restoration; he restores humans to themselves, and humans to each other.

The 12-step program originated with Alcoholics Anonymous. The Christ-centered adaptation that I will use throughout this chapter has been taken from *Rapha's 12-Step Program for Overcoming Chemical Dependency* (McGee et al., 1996). The Word of God has the true principles and precepts we all must live by to be delivered from anything that so easily besets us. Only the Word of God has the power to deliver and reframe us to prevent us from going back to a lifestyle of such pain and hardship. In this chapter, I will give a brief overview of each step. As we examine each step, we will consider how each movement can catapult a person into a life free from addiction. What follows is written in a style oriented primarily toward people who are themselves dealing with addiction. However, occasionally references will be made to the counselor or helper.

STEP ONE

We admit that by ourselves we are powerless over additive substances — that our lives have become unmanageable.

> For I know that nothing good dwells in me, that is, in my flesh; for the wishing is present in me, but the doing of the good is not. (Romans 7:18 NASB)*

---

*All Scripture quotations in this chapter are from the *New American Standard Bible* (NASB) unless otherwise indicated.

The two keys words in step one are *powerless* and *unmanageable*. The addicted person must begin to understand his or her true condition in order to begin to recover. What is crucial in this step is our ability to understand that God through his Word implores us to understand the human heart. Romans 7:18 tells us that nothing good dwells in this flesh apart from God. We may desire to be obedient and to perform the perfect will of God, but we fall short in our own strength. So the first lesson we learn is not to depend on ourselves to accomplish the excellent will of God for our lives. Evidence of our lack of ability to fulfill our desired behavior is the life that is unmanageable. We all must come to that fork in the road in our lives where we recognize that apart from Christ we are powerless to overcome anything in this life.

In examining the case of the Prodigal Son, the Bible says, "and when he came to himself" he began to understand his condition (Luke 15:11–32). The Prodigal Son remembered that prior to his riotous living, his servants lived better than he was currently living. He understood that he had no power. Eating the same food that the swine ate helped him to understand that his life had become unmanageable. He also understood that if he remained in that condition, he would die. The solution was for him to repent and return home. The Prodigal Son left his denial the moment he was able to see his true condition.

The addicted person must look at his condition truthfully in order to begin to work towards recovery. This is not an easy process because the chemicals in the addictive person's body have so effected the central nervous system that it becomes hard for the mind to identify what is truth and what is a lie. After having a history of distorting the truth because of drugs that gave false highs or false lows, discerning the truth becomes difficult.

In short, Step 1 helps us to see our true condition apart from God. Jeremiah 17:9 states, "The heart is more deceitful than all else and is desperately sick; who can understand it?" We have to see our lives as unmanageable and understand the powerless nature of our inner selves to effectively change our condition.

STEP TWO

We come to believe that God, through Jesus Christ, can restore us to sanity.

> For it is God who is at work in you, both to will and to work for His good pleasure. (Philippians 2:13)

In step two, hope invades the scene through Jesus Christ. One must identify Jesus Christ as the only true God who can restore all humankind to sanity. In the traditional AA program, step two asks people to identify a power greater than themselves to restore them to sanity. It is left up to the individual to identify the power source. If the individual has never been introduced to Jesus Christ and does not understand that the Living Word has all power at his disposal, he or she may search for a lifetime and never discover a power greater than him- or herself. As the songwriter says, "I give you Jesus." We must introduce each person to the true and living God. Remember that the void in one's life triggers one's self-destructive patterns of addiction, and only God through Jesus Christ can fill that God vacuum. The Bible tells us that the only way to the Father is through Jesus Christ. Jesus Christ is the way, the truth, and the life. No one comes to the Father but through him.

The counselor must understand how Jesus Christ relates to the addicted person. People who are addicted are looking for peace in their lives. Jesus is the Prince of Peace. People who are addicted are looking to find rest and comfort from a life of turmoil. Jesus is the Comforter who has come to deliver all from the anguish of life. Life for the addicted person can be lonely. Such a person should be directed to have a real encounter with Emmanuel ("God with us"). Everything that people think they need is found in God, because God is! John 3:16–18 tells us that Christ desires a relationship with all who call themselves Christians — a lifelong relationship.

The other work in this step is to separate what the Scriptures say God is from notions of God that originate out of experience with parents or other authoritarian relationships. Those relationships can quite possibly distort one's view of God. An example of this would be the person who believes God is harsh because his parents were very harsh in their dealings with him. To accept a loving God may be easy for this person because he is longing to feel accepted, or he may not want to accept God because he cannot believe that God will love him. Each person must take time to evaluate what part of God's character is hard to accept and then review past relationships that may have produced this belief system about God. We may understand that Jesus Christ can restore us to sanity, but until we can trust him to do so, knowing the cure is fruitless.

STEP THREE

We make a decision to turn our lives over to God through Jesus Christ.

> I urge you therefore, brethren, by the mercies of God, to present your bodies a living and holy sacrifice, acceptable to God, which is your spiritual service of worship. (Romans 12:1)

It is not good enough merely to know that Jesus Christ is a power greater than ourselves; we must accept him as our Savior and the Lord of our lives. We must understand the concept of turning our lives over to God, so he can do with our lives what he chooses. Jesus Christ is our Savior. This underscores God's divine plan for our lives. Christ's death on the cross enables us to present our imperfect, sinful selves to God, just as we are, in need of a Savior. Through repentance we are able to erase the unworthiness of our souls, our worst selves, and exchange it for forgiveness and a promise of a new beginning.

Why must Christ be in charge of our lives? Because he is like the potter and we are like the clay. He created us for a purpose, and outside of him we will never know the reason for our existence on this earth. It makes sense that to give control of our lives to the only one who knows our exact purpose leads to true peace. What a tragedy it is for humans to use and seek other substances to fill the void that can only be filled by the Creator who created it to draw us to him, Jesus Christ the Son of the living God.

STEP FOUR

We make a searching and fearless moral inventory of ourselves.

> Let us examine and probe our ways, and let us return to the LORD. (Lamentations 3:40)

This is one of the most powerful steps because it teaches us to fearlessly look at ourselves and to correct areas in our lives that do not match up to the principles of God. So often people find themselves repeating negative patterns in their lives. Those negative patterns may be the source of their frustrations, but they are not sure how to escape and not reenter the revolving addiction door. Proverbs 28:13 states, "He who conceals his transgressions will not prosper, but he who confesses and forsakes them will find compassion." What we must do is look at ourselves honestly so we can discover those areas in our lives that need to be made whole.

On the other hand, there are things in our lives we do well. We need to acknowledge those areas in our lives and praise God for those areas of victory that we so often overlook. We take areas of victory for granted; as a result, we do not evaluate ourselves with a sense of balance. The things we do well can be a blessing for other people.

Lamentations 3:40 clearly states that if we examine and probe our ways, there will be a need for us to return to the Lord. When we stand beside God and his righteousness, there will always be a need for us to change some area in our lives. There will always be an area in our lives where we do not meet God's standard. We discover those areas through prayer, devotion, and meditation on his word.

In step four we examine our relationships with God and others that significantly influence who and what we are today in relating to one another. People are afraid to look at their past for fear of dragging up something they think they cannot handle. When trying to understand patterns of behavior as they relate to the past, people often say, "Let sleeping dogs lie" or "Let the past stay in the past." But if we really begin to search and make a moral inventory of ourselves, we must approach our self-examination fearlessly and with excitement about discovering healthy ways of truthfully investigating ourselves and improving where we need to improve.

Specifically, we ask about issues of our character that drive who we are and how we relate to God and others. We need to honestly see ourselves for who we are so we can identify those areas in our lives where Satan gets a foothold and encourages negative behavior. The following is a list of character traits that may govern and rule our lives:

☐ Anger	☐ Lying	☐ Impulsiveness	☐ Intolerance
☐ Forgiveness	☐ Selfishnessness	☐ Patience	☐ Tolerance
☐ Resentment	☐ Self-centeredness	☐ Pride	☐ Jealousy
☐ Bitterness	☐ Gratitude	☐ Humility	☐ Acceptance
☐ Honesty	☐ Ingratitude	☐ Fear	☐ Criticalness
☐ Dishonesty	☐ Impatience	☐ Trustfulness	☐ Love
☐ Peacefulness	☐ Laziness	☐ Generosity	☐ Stinginess

As we carefully examine ourselves concerning these characteristics, we must ask ourselves: Which of these characteristics dominate my life and why? Is it a healthy or unhealthy pattern? What does the Scripture say about these characteristics? Do I need to change? The Bible tells us that God is at work in us "to will and to do of his good pleasure" (Philippians 2:13 KJV).

Step four helps us to unearth those areas in our lives that feed our addictions. These are areas of sin that have gone unattended. Victory comes when character defects are truly identified, flushed out, and replaced with spiritual virtues. Consequently, the fallow ground in our lives is broken, replaced by fresh soil and vibrant seed, and cultivated to produce the character of God in each of us. The result? Each of us experiences God's deliverance. Sin bogs us down and does not allow us the freedom to see ourselves as God sees us, sinners in need of a savior. We are imperfect creatures tied to a lifeline of confession and repentance to bring true peace and satisfaction in our lives.

On the other hand, we can rejoice in those areas that we have given over to God for our good and his glory. We can plainly see how God has carefully guided us through sculpting and refining us into his design. Step four gives us the privilege to look at sin-conquered territory in our lives.

STEP FIVE

We admit to God, to ourselves, and to another human being the exact nature of our wrongs.

> Therefore, confess your sins to one another, and pray for one another, so that you may be healed. (James 5:16)

This step releases us from the grip of secret sins in our lives. Individuals resist this step because of the lack of trust they have in people. Many are quick to point to a time in their life when they trusted someone with something about them, and that person betrayed their confidence. There is wisdom needed in choosing whom you confide in; nevertheless, the Word rings true. It is healthy for us to confess to one another so that we can pray together and begin to experience healing and the true forgiveness of God. There is accountability that comes when we confess our sins to one another. We must learn to walk with each other and encourage one another on the narrow road that leads to life.

This step calls for humility on our part. We must ask ourselves this question: Am I more interested in what people think about me, or am I more interested in my healing? If we are more interested in what people think about us, then we will remain in bondage waiting for others'

approval. If we are more interested in our healing, we will humble ourselves and confess our sin to another: "[If] My people who are called by My
name [will] humble themselves and pray, and seek My face and turn from
their wicked ways, then I will hear from heaven, will forgive their sin, and
will heal their land" (2 Chronicles 7:14). God wants to heal all of us of
our diseases and make us whole. Confessing our sins and exposing ourselves leads to life.

STEP SIX

*We commit ourselves to obedience to God, desiring that he remove patterns
of sin from our lives.*

> Humble yourselves in the presence of the Lord, and He will exalt you.
> (James 4:10)

Step four shows us that we have some weaknesses in our lives that
lead us to sin and destruction. Now that we have identified those areas
in our lives, we crucify and commit those areas to God on a regular basis.
We cannot succeed in this life apart from God. Our very existence
depends on our constant dependence on him for life instruction. In
order not to return to old thinking patterns of destruction, we begin to
rely on God for our direction and submit to his every command. In step
six, I become keenly aware that *life is no longer about me,* but about the
God through whom I will live my life. In 1 Samuel 15:22, the Bible says
that "to obey is better than sacrifice." It is better to be obedient to God's
first command than to suffer the sacrifices of life. In her book *Passion
and Purity* (1984), Elisabeth Elliot asks, "What kind of God is it who
asks everything of us? The same God who . . . 'did not spare his own Son,
but gave him up for us all'; and with this gift how can he fail to lavish
upon us all he has to give? He gives all. He asks all" (p. 38). If we are
going to have a heart for God, we must ask him to fix our hearts to long
for only him.

The addict has listened to the voice of destruction, a power greater than
him- or herself. Identifying and listening to the voice of the Lord is self-
empowering. Obedience is being sensitive to the Spirit's nudging every
moment of the day to perform his perfect will in our lives. Only a God who
loves me would require everything from me. God's standard is total and
immediate obedience. He accepts nothing less.

STEP SEVEN

We humbly ask God to renew our minds so that our sinful patterns can be transformed into patterns of righteousness.

> And do not be conformed to this world, but be transformed by the renewing of your mind, that you may prove what the will of God is, that which is good and acceptable and perfect. (Romans 12:2)

What should be our utmost desire? Simply, to live for God every moment of our lives. The Bible tells us that his ways are not our ways, and his thoughts are not our thoughts. Our daily spiritual battle cry should be, "I want to be more like Jesus and less like me." How can we have more of Jesus and less of me? We line our thinking up with the Word of God. Everywhere that our thinking differs from the Master, we submit to his belief system.

How does one begin to think more like Jesus? We have to expose ungodly thoughts. All negative thinking is ungodly thinking that takes away from who we are in Christ. Proverbs 23:7 states, "As [a man] thinks within himself, so he is." All thinking that exalts others over God is false thinking. All thinking that pleases humans rather than God is faulty thinking. Any kind of thinking that destroys your self-image is faulty thinking. Any kind of thinking that traps you into believing you cannot change to become better than you are is faulty thinking.

STEP EIGHT

We make a list of all people we have harmed, and become willing to make amends to them all.

> And just as you want people to treat you, treat them in the same way. (Luke 6:31)

In this step we are simply going to list the people we have harmed in word, deed, or thought and prepare to make amends. We must always maintain right relationships with everyone. Romans 12:17–19 says, "Never pay back evil for evil to anyone. Respect what is right in the sight of all men. If possible, so far as it depends on you, be at peace with all men. Never take your own revenge, beloved, but leave room for the wrath of God, for it is written, 'VENGEANCE IS MINE, I WILL REPAY,' says the Lord." The issue of forgiveness comes front stage in this step. None of us can be whole if we harbor bitterness and unforgiveness in our lives. Addictions feed on this negative thought pattern.

Unforgiveness is the venom that keeps one trapped in addictions. The unforgiving spirit experiences pain and hurt at a very deep level. Quite often drugs and alcohol serve as an escape from the painful reality of our memories.

In *Making Peace with Your Past* (1992), Tim Sledge encourages the reader to understand how painful memories can lie hidden from conscious thought while draining large quantities of spiritual and emotional energy. It is incumbent on us to get and keep ourselves emotionally healthy. Making peace with our past is a great way to move beyond it. Living in the present gives energy and enthusiasm to meet today's challenges.

This step teaches us to begin to consider letting go of the pain. We have harmed ourselves by rehearsing painful memories and reliving them year after year. The rehearsing of the hurts in our lives has caused us to see others in a negative light. Consequently, we must prepare ourselves to ask for forgiveness, even if others have wronged us. The only person we have control over is oneself. It is healthy for us to let go of the bitterness in our lives. If we wait for others to ask for forgiveness, we may wait a lifetime. However, if we choose to let go of the pain today, we will begin to experience freedom from the bondage of pain in our lives.

STEP NINE

We make direct amends to such people where possible, except when doing so will injure them or others.

> "If therefore you are presenting your offering at the altar, and there remember that your brother has something against you, leave your offering there before the altar, and go your way; first be reconciled to your brother, and then come and present your offering." (Matthew 5:23–24)

In this step we are commanded to do something to mend and restore relationships. Right the wrongs that have created distances between others and us. We serve a God that is interested in reconciliation. Our God reconciles humans to humans, and humans to God. God is all about restoring relationships so that everyone can be about the Father's business. We spend far too much time worrying about what others think about us and far too little time being concerned about what God thinks about us. God calls us to be in right relationship with everyone whenever possible. When we are in peaceable relationships, we are freed up to extend our whole selves to others. If we maintain whole relationships, we will waste very little time on self-absorbed movements, and we will spend major time in ministering to and healing others.

STEP TEN

We continue to take personal inventory, and when we are wrong, promptly admit it.

> Therefore let him who thinks he stands take heed lest he fall. (1 Corinthians 10:12)

Step ten represents a lifestyle of discipline. The goal is to deal with sin the moment it enters our lives, as opposed to letting it reign in our lives. Scripture tells us that sin has no dominion over us. Sin separates us from God and creates a disconnection between him and us.

There should be less and less toleration for sin in our lives. The goal in this step is to become so sensitive to the Holy Spirit that he reveals our sinful areas on a continual basis and we are quick to confess and repent. This is evidence that we have developed a heart for God, a heart now bent on pleasing him.

Oh, to God that we all could experience the fellowship that Enoch experienced with God! It was so sweet that God said that Enoch was a pleasure to him. God translated Enoch to continue the fellowship without any earthly distractions. What a testimony! The beauty of this passage is that God is no respecter of persons, and he offers the same relationship to all of us.

STEP ELEVEN

We seek to grow in our relationship with Jesus Christ through prayer, meditation, and obedience, praying for wisdom and power to carry out his will.

> But if any of you lacks wisdom, let him ask of God, who gives to all men generously and without reproach, and it will be given to him. But let him ask in faith without any doubting, for the one who doubts is like the surf of the sea driven and tossed by the wind. (James 1:5–6)

The communication between us and God must be so connected that we seek his voice for our every direction. We should be paralyzed in time until God speaks. God has been so gracious in providing ample instruction for us to live by. The Word of God is the most powerful book on the face of the earth. The Bible continues to be the best selling book of all time. As Christians, the Bible is the bread of life; we cannot survive without it. Apart from God, we have no direction for life.

As part of a disciplined lifestyle, we learn to go to God for direction and to pray for obedience to follow his every command. If we do not develop the habit of having devotions and praying on a daily basis, we do not have a constant source of change. If we are not changing, we are not growing toward God's direction. The more we learn of God's character and power, the more we relax in our ability to carry out his will. When we constantly hear from God for every direction of our lives, we live securely and peacefully, knowing that the God of the universe has ordered our steps. What a powerful relationship! We cannot live apart from him.

STEP TWELVE

Having had a spiritual awakening, we try to carry the message of Christ's grace and restoration power to others who are chemically dependent, and to practice these principles in all our affairs.

> Brethren, even if a man is caught in any trespass, you who are spiritual, restore such a one in a spirit of gentleness; each one looking to yourself, lest you too be tempted. (Galatians 6:1)

Now that you have been and are being delivered, it is your obligation to restore others with gentleness and meekness. When someone gets excited about his deliverance from a substance and understands the impact his deliverance has had on everyone who surrounds him, he is now compelled to share his testimony with others.

There are people who are waiting for you to share your deliverance with them. You hold the key for promise in their lives. You hold the pathway for deliverance for them. God has delivered us so that we in turn can deliver other people. The deliverance chain becomes extended as we offer hope for change in the lives of others.

If you have never experienced the power of being addicted to drugs, alcohol, or anything else, you have been spared one of the most dehumanizing, deteriorating events of a lifetime. No one in their right mind would want to be addicted to a substance that will overpower their fortitude, rule their life, lead to disappointing family and friends, cause them to lose everything, and ultimately hurtle them into being unproductive citizens in this society. However, those who have been delivered can model before humankind that the God of this universe loves us so much that he restores the life of the addicted person through the power of his Word.

CONCLUSION

The Twelve Steps with Godly Principles (see the 12-Step Action Chart below for a summary) have been developed to help the addicted person understand that there is power to deliver them. God's principles can and will deliver us from any addiction. We must be willing to study, love, and live his Word. While the original 12-step programs have assisted others in overcoming their addictions, understanding God's principles for growth and change will deliver people from the *root causes* of the addiction, thus assuring that they are not just exchanging one addiction for another acceptable addiction, but rather freeing themselves totally. God has now, through the power of his Word, become our deliverer.

12-STEP ACTION CHART

Step	Spiritual Discipline	Specific Activity	Scripture
Step 1	Confession	Acknowledging true condition	Romans 7:8
Step 2	Self-examination	Examine beliefs about God	Psalm 139
Step 3	Conversion	Trusting Christ	Romans 12:1
Step 4	Self-examination	Releasing denial	Proverbs 28:73 Luke 15:11–24
Step 5	Confession	Exposing self	James 5:16
Step 6	Obedience	Building faith in God	1 Samuel 15:22 James 4:10
Step 7	Repentance	Renewing the mind by removing false beliefs	Romans 12:2 1 John 1:9
Step 8	Honesty	Identifying broken relationships	Luke 6:31 Romans 12:17–19
Step 9	Forgiveness	Accepting and asking for forgiveness	Matthew 5:23–29
Step 10	Rededication	Walking in the Spirit	1 Corinthians 10:12
Step 11	Sanctification	Spiritual development	Psalm 119:11 James 1:5–6
Step 12	Witnessing	Restore others and share your testimony	Galatians 6:1 Matthew 28:19–20

REFERENCES AND RESOURCES

Elliot, E. 1984. *Passion and purity.* Old Tappan, N.J.: Power Books/Fleming H. Revell.

McGee, R. S., P. Springer, and S. Joiner. 1996. *Rapha's 12-step program for overcoming chemical dependency,* 2d edition. Houston and Dallas: Rapha Publishing/Word, Inc.

Sledge, T. 1992. *Making peace with your past: Help for adult children of dysfunctional families.* Nashville: Life Way Press.

Springle, P. 1990. *Codependency,* 2d edition. Edited by Susan Joiner. Houston and Dallas: Rapha Publishing/Word, Inc.

Summary of Findings from the 1999 National Household Survey on Drug Abuse, Department of Health and Human Services, Substance Abuse and Mental Health Services Administration. On-line: *http://www.samhsa.gov/oas/NHSDA/1999/Highlights.htm.*

Alfred Young Jr.

Chapter 4

Substance Abuse: A Programmatic Approach and Its Blessings

Alfred Young Jr. is a graduate of Union Baptist Seminary in New Orleans, Louisiana, and is founder and senior pastor of the rapidly growing Faith Bible Church of Covington, Louisiana. He is also president and founder of many organizations: Heart to Heart Ministries, which teaches and trains families through radio, workshops, and seminars; Upward Community Services, a nonprofit, multipurpose Christian community development organization that includes a child day-care center empowering welfare mothers and the working poor, a drug and alcohol ministry, and an eight-week summer youth camp; and Urban Impact, a service ministry to youth in the inner-city projects of New Orleans, Louisiana. Pastor Young is a board member of the Children's Advocacy Center and the Youth Service Bureau in Covington, Louisiana; Church Growth Unlimited in Dallas, Texas; and the St. Tammy Parish Commission on Families. He has been the recipient of the Mayor's Service Award (City of Covington, 1995), the Angel Award finalist (Blue Cross-Blue Shield, 1998), and the Alliance for Good Government Civic Award (1999).

Young is a national conference, seminar, and workshop speaker. He is married to Glen Marie, and they have six children.

I magine a new Black church, planted in the heart of the ghetto in a city where the median income for its members is $12,000. The community that the church serves is infested with drug and alcohol abuse, drug dealing, teenage pregnancy, chronic unemployment, excessive high school dropouts, warring street gangs, and so forth.

Nine out of ten children from this twenty-block square and outlying neighborhoods repeat first grade. Housing is a fallback to the 1940s — primarily single-wall shotgun houses without insulation, air-conditioning, electrical upgrades, and green spaces. Bars outnumber churches, crack houses are the offices for the main industry within twenty miles, and nighttime street activity eclipses daytime activity.

The jail is being expanded and judgeships increased. Girls and women are hooked and provide carte blanche sexual services for $3 to $10. Men rotate from the lots, corners, and alleys to the courts, jails, and cemeteries. Most of the boys on all the Little League teams will have a criminal record and jail time by age 20.

The community is extremely limited in its resources, and so is the new church. So what? you say. Sounds like every day in lots of urban communities. Where's the blessing from the topic? How can it help me and my church, class, group, career, or work? The blessing is biblical substance abuse counseling, and if you want to know the how, what, why, who, keep reading as I share the story of the transformation of one church and community from the devastation of substance abuse and show how to do it through biblical counseling.

COMMUNITY CHANGES

Let's look at this same community eight years later. Habitat houses are being moved into and worked on by former crack addicts who are volunteering to help others or doing "sweat equity" for their own homes. *Open* drug dealing and street gangs are nonexistent. The city is constructing sidewalks, and youth are playing in the two parks without harassment or fear from drug users and dealers.

The jail continues to expand, but most of the prisoners are federal detainees from other communities. There are two "drug court" judges who work hand in hand with faith-based organizations who are effecting alcohol and drug rehabilitation. There are only two bars in operation, and they have a 3:00 A.M. curfew. For the first time in years, the majority of the teenagers are graduating from high school. First graders in our community are surpassing their peers because the curriculum has already been presented to them in two of the church-sponsored day-care centers.

Employment is on the rise, crime is declining, families are restored, and many addicts have been clean for five years or more.

CHURCH CHANGES

The church has a full-time paid staff of fourteen as well as part-time staff, and it employs more youth during the summer than anyone in the county. There is a brand-new administrative building with six offices, a conference room, kitchen, reception area, rest rooms, and copy and storage room, all nicely appointed.

A new eighteen-bed alcohol and drug facility is nearing completion, and there are plans under way for another one. There is a gymnasium with tutoring, after-school programs, a day-care center that only charges $25 per week to lower income families, an eight-week summer camp for more than 300 kids, and a host of ministries, two of which are biblical counseling training and lay counseling. The elders, deacons, and ministry leaders of this church are primarily former addicts themselves. How did this happen? All of this change and transformation in the community and church, I believe, can be credited to Bible-based substance abuse counseling.

The impetus for this transformation is Philippians 4:13: "I can do all things through Him [Christ] who strengthens me" (NASB). This verse drives and empowers all that we do. For continual confirmation, we call the substance abuse ministry the "4:13 Ministry." The leadership of the ministry has initiated the development of other drug and alcohol ministries. One of these is located in our city and has more than 150 men and women that are housed, fed, transported, taught, and assisted in every way. In the history of the 4:13 Ministry, we have only had four participants relapse after completing our one-year program. In addition, many of those that did not even complete the program have transformed their lives.

We aspire to use the principles found in the Word of God in designing our program model, since it is our belief that the Bible has all that we need for overcoming life's problems, obstacles, and weaknesses. Philippians 4:13 clearly provides hope for all situations, including destructive addictions and patterns of substance abuse.

INITIAL RESEARCH ON THE PROBLEM

With the extremely high incidence of drug use and its impact on our community, I initially approached the Louisiana Office of Health and Hospitals. My hope was that they could provide resources and assistance to help us stem the tide and assist families. Under their authority and efforts, the director for our region had a number of clinics, support groups, treatment centers, and drug counselors. He was very active in recruiting, marketing, and facilitating state assistance for the drug and alcohol epidemic. There seemed to be no lack of effort or shortage of funding in state programs.

Through interviews with the director, clinic visits, client interactions, and other data-related research, I reached the following conclusions regarding general substance abuse approaches:

- In spite of massive funding, counseling, and facilities, the recidivism rate tends to be 92 percent.
- Clients are usually predominately White, with very few Blacks participating.
- Of the few African American clients that were being treated, less than 10 percent of those were males.
- The counseling models that were being used offered immediate assistance but had little to provide for permanent change and transformation.
- Substance abuse counseling paradigms do not begin with a spiritual emphasis as the core of the problem. Spiritual issues that involved Jesus Christ were not even addressed.
- Behavior modification seemed to be the core approach, with self-created and self-sustained spirituality as the impetus for this modification.

The state director and I agreed that based on the research data and results, a different counseling module and approach was needed to make an impact on substance abuse in our community. We had hosted and completed all of the biblical counseling courses offered through Dr. Willie Richardson and Christian Research and Development. Biblical marital, financial, and family counseling were a great part of our ministry. After a season of prayer and some crises concerning addicted husbands of members of our church, the Lord burdened my heart with Philippians 4:13. He challenged me to prove that the Bible would work on *this* brand of life-dominating sin.

My first step was to meet with three men who were addicts and recruit them to give us an opportunity to help them. Assessment was the easiest part, because on the surface, all of the problems of weight loss, homelessness, stealing, and so forth related to substance abuse were evident.

OUR APPROACH TO THE PROBLEM OF SUBSTANCE ABUSE

Initially, here is what was done:

- A nightly support group was formed, a contract built around Philippians 4:13 was signed, and a commitment was made to learn and live the Bible as the handbook for recovery.
- No meetings were canceled for any reason, including birthdays, Christmas, and other holidays.
- Nightly Bible studies were held that approached addiction as a sin problem along with serious accountability for time, money, and relationships.
- We established a framework for resolving conflicts, addressing concerns, and solving problems. We would not concentrate on what was fair, but rather on what was biblical.
- Each session would open and close with prayer. Men agreed to pray with and for each other during the day.

The theoretical approach was a paradigm that drug addiction was the result of a spiritual problem; the answer, Jesus Christ. If people accepted Christ, applied the Word of God, and allowed the Holy Spirit to control their decisions and day-to-day choices, they would experience not just rehabilitation but re-creation and recovery. In other words, concrete biblical change.

Our assessment at the end of the first year showed us that we were on the right track as evidenced by our first graduate, who had 390 days clean time. Upon investigating him, versus the others who dropped out of the program, we saw a constant theme. Those who were living in crack houses dropped out fairly quickly. Those who established reasonable amounts of clean time lived in stable homes. The difference between him and all others was that he had a stable home that was spiritually supportive of our methods and principles.

From this research we concluded the following:

- The biblical counseling model was working.
- Recovery was very problematic if you lived on the street or in a crack house.
- A living environment that was clean, spiritual, safe, and structured facilitated recovery.

A decision was therefore made to expand the substance abuse ministry to a one-year residency program, and we began looking for a house.

A Christian brother who heard about what we were attempting to do purchased a house for clients to live in for our use. The house at a maximum was in less-than-desirable condition. It cost $7,000.00. We named the house "Bart's House" after a 13-year-old boy who came to us begging for help for his dad.

Church members pitched in, feeding and transporting our initial group of residency clients. The daily intake was Bible, Bible, Bible. The daily format was as follows:

6:00 — 6:30 Personal Hygiene
6:30 — 7:00 Personal Devotions
7:00 — 8:00 Breakfast
8:00 — 10:00 Class
10:00 — 10:30 Break
10:30 — 12:00 Class
12:00 — 1:00 Lunch
1:00 — 4:00 Sweat Equity
4:00 — 7:00 Personal Time
7:00 — 8:30 Support Group
8:30 — 10:00
10:00 — Lights Out

The weekend schedule was modified to allow a day of rest and family visitation on Saturdays. Sundays were for worship most of the day. The evening group was held even on weekends.

During the first year the only book used was the Bible. At the end of that year, seven men graduated and reestablished their lives. One of those men had been the town drunk. He was 34 years old and the father of two daughters. He spent his days sitting on a milk crate playing dominoes and hustling wine at the corner store. In his own words he told how his daughters came to the store one day with some other kids who were buying candy. One of the girls asked him for a quarter. He did not have it. His daughters left the store behind the other kids, crying and begging them for a piece of candy. He felt ashamed and useless.

That evening he came into our program drunk and cursed everybody out, including me. However, the next day he accepted Christ, submitted totally to what was being taught, and became a new man. He was never late for any of the sessions, became a leader and teacher of the group, got his GED diploma, and became involved as a father in his daughters' lives.

His life's dream was to get a commercial driver's license and drive a truck. He got his license and secured a job driving a cement truck. From there he branched out, enrolled in college, bought his first car and a home for his daughters and himself. In the church, he worked his way up to Director of Christian Education, Worship Leader, and Director of Men's Ministries. What was the reference book? You got it — the Bible.

OUR ASSESSMENT OF OUR FIRST YEAR

Based on the evaluation at the end of the first year, the following problems were apparent:

- In addition to Bible study, we needed life skills training.
- Clients who went out for jobs lacked the interpersonal and attitudinal skills for interviews, promotion, and so forth.
- As a result of the client's addiction, their families, especially wives and children, needed counseling as well.
- There was a great need to help female addicts.

Keep in mind that our church is in the heart of the drug zone and that anyone who wanted to could get drugs next door at the corner store. Also, the house where they lived was only a half-block away. Our clients saw the dealers daily; we had no fences up, no locked doors, no guards. Part of the treatment approach was to work their environment from the inside out and not the outside in (2 Corinthians 5:17; Philippians 4:13).

In response to the deficiencies in the program during the first year, we began to gather materials and focus entirely on substance abuse as being, at its core, a spiritual problem. Coordination was made with the local school board to implement an ongoing GED program. Another community group agreed to come in and do literacy training. A nonprofit outreach organization was established called Upward Community Services. This became the vehicle for volunteer recruitment and financial support.

OUR APPROACH IN THE THIRD YEAR

In our third year, a more comprehensive holistic program was started, but it also was based on biblical principles. For example, we did not allow anyone to say of themselves, "Once an addict, always an addict." The Bible says we are born again (John 3) and that in Christ we are a new creation (2 Corinthians 5:17).

The life of Joseph was taught to show them how God can bring us from a pit to prominence. The life of Job was taught to emphasize that life isn't fair, but God is just. We emphasized character versus reputation by using Genesis 37–39 and by asking: "Who are you when no one is looking?" Everyone was trained in evangelism using the "map" of the Roman Road. From the life of Christ in the Gospels, we highlighted selfless living and sacrificial service.

As people approached us for help, they were told, "If all you want is to get off drugs, go somewhere else. If what you want is to get a new life, here is all the work and study that has to be done." They would be referred to people in the community with two or more years of clean time who were living productive lives. A life skills training class was established. In this class, professionals came in to assess our clients' aptitudes, temperaments, and personalities and to help them formulate a plan of advancement. Occupational speakers were brought in to give them exposure and opportunity to what they could do, how to do it, and what skills would be required for various positions. A finance class was implemented using a combination of Larry Burkett and Crown Ministries materials. John Maxwell's "Attitude Determines Altitude" was taught along with Dawson Trotman's "Born to Reproduce." (A list of helpful counseling reference tools can be found at the end of this chapter.) On a weekly basis, family and premarital counseling was implemented. (The primary sources for this are listed at the end of the chapter.)

EXPANSION OF THE PROGRAM

A house across the street from the men's house was rented to expand the program to include women. The house was appropriately named "Gloria's House" in honor of our first female graduate. This graduate was a 46-year-old grandmother addicted to crack. While at her daughter's house begging for money, the television commercial came on showing an egg and the egg frying. The narrator said, "This is your brain on drugs." Her 8-year-old granddaughter said to her, "Ma-Ma, that's you, isn't it." She came in that very day. She is now married, has been clean more than five years, and is working as a nursing assistant. She married one of our male graduates who has helped two of his brothers come into the program. One of his brothers is now the leader of our armor bearer's ministry.

The women particularly needed counseling related to guilt over what they had done to support their habit. There were two major mistakes made with the women:

- They needed a full-time counselor to listen and minister to their needs.
- We comingled them in class with the men, and both groups began to build relationships with each other rather than Christ. Unfortunately, this competed with recovery and focused them on a relationship with others that they at that time were in no way ready for.

THE PROGRAM AND ITS PHASES

The following is an outline of our program and treatment schedule:

- Initial interview
- Intake form (included)
- Intensive ninety days

First Phase

During the first ninety days, clients are limited in phone calls or contacts.

After two weeks in the program, they may place calls.

In the first month, no visitations are allowed and they are confined to the houses and church facility.

The client may not work outside jobs, go on any leaves, or possess any money. They must complete the ninety days, do 300 hours of classes, have a good attitude, complete all written assignments, and connect with a lay counselor before they will be permitted to work and before weekend privileges are granted.

Second Phase

After ninety days they *may* be eligible for employment. During the next ninety days, all monies earned go to pay past due and current upkeep (room and board is $200 per month). They must attend nightly group sessions, spend three hours a week with their counselor, complete all written assignments, and do twenty hours a month in the classroom.

Legal problems and criminal charges are identified and addressed. The courts and district attorney are involved and are asked to help.

Third Phase

During this next ninety-day phase, clients are again evaluated and begin the process of budgeting and directing monies. They are given leadership and mentoring assignments of other clients. Marital and family counseling intensifies, along with extended passes and privileges. In this phase they must submit a ten-year vision for their lives and a detailed three-year plan. Their lay counselor works with them to identify problems and strengthen long-term attitudinal weaknesses. Lifetime commitments to worship, discipleship, Christian service, and Bible study are made. They must also submit a detailed lifestyle plan of their first year after graduation. This plan must be referenced and justified in light of Scripture.

Fourth Phase

The final ninety days are spent with clients handling all of their own money and managing their time, passes, and visitations. Opportunities are provided them to teach classes, lead recruitment efforts, do interviews and assessments, and serve on the discipline committee. They are encouraged to take "Self Counseling" by Dr. Willie Richardson. Most of them make another one-year commitment to attend the nightly group and give back to the program by assisting new clients. At the conclusion of 365 days, they are given a large plaque at a graduation ceremony in the church with family and friends in attendance.

Again, the recidivism rate is very low. The primary reason for this is that biblical counseling seeks and provides solutions to the problems and behavior that people have. It is solution focused. Most other counseling is therapy focused. The differing end results are practical solutions or permanent therapy.

Summary

The first client that graduated from this program is now the full-time director of the substance abuse ministry. He is a very conscientious father and a discipler of men, and he is considering a run for the city council. Many of the families in the church are relatives of those who enrolled in the program. Businesses, nonprofits, foundations, and individuals who have observed the program support it and our church in many ways. For instance, the funding for the classrooms, gymnasiums, materials, summer camp, day care, and land acquisition was provided by people outside the church. The administration building and two lots behind it were built and donated to us by one of the volunteers who counsels in the program. The building was furnished and all utilities, including phones, provided by a local business that sends its employees to us for counseling. This business also pays for a full-time secretary and a receptionist. The same brother who built the administration building is now donating the eighteen-bed residential facility. He and his family have been blessed by the counseling.

Another businessman, who was formerly an alcoholic, purchased two school buses and a van for transportation. Through a foundation that he established, more than forty people are paid up to $5.00 per hour plus books and tuition to go to a local vocational-technical school and learn a trade.

People in the program do all of the maintenance and most of the repairs to the church and ministry facilities. We have learned that all the church needs in order to do ministry and reach its community is in the streets and crack houses.

Other churches in our community and around the country visit with us to study and implement what God has done here. Two African delegations of representatives from countries with similar problems have also visited and studied the programs. After reviewing our initial houses and community, they were convinced that the programs and principles are transferable to anyone.

In short, Biblical Substance Abuse Counseling has been a great blessing to our church and our community.

Reference Resources

God has used Dr. Willie Richardson of Christian Stronghold Baptist Church in Philadelphia as our mentor in counseling, discipleship, and family ministry. Dr. Jay Adams's books and materials have been our basic resource tools. They have proven themselves to be very effective for problems at any level.

COUNSELING RESOURCES

Adams, J. E. 1976. *Christ and your problems.* Grand Rapids: Baker Book House.

Hyles, J. 1962. *Let's go soul winning.* Murfreesboro, Tenn.: Sword of the Lord Foundation.

McGee, R. S., and J. W. McCleskey. 1994. *A Christ-centered 12-step process.* Nashville: LifeWay Press.

Richardson, W. *Making Jesus King.* Men's Discipleship Ministry, Disciple's Workbook. Philadelphia: Christian Research and Development.

RESOURCES FOR FAMILY AND PREMARITAL COUNSELING

Adams, J. E. 1989. *Christian living in the home.* Phillipsburg, N.J.: Presbyterian and Reformed Publishing.

Eyrick, H. A. 1991. *Three to get ready: Premarital counseling manual.* Grand Rapids: Baker Book House.

Richardson, W. 1981. *Communication, love, finances.* Book 1, Marriage Improvement Series. Philadelphia: Christian Research and Development.

_____. 1980. *Pre-marital counseling couples packet.* Philadelphia: Christian Research and Development.

Young, A. Biblical principles of forgiveness and reconciliation. Unpublished manuscript. Faith Bible Church, 19592 Garland Street, Covington, LA 70433.

Part 2

Confronting Family Issues

Kenneth Staley and Sheila Staley

Chapter 5

Domestic Abuse

Dr. Kenneth Staley is an associate pastor of Christian Stronghold Baptist Church, Philadelphia, Pennsylvania. He is a graduate of Villanova University and Miller Theological Seminary and has pursued advanced studies at Westminister Theological Seminary and Penn State University. In addition, he has completed graduate studies with the American Association of Marriage and Family Therapy. Dr. Staley and his wife, Sheila, are the parents of three children.

Sheila Staley is a graduate of Rosemont College and of Antioch College, where she received a masters degree in secondary guidance and counseling. She is a clinical member of the American Association of Marriage and Family Therapy. She is the author of four publications, *Victorious Living as a Single-Parent; Self-Counseling Workbook for Single Parents;* "Single Female Parenting: A Ministry Perspective," in *The Black Family: Past, Present and Future;* and "Bridging the Gap" in *Women to Women.*

D omestic abuse is one of the least addressed issues affecting the Christian family today. To the law enforcement authorities and the social service providers, it appears to be a taboo subject from the pulpit to the pew. To many outside the church community, it seems as if the church and its families are untouched by this problem. Statistics, however, tell a different story.

As the number of reported incidents of domestic abuse increases nationally, so has the percentage of individuals in our congregations directly affected by domestic abuse. This is a natural correlation since, in keeping with the ministry of reconciliation, the church is to be a healing station for sin-sick, broken people.

The concern of pastors and Christian counselors is how to integrate prevention strategies within existing ministries to families as well as how to provide effective counseling intervention to those families affected by domestic abuse without neglecting the teaching of the Bible as it relates to the sanctity of marriage and family life. In our experience, the fear of rejection, shame, and isolation are recurring issues associated with the abused spouse and the abuser. Regardless of the reason for this pattern of thinking, these issues have allowed many an abuser and abused spouse to develop masks and walls to perpetuate a facade of normalcy within the home to outsiders.

The goal of this chapter is to address many of these concerns. The focus will be on domestic abuse between spouses. We will attempt to provide insight into the nature of domestic abuse, its violation of God's plan for marriage, and a biblical response for pastors and counselors.

THE PROBLEM OF DOMESTIC ABUSE

Domestic abuse is not confined to any one religious, ethnic, economic, or educational background. Age, physical abilities, and lifestyle are not determinants. Women are the most frequent victims of domestic abuse, but elder and child abuse are also common. Men of the family are commonly the abusers.

Consider the following statistics.

- More than 50% of all women will experience violence from intimate partners. (National Coalition Against Domestic Violence, 1992)
- 30% of women murdered in the United States are murdered by their husbands, ex-husbands, or boyfriends. (Bureau of Justice Statistics National Crime Victimization Survey, August 1995)
- 22 to 35% of women who seek treatment from emergency rooms are there with injuries related to on-going abuse. (*Journal of the American Medical Association,* 1990)
- Up to 50% of all homeless women and children in the United States are escaping domestic abuse. (Elizabeth Schneider, *Legal Reform Efforts for Battered Women,* 1990)
- Approximately one out of every 25 elderly people is victimized annually. (Candare Heisler, *Journal of Elder Abuse and Neglect,* 1991)

- One out of every four gay couples (24%) experiences domestic violence in their relationship. This represents approximately the same rate as heterosexual couples. (*Family Violence Prevention Trend,* 1996)

The term *battering* is often used to describe the activity associated with domestic abuse. Battering is defined as "a pattern of behavior used to establish power and control over another person through fear and intimidation, often including the threat or use of violence." Battering happens when one person believes they are entitled to control another. Assault, battering, and domestic violence are crimes (National Coalition Against Domestic Violence, 2000).

Four categories are included in the definition of battering:

- **Physical abuse**. Physical abuse is the most recognized. It includes pushing, hitting, beating, and inflicting injury with weapons. It usually begins with what is excused as trivial contacts, which escalate to more serious attacks. These attacks can result in homicide or suicide.
- **Psychological abuse**. Psychological abuse is more than verbal disagreements between family members. Psychological abuse involves the systematic destruction of a person's self-worth through harassment, threats, and deprivation of food and sleep.
- **Sexual abuse**. Sexual abuse in a marriage is marital rape. When an older family member sexually abuses a child/children or teenager(s), it is considered incest.
- **Destruction of property or pets**. Destruction of property or pets demonstrates another form of abusive behavior. The destruction of property is often communicating the message, "This time the property; next time, it may be you."

Too often battering is an activity selected to deal with the stress that has mounted from unresolved problems. These problems may find their origin in economic pressures, work-related stresses, lack of housing, dysfunctional intimate relationships, and family pressures. Battering is a learned behavior. Many abusers have learned in their families of origin that violence is the most effective way to resolve problems. Society has aided in strengthening this method of problem solving through messages from various sources.

Violence is not an outgrowth of the relationship between the abuser and the abused. It is an indication of a lack of tools to deal with conflict and stress. Therefore, for example, if the abuser leaves the spouse and remarries, the abuse will likely continue in the new relationship because the abuser has not developed the tools to deal with the frustrations.

Conflict and stress, over time, build up like a pressure cooker until the pressure becomes unbearable and there is an explosion. The explosion takes the form of abuse. Afterward, the abuser repents and promises "never again" to abuse. The "honeymoon" phase of the relationship has begun. However, in some abusive relationships, the abuser never recognizes or admits to anyone, himself included, that the abuse has taken place. As a result, there is no "honeymoon" phase. In either situation, however, there is a calm period following the violent incident. In time the conflict and stress build up again. The individual will resort to violent behavior when the pressure of unresolved conflict becomes too great. These events that happen in a violent relationship between men and women have been called the "battering cycle" or "cycle of violence" illustrated in the following diagram (based on Rouse, 1984).

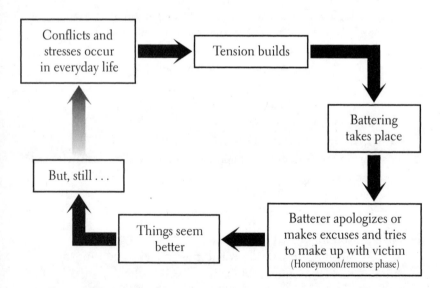

In a marital relationship, the man is usually the perpetrator of domestic abuse. Research, however, does indicate that wives also batter. In those cases, the abuse by wives against their husbands is usually a response to violence by the husband. Overall, men, more than women, practice more dangerous and injurious forms of domestic abuse such as using their fists, knives, and guns.

A man who batters will have one or more of these characteristics:

- Has low tolerance for frustration and stress
- Rarely acknowledges emotions or feelings
- Has low self-esteem with unrealistic goals, which allows him to classify himself as a failure regardless of his success as perceived by outsiders
- Sees himself with poor social skills
- Is extremely dependent on the relationship with his spouse. The man who abuses his wife believes he cannot survive outside the relationship, just as the wife, who is the victim, believes she cannot live outside the relationship
- Is extremely jealous and possessive toward the abused victim
- Is depressed, possibly severely. May threaten to commit homicide or suicide if he fears his abused wife is going to leave or change the situation
- Abuses alcohol. There is a strong correlation between alcoholism and battering in men. Referral to both an alcoholism program and a domestic abuse program may be required to successfully treat his problems.
- Minimizes his violent behavior internally and externally

A man will continue his violent behavior because he sees it as an effective tool for gaining and keeping control over another person — the abused wife. He usually has not suffered adverse consequences for his behavior.

The wife's reasons for not leaving are more complex than any lack in her character. In most cases, it is dangerous for the woman to leave.

- She may fear additional hardships and problems if her financial and social status is tied to her husband.
- She may fear for her life and the lives of her children.
- She may fear harassment at church, at work, and in her community.
- The abused wife is experiencing shame, embarrassment, and isolation. Often she does not have support from her family and friends in leaving.
- She is concerned about the response from the civil authorities and her faith community.

- She may not know how to access a safe place to live and a support network.

Unfortunately, police officers often treat domestic problems as a dispute rather than as a crime of attack. Furthermore, the court system is reluctant to give maximum sentences to the convicted abusers, and pastors and counselors have generally been trained to save the marriage rather than stop the violence.

ASSESSMENT AND RELATED COUNSELING ISSUES

It is extremely important to assess the danger and deadliness of a battering situation. Pastors and counselors in the church community must realize that they have a "duty of case" in the counseling relationship. Legally, a duty of case has been defined as "a special relationship between you as the counselor and the person being counseled — the counselee — to the extent that you are considered to have a responsibility to ensure the counselee's safety and welfare" (Levicoff 1991, p. 83). Legally, this has included the responsibility to prevent the client from harming him- or herself, as well as preventing the client from harming another person. The duty of case is paramount in situations involving domestic violence. We must be diligent to ask clear, direct questions; make necessary referrals, especially in cases indicating alcoholism, drug abuse, and mental illness; and network with law enforcement, secular agencies, and community organizations where appropriate. Everyone in the household is affected by domestic violence — the wife, the husband, and the children. A strong network is needed to address the problem.

When gathering data, ask questions such as these:

- Did you push her? Hit her? Hit her with an instrument? Open hand? Closed fist?
- How often does this happen?
- When was the last time?
- What do you see as the most important problem?
- How would your life be different without the violent behavior?
- How would you change your relationship?

Be focused in your questioning. Create an environment where both the abuser and the abused individual can talk about their problems. As the counselor, you must be willing to confront. A man cannot be allowed to shift the blame for his violent behavior to the relationship or to other factors. A clear message must be given that the violence must stop and that he has the power to stop it. When a man accepts the fact that he has that power, then he is ready to develop alternatives to his behavior.

Hope must be expressed biblically — verbally and nonverbally. In expressing biblical hope, the abuser, his wife, and the family must know that we are concerned and willing to provide counsel and support. However, neither the Bible nor we as pastors and counselors condone violent behavior.

People who abuse others often want another alternative that is as effective as their violent behavior. Physical separation as a "time-out" can be effective in enabling both spouses time to sort out their emotions. This physical separation can range from a short time, such as a long walk, to a longer period of time that allows the abused wife to rest from the abuse and gives the husband time to consider the consequences.

When a man comes in for counseling, it is usually because his wife has left him and he wants her back. He prays that God will give him direction on how to be a better husband and father. Rarely does a man seek out help to stop his violent behavior in the home. Pressure usually must be exerted to make the man come for counseling and to remain until he has successfully completed it. Pastors and Christian counselors must begin to view the criminal justice system as an ally in compelling abusive men into treatment to end violent behavior in the home.

A family that is caught in the cycle of domestic violence has other related problems that must be addressed such as communication skills, conflict resolution skills, assertiveness training, and parenting skills. In the face of a multitude of issues, our first priority as pastors and counselors is to stop the violence. When violence ceases and the threat of violence has been removed from the marital relationship and family, the other counseling issues can be addressed.

THE RELIGIOUS ELEMENTS OF THE PROBLEMS OF DOMESTIC ABUSE

Domestic violence affects every dimension of family life — physical, emotional, mental, social, and spiritual. The spiritual encompasses the family's values and belief system regarding its relationship with God and others, both as individuals and as members of a family. It is the core of the family's life. For the Christian who finds him- or herself in the midst of domestic violence, religious issues and concerns are priority issues to be addressed. They cannot be ignored. The psalmist describes the anguish felt by the abused spouse:

> My heart is in anguish within me;
>> the terrors of death assail me.
> Fear and trembling have beset me;
>> horror has overwhelmed me.
> I said, "Oh, that I had the wings of a dove!
>> I would fly away and be at rest—
> I would flee far away and stay in the desert;
>> I would hurry to my place of shelter, far from the tempest and
>> storm."...
> If an enemy were insulting me,
>> I could endure it;
> if a foe were raising himself against me,
>> I would hide from him.
> But it is you, a man like myself,
>> my companion, my close friend,
> with whom I once enjoyed sweet fellowship
>> as we walked with the throng at the house of God....
> My companion attacks his friends;
>> he violates his covenant.
> His speech is smooth as butter,
>> yet war is in his heart;
> his words are more soothing than oil,
>> yet they are drawn swords. (Psalm 55:4–8, 12–14, 20–21)

Based on their understanding of the Bible, many women do not believe there is an alternative to their violent marriage. Divorce is not a viable option. A single-parent household is unacceptable. A violent father is better than no father. Therefore, they try to preserve the status quo of family at all costs. A misinterpretation of Christ's teachings on marriage in Ephesians, Colossians, and Corinthians has given illicit permission to the abusive husband and has left the abused wife in bondage to guilt, self-blame, and suffering. The abused woman often feels abandoned by God. She views her abuse as punishment for past sins. Suffering is her plight in the marriage.

There are times in the marriage that the husband fulfills her dreams of love. During those times, she perceives her husband as a good man. These "good times" strengthen her position that if she loves him and behaves as the wife described in 1 Peter 3, she can change him. This "double bind" blinds her to the inability of her husband to handle conflict and stress. She is rendered incapable of emotionally and spiritually stepping outside the marriage to seek help. Most importantly, God's teaching on suffering is distorted.

Finally, abused women hesitate to approach their pastors and Christian counselors for fear of their response. When we ask, "Why didn't you come to me sooner?" the response is usually, "I was afraid that you would insist that I stay in the situation."

THE BIBLICAL RESPONSE

Stop doing wrong,
    learn to do right!
Seek justice,
    encourage the oppressed.
Defend the cause of the fatherless,
    plead the case of the widow. (Isaiah 1:16–17)

Marie M. Fortune (1982) outlines two gospel stories that provide a model of compassionate response to the victims of violence: the Good Samaritan in Luke 10:29–37, and the Persistent Widow seeking vindication in Luke 18:1–8. In these parables, the church as the Good Samaritan and the Persistent Widow is called to bind up the wounds of those abused and to confront the abuser. As pastors and counselors we must advocate for the victims of domestic violence. This involves advocating for legal, social, and medical assistance for our counselees.

Questions regarding separation and divorce, family authority and responsibility, suffering, and forgiveness must be sensitively dealt with in counseling. The final step in the initial intervention stage must be to stop the violence, not to preserve the family at all costs. Insistence that individuals avoid separation and/or divorce, and stay in an abusive situation may lead to a life-threatening situation.

Correct biblical instruction and counsel on marriage and on the role of husband and wife must be addressed once the violence has stopped. Marriage is a mature covenant between a man and a woman before God. It is a lifelong commitment based on love, trust, and a mutual giving of self to another. It involves respect and equality between the husband and wife. According to Ephesians 5:21, all Christians, including husbands and wives, are to be mutually subject to one another: "Submit to one another out of reverence for Christ."

Christ elevated the relationship between husband and wife to a higher level. A Christian marriage is to be a visible representation of the relationship between Christ and his church (Ephesians 5:23–24). Throughout his ministry, Christ's relationship with his disciples was one of a servant-leader. Thus, the relationship of a husband to his wife is not one of dominance or authority, but one of a servant-leader. In 1 Peter 3:7, husbands are warned to be considerate of their wives and to treat them with respect as heirs with them of eternal life so that the husbands' prayers will not be hindered. Christ's teachings in regard to women and children are based on love and protection, not abuse. "Wives, submit to your husbands as to the Lord" (Ephesians 5:22) teaches that a wife is to be sensitive, flexible, and responsive to her husband. This verse is not a license to abuse.

Adultery is seen as a betrayal in the marriage relationship; the marital covenant has been broken. The same is true of domestic abuse in a marriage. Betrayal has taken place. The marital covenant has been broken. Trust has been shattered. It will take time to rebuild trust. The healing process can begin once the abuser is willing to admit that he has inflicted his violent behavior on his wife and family. With genuine effort to change, the marriage covenant can be renewed and the marital relationship restored. There must be a commitment to nonviolence, however.

In a marriage where one spouse is an unbeliever, 1 Corinthians 7:15 states, "If the unbeliever leaves, let him do so. A believing man or woman is not bound in such circumstances: God has called us to live in peace." When the abuser is a nonbeliever and shows no sincere effort to stop and seek treatment for his violent behavior, he has broken the trust. The wife, upon thoroughly discussing her perception of the marriage and her goals in light of God's work, may decide to leave. In most cases we have discovered that the unbelieving spouse has already emotionally left.

Many times the abuser is more ready to seek forgiveness than those abused are willing to give it. The abused individual should not be pressured to forgive. Timing is important. They should be counseled to understand that forgiveness does not mean to forget or to pretend that abuse never happened. Extending forgiveness is for the abused individual's well-being and healing process, as well as the abuser. For the abused individual, granting forgiveness may initially be an act of the will in obedience to God's command (Matthew 18:21–22; Luke 17:4). Over time, the granting of forgiveness will allow the abused individual to give her hurts to God and to pray for her abuser. Forgiveness of the abuser is the late stage of letting go of the abuse and moving on with life.

God's love and care must be emphasized throughout the counseling. The abused wife's explanation of suffering as "God's will" or "part of God's plan for me" depicts God as stern and harsh, not loving, merciful, and concerned for the well-being of his children.

When a Christian woman chooses to remain in an abusive relationship with the hope of changing the spouse, this is unrealistic and the abuse usually continues — even escalates. Even in the abuse situation, however, God's love and concern is present:

> For I am convinced that neither death nor life, neither angels nor demons, neither the present nor the future, nor any powers, neither height nor depth, nor anything else in all creation, will be able to separate us from the love of God that is in Christ Jesus our Lord. (Romans 8:38–39)

Both the abusive husband and the wife must be counseled to see God's divine care and plan for them and their family, which includes a future and hope (Jeremiah 29:11).

Domestic violence is sin and outside of God's design for marriage.

SUMMARY

We have attempted to address the problem of domestic violence and its impact on Christian marriages and families as well as the need for a biblical response in counseling. For too long pastors and lay leaders have not given permission through sermons, classes, and seminars that the church is the place to bring the problem of domestic abuse.

As with other societal ills, our communities are crying out for a light in the darkness. Law enforcement authorities, social service agencies, and community organizations are unable to meet the deepest hurts of families caught in the cycle of domestic violence. Pastors and counselors must become more knowledgeable about the problem of domestic violence and equipped with the counseling tools to bring healing. We are Christ's ambassadors. We have at our disposal the mandate to be his ministers of justice and grace.

REFERENCE RESOURCES

Fortune, M. M. 1982. The church and domestic violence. *Theology, News and Notes,* Fuller Theological Seminary, 29, no. 2 (June): 17–22.

Fortune, M. M., and J. Hertz. 1980. *A commentary on religious issues in family violence.* Seattle: Center for the Prevention of Sexual and Domestic Violence.

Fortune, M. M., and D. Harman. 1980. *The person who batters.* Seattle: Center for the Prevention of Sexual and Domestic Violence.

Levicoff, S. 1991. *Christian counseling and the law.* Chicago: Moody Press.

National Coalition Against Domestic Violence (NCADV). 2000. *Information Bulletin* (September). Website: www.ncadv.org/problem/problem.htm.

Rouse, Linda P. 1984. *You are not alone: A guide for battered women.* Holmes Beach, Fla.: Learning Publications.

Walker, L. E. 1979. *The battered woman.* New York: Harper & Row.

ADDITIONAL RESOURCES

Books

Adams, C., and M. M. Fortune. 1996. *Violence against women and children: A Christian theological sourcebook.* New York: Continuum Publishing Group.

Burns, M. C., ed. 1986. *The speaking profits us: Violence in the lives of women of color.* Seattle: Center for the Prevention of Sexual and Domestic Violence.

Fortune, M. M. 1995. *Keeping the faith: Guidance for Christian women facing abuse.* San Francisco: HarperCollins.

_____. 1991. *Violence in the family: A workshop curriculum for clergy and other helpers.* Cleveland: Pilgrim Press.

Videos

Broken Vows: Religious perspectives on domestic violence. Center for the Prevention of Sexual and Domestic Abuse, 936 N. 34th Street, Suite 200, Seattle, WA 98103.

Provides information on domestic violence; provides interviews with clergy, psychologists, and shelter workers; discusses theological issues

Wings like a dove. Center for the Prevention of Sexual and Domestic Violence, 936 N. 34th Street, Suite 200, Seattle, WA 98103

Provides hope and healing to abused women; provides information for religious and community groups

Referrals

If you know someone in a physically or psychologically abusive situation, the following referrals can assist in obtaining immediate help:

- For immediate assistance, dial 9-1-1
- The National Domestic Violence Hotline: 1-800-799-7233
- The Rape, Abuse and Incest National Network: 1-800-656-HOPE (4673)
- The Center for the Prevention of Sexual and Domestic Violence provides information about issues of religious and sexual and domestic abuse:
    936 N. 34th Street, Suite 200
    Seattle, WA 98103
    Phone: (206) 634-1903
    Fax: (206) 634-0115
    E-mail: cpsdv@cpsdv.org

Deborah G. Haskins

Chapter 6

Sexual Abuse and Incest

Deborah G. Haskins is Director of Masters Education and Field Education in Psychology at Loyola College in Maryland and is a Licensed Clinical Professional Counselor in Maryland. She is also a National Certified Gambling Counselor and provides problem gambling counseling and clinical supervision for counselors seeking problem gambler certification. Her counseling expertise includes sexual abuse recovery for adolescent females and women, substance abuse aftercare treatment, grief and loss, identity problems, and the role of religion and spirituality in human functioning. She specializes in incorporating cultural diversity into counseling and clinical practice and trains human services professionals in this.

Dr. Haskins holds a bachelor of science degree from Rider University, a master of arts degree in counseling service, and a doctor of philosophy degree in pastoral counseling from Loyola University in Maryland. She has published research on sexual abuse attitudes among African Americans and psychotherapy with African Americans. She is Coordinator of Health and Wholeness at her church and assists congregations and communities in mental health prevention and support. She is married to Bruce, a minister, and they have three children, Jason, Joy, and Joseph.

Incest and child sexual abuse have received wide attention in the United States during the last twenty years. While there are varying definitions of incest and child sexual abuse described in the literature, sexual abuse includes any contact or interaction between a child and an adult in which the child or adolescent is either sexually stimulated or is used for the sexual stimulation of another individual. Sexual abuse includes fondling, exhibitionism, forcible rape, sexual exploitation, and prostitution (Veltkamp and Miller 1994). In 1999, Child Protective Service (CPS) agencies reported that an estimated 826,000 children were victims of substantiated or indicated child abuse and neglect (U.S. Department of Health and Human Services 1999). The number of children reported annually to state CPS agencies has tripled during the past seventeen years for which data has been recorded. Because many cases go unreported, it is estimated that the true numbers are much higher (U.S. Department of Health and Human Services 1996).

Child abuse is a problem that affects many families and communities, regardless of ethnicity, income level, educational status, or religious affiliation. Fortune (1991) identified several religious aspects of the problem. Scriptures are often used inappropriately to justify the abuse of children (e.g., "Spare the rod and spoil the child"); and religious traditions have frequently taught children to "honor" their parents and not question their actions, even when it hurts them. As a result of unhealthy religious obedience, children may not report child sexual abuse and may suffer long-term effects if no professional or legal intervention occurs. Often these children grow up to be adults still struggling to recover from the psychological and spiritual pain. Many may seek professional help as adults, but many others do not.

Despite increased public awareness, incident reporting, and support for psychological treatment for child sexual abuse, there is still a discrepancy between the numbers of occurrences and reports filed, particularly among ethnic communities. Reports from the states to the National Center on Child Abuse and Neglect in 1994 found that forty-seven states provided data on race and ethnicity when reporting abuse. Caucasian victims constituted almost 56 percent of all victims, while African American victims represented the second largest group at about 26 percent (National Committee to Prevent Child Abuse 1995). Professionals and researchers have discovered that ethnic individuals, such as African Americans, are not as likely to report abuse events and do not seek psychological services due to a general mistrust of social agencies (McAdoo 1982; Pierce and Pierce 1984; and Ganns 1991).

Limited knowledge exists as to how African Americans perceive incest and child sexual abuse and sexual abuse treatment. The degree to which an African American views child sexual abuse as exploitive, is willing to report the incident to CPS, and seeks psychological services may be related to a number of factors. African Americans have historically relied on their religious and spiritual faith to overcome oppression and offenses. Many African American families who suffer effects of child sexual abuse may use their own religious and spiritual resources to overcome sexual trauma;

therefore, it is important for African American families, Black churches, and lay and professional people working with African Americans to integrate cultural values and resources into prevention and mental health programs. African Americans and religious people are no less immune to occurrences of incest and sexual abuse.

CURRENT STATUS OF INCEST AND CHILD SEXUAL ABUSE
Sexual Abuse Theories
Research on child sexual abuse identifies the experience of sexual exploitation as a traumatic incident. What happens when a child, adolescent, or adult has been exploited for the sexual gratification of another when consent was not given? Van der Kolk (1987) states that the human response to overwhelming and uncontrollable life events is consistent. While the nature of the trauma, age of the victim, predisposing personality, and community response have an important effect on how the individual adapts to the trauma, the core features of post-traumatic syndrome are fairly constant across these variables. The American Psychiatric Association developed a separate category for this human response to overwhelming life events under the heading of "Post-Traumatic Stress Disorder" (PTSD) (DSM-III 1980). Six factors affect the long-term adjustment to traumatization: severity of the stressor, genetic predisposition, developmental phase, a person's social support system, prior experiences of traumatization, and preexisting personality (van der Kolk 1987).

First, the severity of the stressor is a major factor and may create psychiatric disturbances, cognitive disturbances, persistent nervousness and irritability, and sleep disturbances. These disturbances have been found in concentration camp survivors as well as among rape victims (Kilpatrick, Veronen, and Best 1988).

Second, sexual abuse victims possessing genetic vulnerabilities may be likely to develop chronic stress responses.

Third, there is a relationship between the developmental phase during which the sexual trauma occurs and the victim's psychological response. For example, researchers and clinicians observe that adults who possess a solid identity and good social supports (for example, family and church support) are typically protected against psychological trauma as compared to children (Hendin and Pollinger 1984). Because children have not developed a variety of coping behaviors, they may be more vulnerable to child sexual abuse (Green 1983).

Fourth, a person's social support system affects the individual's ability to survive the effects of psychological trauma. In particular, when child sexual abuse occurs by a person known to the child — an individual that the child has trusted and depended on — the child inevitably struggles with trust. This lack of trust often contributes to poor future intimate relationships because the child has learned early on that one cannot trust others (Green 1983). Also, the child often develops rage that may be directed toward self, by using drugs and alcohol, for example, or toward others, by assaulting siblings or peers.

Fifth, individuals with a previous history of traumatic experiences are likely to develop long-term symptoms in response to later traumas (Finkelhor 1984). For example, children who have been physically abused and are later sexually abused are at risk for developing long-term symptoms. If psychological treatment was not provided during the earlier traumatic experience, the person's symptoms and psychological well-being may deteriorate. Although many victims of sexual abuse suffer long-term effects, many individuals seek psychological services after victimization and recover. Many others do not seek psychological treatment, and little data exists as to whether they recover or not. Harvey (1996) notes that much of the literature reports how people seeking mental health services fare psychologically; but many victims may access support systems in their environments, and sexual abuse literature may not report the outcomes of this segment of the victim population. Many sexual abuse survivors may heal from the abuse if they have resources, such as family, friendship, and religious and spiritual support, and may not develop long-term symptoms. It is clear that some type of response is vital to the psychological recovery after a sexual assault experience.

Finally, researchers concluded that there is a strong relationship between preexisting personality factors and chronic PTSD symptoms. Burgess and Holstrom (1979) studied the long-term effects of rape and found that 29 percent of the rape victims who had not recovered after five years were women with a poorer pre-trauma adjustment than the 39 percent who had recovered after six months. It appeared that the women with preexisting personality difficulties became fixed in a consistent state of help-lessness and developed chronic anxiety and phobic behavior after the rape.

Post-traumatic stress symptoms, therefore, are common outcomes of incest and child sexual abuse. In order to continue living, the victim often alternates between numbing and denial of the event as recollections of the sexual event surfaces (Veltkamp and Miller 1994). Whenever memories of the sexual assault intrude into the mind of the victim, he or she may develop a host of behaviors to numb or eliminate the intrusive thought or experience. Researchers and mental health professionals document that often victims of sexual abuse will consume alcohol or drugs as a coping strategy to numb the intrusive sexual memories. The addicted person may be misunderstood and labeled solely as an addict and may not receive attention to the underlying problem, which may be the traumatic event. Many substance abuse patients are depressed and struggle to recover from the sexual violence (Evans and Sullivan 1995).

Another at-risk child sexual abuse group is the adolescent. The American Humane Association (1988) documented that of approximately 1.7 million cases of child abuse, 24 percent involved youths between 12 and 17 years of age. Hibbard, Ingersoll, and Orr (1990) found that in a study of 3,998 students who were not seeking clinical treatment and did not officially report the sexual abuse, 20 percent claimed to have endured some form of physical or sexual abuse; more girls did than boys. Wyatt (1988) reported that many adolescents who are survivors of incest and child sexual abuses are promiscuous, become teen parents, and develop other at-risk behaviors. Many abused teenagers run away, steal, perform poorly in school, abuse drugs, set fires, or enter the juvenile justice system (Gil 1996). Unfortunately, many of these adolescent teenagers are survivors of child sexual abuse who become sexually active as a result of the sexual exploitation, and yet they may never receive an accurate assessment and treatment. Many parents, school professionals, and law enforcement agencies focus on the acting-out behavior but rarely consider that there may be underlying problems such as sexual victimization.

Current Research

While there is a dearth of psychological research regarding the definition, prevalence, and phenomenon of child sexual abuse, there is a greater gap in the literature regarding the experiences of African American survivors of child sexual abuse (Wyatt 1990; Pierce and Pierce 1984; Abney and Priest 1995). Current research describes the experiences of ethnic members and religious people who suffer sexual violence (Fontes 1995; Fortune 1991). Pierce and Pierce (1984) noted that in the past, a color-blind attitude in the broad field of research and clinical practice was highly valued. However, according to Cooper (1973), "such an attitude is not totally possible, realistic, or useful" (p. 129). Pinderhughes (1982) explained that effective intervention with families requires knowledge of ethnic factors as they influence family functioning. Pinderhughes further explained that more focus on the relationship between race and child sexual abuse in general, and incest in particular, will increase the understanding of this sensitive issue and improve the quality of services offered to children and families.

Abney and Priest (1995) stated that research regarding childhood sexual victimization in African American communities is sparse. Additionally, they note that significant segments of the African American community have taken a twofold thematic variation of "see no evil, hear no evil." Why? First, sexually abusing children is something other ethnic groups do; and second, if African Americans do engage in incestuous acts or other sexually abusive behavior with children, it should be silenced because acknowledging the abuse may be used to further exclude African Americans from the American mainstream. This failure to admit that child sexual abuse exists within African American culture ultimately results in survivors with this psychological injury not being supported.

In order to provide psychological services to African Americans, researchers document that it is important to understand the sociopolitical history of African Americans in American culture, such as the history of slavery, racism, poverty, and oppression (Baldwin 1985; Pinderhughes 1982). Often African Americans are stereotyped or "pathologized"; yet African American families possess tremendous strengths. These cultural strengths may buffer the effects of sexual abuse and may also sometimes be a potential risk factor. Often when there is a sexual abuse crisis, the family may problem-solve by relying on their own family and friends' support. This reliance on family and friendship — extended family networks — is a major strength in African American families (Littlejohn-Blake and Darling 1993; McAdoo 1982). Blood relatives and non-blood relationships (i.e., godparents, close family friends) comprise this extended family network and often assist the parents and caregivers in providing support to the family, especially during crises. While extended family networks are a notable strength, it may also create opportunities for increased incest and sexual abuse.

Wyatt (1985) found in her study of sexual abuse of African American and Caucasian women in childhood that young African American preteens were more likely to experience sexual abuse in their homes, by mostly African American male perpetrators who may be nuclear or extended family members. In addition, African American women were slightly less likely to report child abuse incidents to nuclear family members and to the police. While Wyatt did not find significant differences between the African American and Caucasian research participants, she did discover that

African American women were slightly more likely to cite fear of consequences as the reason for not disclosing abuse incidents. Wyatt explained that African American women were more concerned about the financial hardships if the stepfather or boyfriend were removed from the home. In addition, the stronger family ties could make it more complicated to disclose abuse incidents involving male relatives. Young children may be more fearful to tell an adult family member about the abuse if the abuser is another family member who has close contact with the family. The child may be fearful of disrupting family relationships. So while there are tremendous strengths in the extended family relationships, when abuse occurs, these family networks may serve as a barrier for African American women to heal the traumatic event.

Moreover, Abney and Priest (1995) document that reporting of sexual abuse by African Americans is further complicated by the realization that a significant number of African Americans have experienced negative encounters with the police, criminal justice system, or social service agencies. Individuals who have such experiences may be unlikely to report sexual abuse incidents to the same agencies where they have experienced negative or dehumanizing treatment.

Another notable strength of African American families is the reliance on religion and spirituality. Veroff, Douvan, and Kulka (1981) found that African Americans depend on prayer, personal spirituality, and religious resources (i.e., pastors) to a greater degree than do Caucasian Americans. Because many African Americans may rely on ministers, the church is in a great position to provide education and intervention for sexual victimization. However, Fortune (1991) states that it is important for clergy to receive appropriate training regarding sexual abuse in order to effectively respond to victims in their congregations and communities. She emphasizes that for a religious person, personal faith can provide much-needed strength and courage to survive a very painful experience; churches can provide a network of community support for victims, abusers, and their children.

BIBLICAL VIEW OF CHILD SEXUAL ABUSE

Much has been written about incest and child sexual abuse and the societal taboo regarding this devastating trauma. Theorists have speculated that there is a universal incest taboo throughout many cultures, past or present (DeMause 1988); yet there is really little evidence of a universal barrier against incest.

There is biblical evidence forbidding incest and child sexual abuse, however. In Leviticus 18:1–17, the Lord instructs Moses to speak to the Israelites and tell them to refrain from the practices they used in Egypt and not take them into Canaan where the Lord directed Moses to go with his people:

> No one is to approach any close relative to have sexual relations. I am the LORD. Do not dishonor your father by having sexual relations with your mother. She is your mother; do not have relations with her. Do not have sexual relations with your father's wife; that would dishonor your father. Do not have sexual relations with your sister, either your father's daughter or your mother's daughter, whether she was born in the same home or elsewhere. Do not have sexual relations with your son's daughter or your daughter's daughter; that would dishonor you. Do not have sexual relations with the daughter of your father's wife, born to your father; she is your sister. Do not have sexual relations with your father's sister; she is your father's close relative. Do not have sex with your mother's sister, because she is your mother's close relative.

It is clear from these Scriptures that the Lord did not view sexual relations with any close relative as appropriate.

Although the Bible does admonish Christians to refrain from incest and child sexual abuse, there is evidence that some Christians do sexually exploit children. Butman (1983) writes about the prevalence of incest in Christian homes. He states that child sexual abuse may be unreported in religious homes because many parishioners may fear losing social status and acceptance because they have been looked up to as strong religious people. He indicated that there are two factors that contribute to the prevalence of incest in Christian homes: (1) many religious families have trouble discussing sexual matters and intimacy openly; and (2) these families tend to have authoritarian leaders — the men believe they "own these women" (p. 21). Butman affirms that Christian faith may contribute to one's emotional well-being, but it does not guarantee psychological perfection. If religious families feel restricted regarding sexual matters, it seems highly unlikely that they will report or even seek psychological or spiritual healing for child sexual abuse trauma for themselves or family members. Religious African American families, like other ethnic groups, may postpone responding to sexual abuse.

Gil (1988) studied childhood sexual abuse experiences of thirty-five adult women (some of them African Americans) who were raised in conservative Christian homes and described themselves as victims of father-daughter incest. The women completed a structured questionnaire and were interviewed about their abuse histories. Gil discovered that natural fathers abused the daughters more than stepfathers, unlike other incest studies, which show stepfathers committing abuse more than natural fathers. Gil also found that 42 percent of fundamentalist Christian fathers were considered strict and legalistic by their daughters, whereas the majority of Reformed/Mainline and Baptist fathers were perceived as less legalistic. It appears that patriarchal fathers were more rigid and more likely to exert control over the daughter in fulfilling sexual gratification. The adult women in the study also cited financial problems, breakdown in parental communication, family crisis, and decline in religious commitment as issues facing the family at the time of the abuse. It is obvious that religious families may experience similar threats to the family as do those nonreligious families and could react in a dysfunctional way to personal conflicts in the couple's intimate relationship by satisfying their intimacy needs through the child.

Because African Americans commonly lag in seeking professional mental health services, it is important for Black churches to take an active leadership role in teaching the biblical view of incest and child sexual abuse. Additionally, when church leadership learn of incidents of sexual abuse, it is vital that they have accurate sexual abuse education so that families and perpetrators of abuse will receive appropriate attention. Moreover, since African Americans are likely to seek support from the pastor or laypeople at some time, knowledge of the assessment and treatment of sexual abuse will enable church leaders and laypeople to respond appropriately.

ASSESSMENT OF INCEST AND CHILD SEXUAL ABUSE

There is a tremendous amount of literature regarding assessment of sexual abuse among children and adults. Additionally, there are specific assessments to evaluate special considerations such as those of children (Veltkamp and Miller 1994) and adults (Herman 1981; Davies and Frawley 1994); adolescents (Gil 1996); addicted survivors of trauma (Evans and Sullivan 1995); and religious concerns (Fortune 1991). Because psychological effects of sexual abuse typically continue into adulthood, many victims seek help from mental health professionals. First, professional helpers need to inquire about sexual abuse when they conduct a sexual history during the intake session. Herman (1981) states that questions about sexual abuse should be incorporated into any clinician's ordinary history taking.

Herman (1981) notes that often male and female therapists are resistant to raising questions about sexual abuse with their patients. Yet asking about incest and sexual abuse is similar to asking about other taboo topics such as alcoholism, violence, and suicide. Herman emphasizes that the patient will be comfortable answering questions about sexual abuse if the helper is reasonably comfortable asking the question. Most professional clinicians use the DSM-IV (1994) to assess PTSD, depression, chronic stress disorders, and other primary or secondary disorders to assess the victim's post-trauma symptoms and behaviors. There are formal sexual abuse questionnaires such as the *Trauma Symptom Checklist for Children* (Briere 1996) and the *Trauma Symptom Inventory for Adults* (Briere 1995). The helper can ask a standard question such as, "Discussing sexual experiences are often uncomfortable for people; however, this information can be important during the helping process. Have there been any prior experiences in which you were inappropriately touched in a sexual manner?"

Religious helpers need to be aware that sexual abuse often affects the person's spiritual and religious identity. Fortune (1991) reports that when confronted with a personal experience of family violence, many survivors of sexual abuse will experience a crisis of meaning in their lives. Basic life questions surface, such as, Why is this happening to my family and me? or Why did God let this happen? These are examples of the survivor's search to understand and make sense of the abuse event. Fortune states that questions of meaning may be expressed in religious terms; therefore, the victim's religious and spiritual experiences may also need careful assessment and response.

Sexual abuse assessment is an arena that requires specialized education and training. Clergy and lay counselors should consult with professionals who are trained to assess sexual abuse to ensure proper problem identification; diagnosis of symptoms and behaviors; and potential psychological, medical, or legal intervention. Most important is that the assessment of a sexual abuse experience will influence whether the victim, family, and perpetrator ultimately receive attention. Most states consider sexual abuse to be a criminal act, and many states require mandatory reporting to CPS and law enforcement when any professional has suspicion or knowledge of the sexual exploitation of a child. Clergy and pastoral laypeople should become familiar with the child abuse statutes in their jurisdictions because mandatory reporting statutes may also bind them.

TREATMENT OF INCEST AND CHILD SEXUAL ABUSE

A variety of psychological and mental health treatment models exist for incest and child sexual abuse. Van der Kolk (1987) posits that unresolved trauma can cause behavioral reenactments, compulsive behaviors (e.g., excessive hand washing), PTSD symptoms, and physiological responses (e.g., ulcers, urinary tract problems) that can debilitate individuals or cause global impairment. Herman (1992) states that generic PTSD does not completely coincide with her identification of "complex PTSD," which is experienced by survivors of chronic, repetitive, and severe abuse. Gil (1996) notes that there is a consensus among clinicians working with trauma that the traumatic experiences must be brought into conscious awareness and processed, and Cuffe and Frick-Helms (1995) state that "the trauma-specific phase of treatment should focus on the traumatic aspects of the abuse, allowing expression of emotions and working through of traumatic memories" (p. 235). But, as Gil (1996) states, "Sexual abuse treatment must be done with tremendous caution in a structured, purposeful fashion and not begun until the victim has sufficient ego strength and an expanded collection of coping strategies."

Gil also notes that because sexual abuse often occurs within the context of family interactions, it is helpful to use a systemic approach in which both the child victim and the family members affected by parental maltreatment receive treatment. Children, adolescents, and adults should receive specialized treatment targeted for their specific developmental stage. For example, many children will engage in play therapy to process their emotions regarding the sexual violation (Gil 1991). Adult survivors of sexual abuse will benefit from a different treatment approach, particularly because they may also be negotiating a host of other problems, such as engaging in intimate relationships, parenting, and creating successful vocational and personal identities.

Finally, because many victims of sexual abuse will face an existential crisis in their religious and spiritual identity, they may also benefit from pastoral treatment. However, clergy and pastoral laypeople must approach the victim with tremendous sensitivity and be careful not to provide scriptural and theological prescriptions, such as "God can take care of any pain," without also providing an atmosphere where the victim can express the pain. Fortune (1991) states that often the minister or counselor's need for the victim to finish and resolve the abusive experience leads the helper to push a victim to forgive the abuser. She emphasizes the importance of victims' forgiving at their own pace and not being pushed by others' expectations of them. Timing is an important treatment concern, and the victim's timing in the healing process must be respected. Helpers must be careful not to take the victim's power away by prescribing the manner and pace of psychological and spiritual healing.

CASE EXAMPLES

Three cases will describe common sexual abuse incidents. These scenarios are fictitious but are representative of clinical experiences this author has encountered during ten years of providing professional counseling to victims of incest and sexual abuse. A child, adolescent, and adult victim case will be described.

Child Victim

Amy is an 8-year-old African American female living with her 30-year-old mother and 32-year-old father. Amy is an only child. Amy's paternal uncle began baby-sitting her when she was 7. He became unemployed and sought shelter with his brother's family. He offered to baby-sit Amy and would tell her parents that "the least I can do to show my gratitude is watch Amy so that you can go out and have fun." One evening, Amy's uncle told her he wanted to play a "game" with her. He stated, "In return for playing this game, I will let you have some candy." Amy loves candy and loves to play games. Her uncle tells her to take off her clothes and he will pretend to be a doctor and give her an examination. Amy complies and the uncle begins rubbing her stomach and eventually her vagina. Amy feels uncomfortable and tells the uncle to stop. Her uncle stops but tells Amy, "You must not tell anyone about our secret."

This scenario is a typical scene among child victims of sexual abuse. Often the offender is someone the child knows and trusts. The offender knows that the child will trust him or her and typically tells the child never to tell. Amy's parents begin noticing that when they go out socially, Amy asks to go or becomes very sullen. When they ask Amy what is wrong, she withdraws. Typically, it is not apparent to the parents or caregivers that the child has been violated, but the child's behavior at home and at school may change. Often children become very sad, withdrawn, or aggressive; there may be changes in their academic behavior. The child may become depressed, but depression is expressed differently among children as compared with adults. Children experience changes in their behavior, and often adults do not identify changes in their children's mood.

Adolescent Victim

Sherry is a 16-year-old African American female being raised by her 45-year-old mother. Sherry has one brother who is 18 years old. Her father died one year ago, but her parents had divorced when she was 10. Sherry's mother brings her in for counseling because her grades have dropped in school. She seeks support from her pastor, and the pastor gives her a counseling referral. He has spoken to Sherry several times, but he cannot get her to open up with him. Her mother reports that "Sherry is depressed and is still struggling with the death of her father." Following the initial counseling interview, Sherry reveals that she and her mother are not that close, and she has a hard time talking to her mother. She talks about her lack of interest in school and friendships along with her sadness about her father. However, Sherry reveals that while she is sad about her father, she is coping with his loss. The counselor has a difficult time identifying why Sherry is unmotivated and withdrawing. After the third counseling session, Sherry finally admits that she was sexually molested by two of her brother's friends two years ago. Sherry reports that her brother's friends often came over while her mother was at work after school. One day when her brother was in one part of the house, her brother's friend held her down on the ground and tried to have intercourse with her. Sherry reports screaming for her brother but his stereo music drowned out her screams. Sherry reports that she has never told her brother or mother. "I do not think they will believe me," she states. "My mother never believes anything I say."

What becomes apparent is that Sherry is depressed and has been experiencing a depressed mood for the past two years. She has functioned, but over the course of the past two years her motivation is waning. It becomes increasingly difficult for Sherry to keep this secret. She does not feel supported by her mother. It will be important for Sherry to feel safe during the counseling relationship and for the counselor to provide family intervention. Because Sherry is a minor, the counselor will also have to report the incident to CPS, and she knows this will be a troubling experience for Sherry.

Adult Victim

Sandy is a 35-year-old African American and married to Dan. Sandy and Dan dated for three years before marriage. They have had many marital conflicts, and these appear to revolve around "Sandy's inability to trust men" as reported by Dan. He reports that Sandy hesitates when he touches her, and after three years he reports his frustration. Dan tells Sandy that unless she seeks professional help, he cannot continue in the marriage. Sandy reports loving her husband and seeks professional counseling. In the first session, she admits that her mother's boyfriend sexually abused her between the ages of 10 and 15. Sandy reveals that she has never told anyone but is concerned that she may lose her husband.

It is apparent to the counselor that Sandy's inability to engage in a close, intimate relationship with her husband is related to her prior experiences of sexual abuse. Her inability to heal from the earlier abuse affects her ability to trust men in general, including her husband. Sandy admits being afraid to share the sexual abuse experiences but emphasizes that she does not want to lose her marriage. The counseling intervention will focus on slowly exploring the traumatic sexual abuse experiences and assisting Sandy in separating her current relationship with her husband, who does not hurt her, from her psychological associations with the perpetrator. It is very common for adult survivors to function until they are faced with a close interpersonal relationship that unconsciously represents the possibility of their being victimized again by a trusted person. Often the adult survivor of sexual abuse will seek help from professionals or clergy when they can no longer function psychologically and interpersonally.

SUMMARY

Sexual abuse is prevalent among all races and ethnic groups. African Americans are not immune and neither are religious communities. It is important for African Americans to receive education and to dispel myths about sexual abuse. It is equally important for the religious community to provide sexual abuse prevention to decrease the prevalence of sexual abuse among African American families and communities. Clergy and religious laypeople will benefit from increased training and education regarding sexual abuse so that members of their communities may receive proper education, assessment, and treatment.

REFERENCES

Abney, V. D., and R. Priest. 1995. African Americans and sexual child abuse. In *Sexual abuse in nine North American cultures,* edited by L. A. Fontes, 11–30. Thousand Oaks, Calif.: Sage Publications.

American Humane Association. 1988. *Highlights of official child abuse and neglect reporting: Annual report.* Denver: American Humane Association.

Baldwin, J. A. 1985. African self-consciousness and the mental health of African Americans. *Journal of Black Studies* 15, no. 2: 177–94.

Briere, J. 1996. *Trauma symptom checklist for children.* San Antonio: Psychological Corporation.

———. 1995. *Trauma symptom inventory.* San Antonio: Psychological Corporation.

Burgess, A. W., and L. Holstrom. 1979. Rape trauma syndrome. *American Journal of Psychiatry* 131: 981–86.

Butman, R. E. 1983. Hidden victims: The facts about incest. *HIS:* 20–23.

Cooper, S. 1973. A look at the effect of racism on clinical work. In *Dynamics of racism in social work practice,* edited by J. Goodman, 127–40. New York: National Association of Social Workers.

Cuffe, S. E., and S. B. Frick-Helms. 1995. Treatment interventions for child sexual abuse. In *Handbook of child and adolescent sexual problems,* edited by G. A. Rekers, 232–51. New York: Lexington Books.

Davies, J. M., and M. G. Frawley. 1994. *Treating the adult survivor of childhood sexual abuse: A psychoanalytic perspective.* New York: Basic Books.

DeMause, L. 1988. What incest barrier? *Journal of Psychohistory* 15, no. 3: 273–72.

Diagnostic and statistical manual of mental disorders, 3d edition. (DSM-III). 1980. Washington, D.C.: American Psychiatric Association.

Diagnostic and statistical manual of mental disorders, 4th edition. (DSM-IV). 1994. Washington, D.C.: American Psychiatric Association.

Evans, K., and J. M. Sullivan. 1995. *Treating addicted survivors of trauma.* New York: Guilford Press.

Finkelhor, D. 1984. *Child sexual abuse: New theory and research.* New York: Free Press.

Fontes, L. A., ed. 1995. *Sexual abuse in nine North American cultures: Treatment and prevention.* Thousand Oaks, Calif.: Sage Publications.

Fortune, M. 1991. *A commentary on religious issues in family violence.* Seattle: Center for the Prevention of Sexual and Domestic Violence.

Ganns, J. A. 1991. Sexual abuse: Its impact on the child and the family. In *The Black family: Past, present and future,* edited by L. N. June. Grand Rapids: Zondervan.

Gil, E. 1991. *The healing power of play: Working with abused children.* New York: Guilford Press.

———. 1996. *Treating abused adolescents.* New York: Guilford Press.

Gil, V. E. 1988. In my Father's house: Self-report findings of sexually abused daughters from conservative Christian homes. *Journal of Psychology and Theology* 16, no. 2: 144–52.

Green, A. H. 1983. Dimensions of psychological trauma in abused children. *Journal of American Association of Child Psychiatry* 22: 231–37.

Harvey, M. R. 1996. An ecological view of psychological trauma and trauma recovery. *Journal of Traumatic Stress* 9, no. 1: 3–20.

Hendin, H., and H. A. Pollinger. 1984. Combat adaptations of Vietnam veterans without post-traumatic stress disorder. *American Journal of Psychiatry* 141: 956–60.

Herman, J. L. 1981. *Father-daughter incest.* Cambridge, Mass.: Harvard University Press.

———. 1992. *Trauma and recovery.* New York: Basic Books.

Hibbard, R. A., G. M. Ingersoll, and D. Orr. 1990. Behavioral risks, emotional risk, and child abuse among adolescents in a non-clinical setting. *Pediatrics* 86: 896–901.

Kilpatrick, D. G., L. J. Veronen, and P. A. Resick. 1981. Effects of the rape experience: A longitudinal study. *Journal of Social Issues* 37: 105–22.

Kilpatrick, D. G., C. L. Best, and L. J. Veronen. 1985. Effects of the rape experience: A longitudinal study. *Journal of Social Issues* 37: 105–22.

Littlejohn-Blake, S. M., and C. A. Darling. 1993. Understanding the strengths of African American families. *Journal of Black Studies* 23, no. 4: 460–71.

McAdoo, H. 1982. Stress absorbing systems in Black families. *Family Relations* 31: 479–88.

National Committee to Prevent Child Abuse. 1995. *Current trends in child abuse reporting and fatalities: The results of the 1994 annual fifty-state survey.* Chicago: National Committee to Prevent Child Abuse.

Pierce, L. H., and R. L. Pierce. 1984. Race as a factor in the sexual abuse of children. *Social Work Research and Abstracts* 20: 9–14.

Pinderhughes, E. 1982. Afro-American families and the victim system. In *Ethnicity and family therapy,* edited by M. McGoldrick, J. Pearce, and J. Giordano, 108–22. New York: Guilford Press.

U.S. Department of Health and Human Services, National Center on Child Abuse and Neglect. 1999. Child maltreatment 1999 reports from the states to the national child abuse and neglect data system. Washington, D.C.: U.S. Government Printing Office, 2001.

Van der Kolk, B. A. 1987. *Psychological trauma.* Washington, D.C.: American Psychiatric Press.

Veltkamp, L. J., and T. W. Miller. 1994. *Clinical handbook of child abuse and neglect.* Madison, Conn.: International Universities Press.

Veroff, J., E. Douvan, and R. A. Kulka. 1981. *The inner American.* New York: Basic Books.

Wyatt, G. E. 1985. The sexual abuse of Afro-American and White-American women in childhood. *Child Abuse and Neglect* 9: 507–19.

_____. 1988. The relationship between child sexual abuse and adolescent sexual functioning in Afro-American and White-American women. *Human sexual aggression: Current perspectives,* 111–12. New York: New York Academy of Sciences.

_____. 1990. The aftermath of child sexual abuse of African American and White American women: The victim's experience. *Journal of Family Violence* 5, no. 1: 61–81.

RESOURCES

Referral Process. Clergy and religious laypeople should develop a referral resource list of mental health professionals, pastoral counselors, CPS agencies, domestic violence shelters, and agencies specializing in the assessment, treatment, education, and prevention of sexual abuse so that when an incident of sexual abuse is brought to their attention, they can consult with experienced professionals and provide timely referrals to individuals and families. When faced with an incident, clergy and religious laypeople should consult with a trained professional before intervening. Trained professionals can assist clergy and laypeople to make appropriate responses and referrals. The following resources are useful references to assist clergy and laypeople:

American Association of Pastoral Counselors: To obtain information about the role of a pastoral counselor and referrals to pastoral counselors across the United States. On-line: *http://www.aapc.org.*

American Psychological Association: To obtain education and prevention materials regarding sexual abuse and referrals to psychologists. On-line: *http://www.apa.org.*

American Counseling Association: To obtain education and prevention materials regarding sexual abuse and referrals to professional counselors. On-line: *http://www.aca.org.*

Center for the Prevention of Sexual Abuse and Domestic Violence (936 North 34th Street, Suite 200, Seattle, WA 98103): An interreligious, educational resource that is an international, private, nonprofit organization headquartered in Seattle, Washington. Founded in 1977 by the Rev. Dr. Marie M. Fortune, the center addresses issues of sexual and domestic violence. Its goal is to engage religious leaders in the task of ending abuse, and to serve as a bridge between religious and secular communities. Their emphasis is on education and prevention. E-mail: *cpsdv@cpsdv.org.* Web site: *www.cpsdv.org.*

Paris M. Finner-Williams

Chapter 7

Divorce Recovery: Grief and Loss

Paris M. Finner-Williams is a licensed psychologist and attorney and the founder and chief executive officer of the Detroit-based Finner-Williams and Associates Psychological Services, created in 1979, and the legal professional association of Paris M. Finner-Williams, Esq., P.C., created in 1991. She was born and raised in Detroit and holds a bachelor of arts degree in psychology from the University of Detroit, a master of education degree in educational psychology from Wayne State University, a doctor of philosophy degree in psychological counseling from the University of Michigan, and a juris doctorate from the Detroit College of Law. A popular guest on radio and television, she addresses male-female relationship and motivational issues. Her counseling and legal services include these issues as well as family law and probate matters. An advocate of church-based Christian counseling, she is a founder and the first chairperson of the Black African-American Christian Counselors Division of the American Association of Christian Counselors.

Finner-Williams worked a combined twenty-three years for local, county, and state government as a Mental Health Department administrator. She provides consultation and training to both public and private agencies and organizations in the areas of group dynamics, client assessment, and mental health treatment. She is a member in or officer of numerous professional organizations and has received local and national recognition for her contributions and leadership in the mental health field. Her husband, Robert D. Williams, is a clinical psychiatric social worker, addiction counselor, and licensed marriage and family therapist. They work together in their private practice to preserve families and couples and help individuals. They are the coauthors of *Marital Secrets: Dating, Lies, Communication and Sex* (2001), which is available through their own publishing company, PR Publishing. They are members of Holy Hope Heritage Church—Baptist in Detroit, Michigan.

n legal practice, the pivotal common question and language written in most divorce judgments is whether

> the Plaintiff having appeared in person and by attorney, and after hearing the proofs in support of the allegations contained in Plaintiff's complaint for divorce; and the court having considered such proofs and being duly advised in the premises and finding that the material facts charged in Plaintiff's complaint are true, and that the court has jurisdiction of this cause and of the parties hereto and of the subject matter hereof, and that there has been a breakdown of the marriage relationship to the extent that the objects of matrimony have been destroyed and there remains no reasonable likelihood that the marriage can be preserved. . . . It is ordered and adjudged that this court, by virtue of the authority therein vested and in pursuance of the statutes in such cases made and provided, in the exercise of its discretion, does hereby order and adjudge that the marriage between the said Plaintiff and the said Defendant, be dissolved and the same is hereby dissolved accordingly, and the said parties are, and each of them is, free from the obligations thereof.

This civil law language is indeed in direct conflict with God's original intent and purpose for marriage. The terms and conditions for divorce are in direct conflict with the beautiful wedding invitations that initially invited family, friends, and the community to bear witness to, and share in, the sacrament of holy matrimony between the now divorced parties. There is nothing holy about either a limited or an absolute divorce. An absolute divorce is based on state statute and marital misconduct, and it renders the parties single. A limited divorce, or separation, serves to address cohabitation rights and maintains the status quo between the parties.

God hates separation and divorce. According to Jesus' answer to the Pharisees in Matthew 19:4–6:

> Have ye not read, that he who made them at the beginning made them male and female, And said, For this cause shall a man leave father and mother, and shall cleave to his wife: and they twain shall be one flesh? Wherefore they are no more twain, but one flesh. What therefore God hath joined together, let not man put asunder. (KJV)

And Malachi 2:16 tells us

> For the Lord, the God of Israel, says: I hate divorce and marital separation and him who covers his garment (his wife) with violence. Therefore keep a watch upon your spirit (that it may be controlled by my Spirit), that you deal not treacherously and faithlessly (with your marriage mate). (Amplified Bible)

The Word of God appears to be in conflict with the required language of the absolute divorce decreed in several ways. The decree states that

- The court is satisfied with the proofs before them, and the material facts charged in the plaintiff's complaint are true.
- The court has authority and the jurisdiction over the marriage and can dissolve the marriage.
- There remains no reasonable likelihood that the marriage can be preserved.

But the Bible tells us in Isaiah 33:22, "For the LORD is our judge, the LORD is our lawgiver, the LORD is our king; he will save us" (KJV). It is important that Christians remain mindful of the fact that every knee shall bow before him and that every tongue shall swear allegiance to him (Philippians 2:10–11). Thus, it is important to be honest about the allegations set forth in their complaint, including the fact that every effort has been made to forgive and reconcile with their spouse.

The grief experienced after divorce can be viewed as a therapeutic response. Grief during the divorce recovery period is often seen as a period of bereavement. Divorce recovery feels like the suffering experienced with the death of a dream. The grief and loss of divorce is the manifestation of sadness, anguish, guilt, remorse, misery, deep distress, and regret over the loss of something loved. It is the loss of the attachment to another; the loss of companionship; the familiar lifestyle, routine, and sexual partner, regardless of the quality of the relationship. It is a change in the rhythm of life as one knows it. It is often filled with the deep disappointment and fruitless longing for what the ex-spouse refuses to give the hurting divorcée.

CURRENT STATUS OF DIVORCE

According to Gallagher (1989), 65 percent of new marriages fail. Since 1970 the divorce rate has increased to about 40 percent. The National Center for Health Statistics (2000) reported the United States divorce rate as 0.41 percent per capita per year (or 4.1 per 1,000 population) and stated that 10 percent of adult Americans are currently divorced and have not remarried. The Barna Research Corporation (2000) reported that 23 percent of born-again Christians have been divorced at some time in their lives compared with 26 percent of the general population.

Barna (1999) stated in an earlier report that in the total adult population of the United States, 11 percent (compared with the 10 percent reported by

Gallagher) was divorced and had not remarried. However, the divorce rate, which includes both Christians and non-Christians, has remained stable across the last several years. For the most part, this stability has contributed to the enactment of no-fault divorce laws.

Previously, parties were duty bound by common law to disclose in writing and swear to in court about a marked number of unpleasant, dishonorable, degrading, and disgracing personal incidents in order to prove that the marriage could not be preserved and the parties could not reconcile. Thus, many states enacted no-fault divorce statutes that eliminated the embarrassment of such public self-disclosure. However, the Family Research Council (1999) has indicated that the divorce laws in almost every state give greater legal rights to spouses who want to end the marriage than to spouses who want to try to work out their marital problems. The council also stated that more than half (55 percent) of the American public want to see these laws modified to offer greater protection to spouses interested in saving the marriage. This aftermath of the no-fault divorce law reflects the fact that the number of divorced people has more than quadrupled (426 percent), from 4.3 million in 1970 to 18.3 million in 1996, in comparison with the marriage rate, which has grown by only 23 percent, from 95 million to 116 million, during the same time period (for statistics, see Saluter and Lugaila 1996).

According to Ahlburg and DeVita (1992), only one-third of Black children have two parents in the home — a lower rate than a half-century ago. Only 18 percent of Black women who married in the 1940s eventually divorced, a rate only slightly higher than that for White women in that era. By 1960, according to More and Winship (1991), only 60 percent of Black women ages 25 to 29 were married. Ahlburg and DeVita note that "of the Black women who married in the late 1960's and early 1970's, 60 percent have already divorced." But compare these facts with the following: In 1990 only 62 percent of White women ages 25 to 29 were married (More and Winship); further, the average White woman will spend only 43 percent of her life married, very close to the 40 percent a Black woman spent in marriage in 1950. Thus, the number of unsuccessful marriages among White and Black women is relatively the same.

A BIBLICAL VIEW OF DIVORCE

There are differing opinions among Christians and theologians on the biblical grounds for divorce. One school of thought is the fundamental belief that God's holy Word does not recognize divorce under any circumstances.

They characterize divorce as a worldly matter for Christians not to espouse, for it is against the will of God. Romans 12:2 supports that position when it states, "And be not conformed to this world: but be ye transformed by the renewing of your mind, that ye may prove what is that good, and acceptable, and perfect, will of God" (KJV).

The statues that the Lord commanded Moses speaks clearly that "if she had at all an husband, when she vowed, or uttered aught out of her lips, wherewith she bound her soul; And her husband heard it, and held his peace at her in the day that he heard it: then her vows shall stand, and her bonds wherewith she bound her soul shall stand" (Numbers 30:6–7 KJV). This passage further demonstrates that the wife and husband shall stand on their oath, vows, and bonds of marriage if the father, wife, or husband held their peace on the day that any of them heard the vows (Numbers 30:1–6 KJV).

In the New Testament, Jesus states in Matthew 19:8 that "Moses permitted divorce as a concession to your hard-hearted wickedness, but it was not what God had originally intended. And I tell you this, a man who divorces his wife and marries another commits adultery — unless his wife has been unfaithful" (NLT). The holy Word further instructs in 1 Corinthians 7:10–16 that "if she (the wife) does leave him, let her remain single or else go back to him. And the husband must not leave his wife" (v. 11 NLT). This view firmly holds that a man and woman are married to each other until death do they part. Blankehorn, Bayme, and Bethke (1990) tell us that almost three-quarters of adult Americans believe marriage is a lifelong commitment that should not be ended except under extreme circumstances. Even 81 percent of divorced and separated Americans still believe in marriage.

The alternative school of thought is that the Bible discusses five circumstances under which God allows divorce: adultery, fornication, desertion (nonsupport), unequally yoked marriages, and abuse. This school of thought holds that God does not command divorce under any of these exceptions but that God will allow divorce and forgive the plaintiff divorcée who commences the divorce proceedings. Let us explain each one briefly.

First, generally speaking, *adultery* is a sin of the heart, soul, and mind; and it covers the sins of infidelity, sexual immorality, and unfaithfulness by a married person. The sexual immorality is also a sin of the physical body. It is believed that one is released from one's marital vows and free to remarry under these conditions: (1) the spouse is unfaithful, (2) there is a pattern of recurrent unfaithfulness by the adulterous spouse, (3) there is a pattern of repeated forgiveness by the believer, and (4) the couple fails to reconcile and renew their marriage even when the adultery has stopped. Matthew 5:31 teaches, "It hath been said, Whosoever shall put away his wife, let him give her a writing of divorcement" (KJV).

Second, *fornication* is often seen as a subcomponent of the sin of adultery. Many distinguish it from adultery by viewing it as a sin of pure lust, illicit intercourse, sexual immorality, and unfaithfulness without the investment of the strayed spouse's heart and spirit. Fornication is often viewed as those immortal acts that may occur once with a stranger and for those single acts of sexual sin that may result in the conception of children outside of the marriage. The holy Word often discusses the children born out of wedlock as those "born of fornication" (e.g., John 8:41 KJV). And Paul answers the church in Corinthians: "Nevertheless, to avoid fornication, let every man have his own wife, and let every woman have her own husband" (1 Corinthians 7:2 KJV).

Third, *desertion and nonsupport* is also often seen as a subcomponent of the sin of adultery. Theologians discriminate it from adultery by regarding it as a sin of abandonment, or "putting away of the spouse" without financial, emotional, or physical support. Some also believe there is a sin of desertion and nonsupport when there has been adultery by a spouse with no sexual relationship with another, or when the partner elects to love someone other than the spouse. But Paul clearly instructs us in 1 Corinthians 7:3: "Let the husband render unto the wife due benevolence: and likewise also the wife unto the husband" (KJV).

Fourth are the *unequally yoked marital relationships*. This happens when one spouse is a Christian believer and the other is not. The Scriptures allow divorce and support the divorcée receiving forgiveness from Christ if the unbeliever elects to withdraw from the marriage and abandon spousal rights, vows, and marital oath (1 Corinthians 7:10–16; see also Matthew 19:3–9). If the nonbeliever withdraws his or her spousal rights, then the believer is released of the marital covenant and is free to remarry.

Finally, fifth is the sin of *mental, emotional, physical, or psychological abuse*. God views our bodies as a temple and vessel of holiness. It is a spousal right to expect physical and mental safety with their partner and have a life free of harm and damage. Spouses have a God-given right to life, freedom, and prosperity. The Scriptures advise us not to nurse hatred in our hearts (Leviticus 19:17), but instead to rebuke those that harm us (Luke 17:3), utilize confrontation strategies as discussed in Matthew 18:15–17, repeatedly forgive them, and reconcile. But if the abuser refuses to seek, accept, and/or benefit from help to eliminate the abusive behavior, then, it is commonly believed, his behavior has communicated that he is not a Christian, is not of the faith, and wants a divorce. By continuing the abuse, the person has abandoned his marital vows and breached his covenant. The failure to renew his or her mind, to repent, and to make behavioral changes is an indication that he or she is not a Christian believer and not living within the will of God. Those that hold this view usually support that divorce is appropriate and that the believer should divorce the abuser and let him go. If the abused becomes psychologically or physically incapacitated, he or she would not be a vessel available to serve in the kingdom of God.

A covenant is a contract between two parties. Free will is a gift from God. If a spouse exercises free will to dissolve the marital covenant and to divorce, then the bonds of matrimony are broken. It is possible after divorce that parties can forgive each other for any mistreatment and then establish a peaceful reconciliation but still make a reasonable decision not to restore the bonds of marriage. It is possible that man or woman can put asunder what God has joined. But God is merciful and will forgive us for our sins, for God judges us by our hearts. During the divorce proceedings and divorce recovery, the believer should pray for a clean heart, mercy, and forgiveness. God loves every divorcée, and he will renew their spirits. God has left us a peaceful comforter — the Holy Spirit.

ISSUES FOR DIVORCÉES TO ASSESS

"Therefore shall a man leave his father and his mother, and shall cleave unto his wife: and they shall be one flesh" (Genesis 2:24 KJV).

Separation of flesh, whether by trauma or under surgical procedures, is painful. Divorce is like undergoing a spiritual surgical procedure, and it is painful, intrusive, and unnatural to God's natural order and intent for two to become one unit and then for their flesh to become disunited or put asunder.

There are at least ten problems and issues that divorcées may express during their recovery.

1. **Regretting family-oriented holidays.** A holiday is usually a time of joy, fun, family stories, mutual warm regard, and being grateful for our lives. However, the first full year of holidays will be difficult for new divorcées. It is often a holiday (especially New Year's Eve, Thanksgiving Day, Christmas Eve, and Christmas Day) that will pierce the romantic veil of hope that they still have a partner.

2. Thoughts of death, suicide, or homicide. Divorcées should be reminded that Jesus Christ died on the cross so that they need not die but instead have an open spirit to receive this new opportunity to develop a happier lifestyle. Life is not over, but instead they are transformed into new creatures in the will of God. It will be important to ask if they have a specific plan, opportunity, or means of harming themselves or others. If the answer is positive, then an immediate referral to an experienced Christian counselor or qualified mental health provider is recommended.

3. Depressed mood, sadness, and emotional mood swings. Divorcées will usually experience uncontrolled crying. Episodes may start from the end of their work shift on Friday until the commencing of the next work-week. This is because of the void they feel in their life and routine. The crying periods vary and may reoccur after significant periods of emotional remission and no crying. The recurrence could merely be hearing the first song played at their wedding reception or their favorite song. A divorcée's mood and affect may often appear to be sad, despondent, distraught, and remorseful. She may feel overwhelmed and hopeless. He may feel a variety of feelings at one time.

4. Extreme anger. Anger can be projected outward and directed toward the ex-spouse and those perceived as supporters of the ex-spouse. Divorcées may even become angry toward God for his being silent; not answering prayers; allowing the pain, harm, and divorce to actually occur; and causing them to be alone once again.

5. Feelings of worthlessness or excessive or inappropriate guilt. Divorcées often feel guilty and worthless in whatever role they play in an intact family, be it wife, mother, husband, or father. The insensitive verbal and nonverbal behaviors of the ex-spouse and others may have a further negative impact on the divorcées. This is a difficult burden to bear.

6. A sense of loss and emptiness. Divorcées feel a sense of casualty, experiencing a void in the present while living under the restrictive terms and conditions of a divorce judgment that speaks about their future — a future that they can't even conceptualize happening. The death of a spouse often is viewed as more acceptable and manageable than the aftermath of a divorce. The pain of the unknown can be crippling.

7. Significant change in appetite, sleeping patterns, and weight. Divorcées often lose or gain more than 5 percent of their pre-divorce body weight in a month. They may experience sleep disturbance, excessive sleepiness, sleep disruption, insomnia, restlessness, nightmares, and a variety of other serious clinical sleeping problems.

8. Diminished ability to think, concentrate, control normal functions or be decisive. Divorcées may be so preoccupied with their new status and adjustment problems that their margin of errors may increase. There will be a need to redirect and refocus on tasks.

9. Grandiose, high-strung, hyperactive, or manic behaviors. Divorcées may have a decreased need for sleep, be more talkative, be easily distracted, and have excessive laughter and involvement of pleasurable activities. Signs of maladjustment may be unrestrained shopping, sexual indiscretions, poor insight into problems, or poor judgment in business decisions. Often divorcées may experience relief from the trauma and stress they were under during the dysfunctional marriage.

10. Inability to forgive the former spouse. Divorcées labor inappropriately under the belief that to forgive the ex-spouse would mean to sanction and approve their sin. Those divorcées need to learn that failure to forgive hardens their heart and leads to wrath and other ungodly feelings.

In summary, divorcées should be encouraged and, when appropriate, reminded of the following:

- These feelings are normal and take time to heal.
- Seek help from a Christian counselor or qualified mental health professional.
- Be in control of your feelings and thoughts; you can take control with the aid of God.
- God does love you and has a purpose for you to fulfill during your lifetime.
- God is not like us humans. When you seek forgiveness from God with a pure heart, it is given. If you ask forgiveness from God, your former spouse, or those who have been offended, God will forgive even if others won't.
- Forgiveness is initially an intellectual act. If you forgive your ex-spouse with your mouth and mind, your heart will follow.
- Carefully consider reconciliation and seek wisdom and God's direction.
- Do not make too many changes in environment and enter into a new relationship too soon.
- Seek the face of God, pray consistently, ask for the peace that he has promised in his holy Word, pray for your ex-spouse, and keep your prayers mostly focused on God.
- Take one day at a time.

- It is all right to feel giddy, happy, hopeful, and relief from the painful bonds of the marriage.
- Seek advice and counsel from a debt elimination specialist and financial planner.
- Set a limited time for "depression" — a time when you will refuse to cry anymore. Of course, you may fail to comply with your self-imposed deadline, but when we fall, God will help us up again and again. Do not embrace and find comfort in a lifestyle of depression and a spirit of doom.
- Get help with establishing an alternative holiday style that will allow you to be around more single people instead of married couples and experience joy, laughs, humor, physical hugs, touching, peace, and blessed assurance. First Thessalonians 5:16–18 says, "Rejoice always; pray without ceasing; in everything give thanks; for this is God's will for you in Christ Jesus" (NASB).
- Sin not, but rather take advantage of this time for self-examination and correction.
- Children need to consistently be told that they are not at fault for the divorce. Pay child support, and never speak to the ex-spouse through the children or speak of your former spouse negatively to the children. Encourage liberal parenting time by your former spouse with your children. Do not allow your children to become your caretaker.
- Treat yourself to recreation, relaxation, and luxuries (such as massages and vacations).
- Do not substitute other dependencies such as drugs, gambling, excessive shopping, coffee, sex, gambling, or physical exercise for marriage and love.
- Meditate daily on Scriptures that will change your mind and spirit, such as 1 Peter 5:7–8; Galatians 5:25–26 and 1:10; Romans 8:3–13; 1 John 5:4; Philippians 4:8; Colossians 3:7–9; Psalm 51:10; Matthew 12:34–37; and Ephesians 4:23.

One can live to love again in a New Testament relationship with Jesus Christ. There is hope for each of us. God can restore all that we have lost if we accept the invitation of God to heal our broken hearts, withered dreams, shattered lives, and wounded spirits.

CASE EXAMPLES OF DIVORCÉES

The two heartfelt testimonies that follow illustrate reasonable approaches to helping people who have endured divorce. (Names and details have been changed.)

John

John is a 32-year-old male working as a technician in a local automobile manufacturing company. He has a high school diploma and a vocational certificate and is attending a local university part-time as he pursues a bachelor degree in accounting. When asked why he was seeking a divorce, he wrote:

> I believe that the true sanctuary and meaning of the marriage vows were not enforced in her life. I also believe that our marriage was based on money and physical attraction, rather than spiritual content. The wants and influence of her mother dominated rather than our joint united bond to overcome any obstacles. She also carried some of her previous marriage baggage into ours! She has been holding my baby girl hostage to punish me for the problems between us that we could not work out separated from each other.

John was experiencing depression, anger, and poor concentration. After the divorce, he would not attend his academic classes or go to work on Monday and Friday after having had a near-perfect attendance record. He started self-medicating with beer and became socially withdrawn. It was necessary to assist John with identifying, recognizing, and accepting his own emotional baggage, his role in failing to marry for the right reasons, and his behaviors that contributed to the dissolution of the marriage. He examined his feelings and thoughts about his former in-laws. He was directed to Scriptures regarding forgiveness, was taught effective parenting and conflict resolution skills. Repeated behavioral modeling and role playing exercises were used extensively. Weekly homework assignments were geared toward better managing his relationship with his ex-wife and daughter. He was given leads to focus on strengthening his ego, self-esteem, and self-concept. He was required to attend Alcoholics Anonymous meetings every Wednesday and Saturday. He was persuaded to return to his academic studies, attend his church worship service each Sunday, and join a father's support group. John's instability improved as he witnessed how the parenting time and child support provisions of the divorce judgment would protect his opportunities to bond with his daughter. He also gained peace and composure as he learned how to enforce the terms of the divorce judgment and focus on improving his relationship with God while studying the Word of God in a structured manner.

Jane

Jane is a 55-year-old female with twenty years of experience in the local school system, working as a certified master's level prepared teacher. She was married to a man who worked as a newspaper editor for a local Black paper and later became an attorney for thirty-four years. After obtaining her two degrees and raising their children, she worked two teaching jobs so that her husband could complete his law degree and become a licensed attorney. He insisted that she not work while their three children were under the age of twelve, but he did support her attending college classes while the children were in school.

When asked why she was seeking a divorce, she wrote:

The reasons I believe my marriage went wrong:

1. I am a "born again" Christian and I must write from that perspective. This is my second divorce. I did not consult God for my mate in either case. My first divorce was based on God's Word — fornication. My second divorce is also based on God. My marriage was entered into by deceit of my husband and God told me that "a contract entered into by deceit on the part of either one was not binding." Deceit — he didn't love me for myself and he sought to take advantage of that for his gain.

2. Being there faithfully and giving him all the space that I thought he should have, that means that I stayed home and in the house taking care of children when I wasn't working.

3. I stood by him without question when he was right or wrong. That included times when he was doing drugs, something that I was totally against.

4. Him being unfaithful, in other relationships and having children outside of the marriage.

For the first nine months after the stormy divorce proceedings, she was experiencing homicidal ideation and emotional mood swings ranging from anger to solitude. She dreaded family-orientated holidays, always overcooked, and overate in the former marital home alone. For the first time in her career she received oral and written reprimands for unacceptable work performance that she attributed to impaired concentration, preoccupation with her memories, and inability to obtain an acceptable answer to the question, Why has this divorce happened to me at this time of my life?

It was necessary to provide Jane with legal advice and counsel relative to personal assault charges and charges that could arise from damage caused to personal property by her ex-spouse. This appeared to be an effective detriment to any planned criminal or misdemeanor acts. She was encouraged to renew healthy relationships with never-married and divorced Christian friends from her church, sorority, and at work. She was referred to a board-certified psychiatrist for a medication review and consultation, given the delusional themes of persecution and tactile hallucinations when she became physically exhausted from excessive working hours.

Jane eliminated her second job, limited work to eight and a half hours a day, and joined a healthy Saturday night eating/cooking club that rotated to her home every six to eight weeks. Given her spiritual gift of teaching, she joined the tutorial section of her church's Christian Education Department. We worked on preplanning her holidays, some with and without her adult children, who presented with domineering and control problems toward her since the divorce. She was given Scriptures and therapeutic assessments to complete between counseling sessions that would assist her with improving her spirit, establishing an identity separate from her ex-spouse, and viewing God as her husband. She was asked to identify which gospel or hymn would best described her mood and feeling every two or three sessions, and she was asked to sing a portion of it during each session. This was a good way to gauge her mood and to assess when her affect was improving. She was taught anger management, stress reduction, assertiveness, and cognitive restructuring skills (similar to the renewing of the mind and spirit). She was granted a six-week medical leave from her job for stress, and she returned with improved concentration and significantly reduced performance errors.

Within twelve months, Jane's clinical presentation was much improved, and she was able to express thoughts and feelings of thanksgiving for a quality of life absent of deceit, superficiality, and emotional detachment. She acknowledged that the strongholds of anger, homicidal ideation, solitary overeating, and remorse were broken by the blood of Jesus and the anointing of the Holy Spirit on her new life.

ISSUES OF REFERRAL, CONSULTATION, AND TERMINATION

As African American professionals, pastors, lay counselors, and Christian counselors, we will be faced with a variety of ethical problems that arise from different human problems that affect the life of divorced adults and their children, ex-spouses, and families. As helpers and caregivers we should acknowledge that the first rule is to do no harm to those we serve, to the significant others of clients, and to those we are affiliated with or are required to relate to on behalf of a client.

When considering making a referral, this should not be done until after obtaining the client's consent and providing the client with informed choices among referral sources. One should maintain good insight about one's own personal problems and reduce or restrict the counseling ministry so that clients are not adversely affected by the counselor's personal circumstances. If any of the following is true for the person one is working with, one should make a referral:

- The person is a current or former sexual and/or marital partner.
- There is a dual or multiple relationship where two or more roles are mixed in a manner that can harm the counseling relationship.
- You cannot resolve all counseling conflicts in the client's best interest.

Consultation with others should be considered if:

- You are tempted to resolve a client's manner in harmful ways.
- You are faced with difficulties beyond your experience, or the client-counselor relationship deteriorates to the level of possible harm to the client.

The overall intent is to keep the client's best interest in focus and that harm is avoided.

With consent of the client, you should take proper action against the harm done to that client by other counselors and pastors. This may include assisting the client with filing an administrative complaint with licensing boards or professional organizations, or initiating litigation against the counselor. Nearly 40 percent of the states require such assertive acts.

CONCLUSION

Colossians 3:12–13 states: "And so, as those who have been chosen of God, holy and beloved, put on a heart of compassion, kindness, humility, gentleness and patience; bearing with one another, and forgiving each other, whoever has a complaint against anyone; just as the Lord forgave you, so also should you" (NASB). And 1 Thessalonians 2:7 says, "But we proved to be gentle among you, as a nursing mother tenderly cares for her own children" (NASB).

REFERENCES

Ahlburg, D., and C. J. DeVita. 1992. New realities of the American family. *Population Bulletin* 47, no. 2: 1–44. *http://www.divorcereform.org/rates.html*

Barna Research Online. 1999. Christians are more likely to experience divorce than are non-Christians. Barna Research Corporation. *www.barna.org/*

Barna Research Online. 2000. Church demographics. Barna Research Corporation. *www.barna.org/*

Divorce rates and marriage rates—what happened. *www.divorcereform.org/rates.html*

Family Research Council. 1999. Marriage and family. *www.frc.org*

Gallagher, M. 1989. Recent trends in marital disruption. *Demography* 26: 37–51.

More, R. D., and C. Winship. 1991. Socioeconomic change and the decline of marriage for Blacks and Whites. In *Urban underclass,* edited by Christopher Jencks and Paul E. Peterson, 120. Washington, D.C.: Brookings Institution, 1991.

National Center for Health Statistics. 2000. Divorce. *www.cdc.gov/nchs/fastats/divorce.htm*

Saluter, A. F., and T. A. Lugaila. 1996. Marital status and living arrangements: March 1996. *Current Population Statistics.* Washington, D.C.: U.S. Bureau of Census.

Suggested Resources

Adams, J. E. 1980. *Marriage, divorce and remarriage.* Phillipsburg, N.J.: Presbyterian and Reformed Publishing.

Gallagher, M. 1996. *The abolition of marriage: How we destroy lasting love.* Washington, D.C.: Eagle Publishing.

Other Resources

Divorce Care Video Series is a powerful tool for divorce recovery ministries, professionals, pastors, lay counselors, and other individuals. It is an effective resource for hurting people struggling with the pain of separation and divorce. To order, contact Divorce Care at (800) 489-7778 or write them at P.O. Box 1739, Wake Forest, NC 27588-1739.

Simmons, Curt (*curtsimmons@nortevinfo.net*). *The Broken Circle Newsletter.*

Willie Richardson

Chapter 8

Blended Families

Willie Richardson is the founder and president of Christian Research and Development and of Resources for Better Families. The main objective of both organizations is to research needs and methods as well as to develop materials for family and church ministry training. He is also the founder and pastor of Christian Stronghold Baptist Church, Philadelphia, Pennsylvania, which has grown from six people to 3,500 active members. Dr. Richardson is a graduate of Philadelphia College of Bible. He has studied at Temple University and has a doctorate of divinity from Geneva College.

Dr. Richardson, a former design engineer, also has thirty-seven years experience in biblical teaching and counseling. He is the author of several workbooks and books, the latest of which is entitled *Reclaiming the Urban Family* (Zondervan 1996). Richardson has been invited to the White House on three different occasions: by former presidents Ronald Reagan and George Bush, and recently by President George W. Bush when he introduced his Faith-Based Initiative in January 2001.

Dr. Richardson and his wife, Patricia, have been married for more than thirty-seven years and are the parents of four adult children and have five grandchildren.

As a pastor and counselor, I want to sound the alarm that we need to prepare and train people for family life. In particular, a relatively new family type, the "blended family" has become very prevalent in the last thirty years. Whitehead (1993) states:

> Divorce and out of wedlock childbirth are transforming the lives of American children. In the postwar generation more than 80 percent of children grew up in a family with two biological parents who were married to each other. By 1980 only 50 percent could expect to spend their entire childhood in an intact family. If current trends continue, less than

half of all children born today will live continuously with their own mother and father throughout childhood. Most American children will spend several years in a single-mother family. Some will eventually live in stepparent families, but because stepfamilies are more likely to break up than intact (by which I mean two biological-parent) families, an increasing number of children will experience family breakup two or even three times during childhood. (p. 47)

I don't know the origin of the term "blended family," but the last thing these families are doing is blending. However, the term "stepfamily" has become a stigma for some people because it suggests unnatural relationships, so blended families is used instead. Pratt (1995), an expert on blended families, reports that 70 percent of stepfamilies dissolve within ten years. I believe that with better training we can turn this statistic around. Our goal as caregivers, counselors, or members of such families is to get them to become intact, wholesome blended families.

GETTING BEYOND IGNORANCE AND DENIAL

Most of us are ignorant of the destructive issues of blended families. This should not be an insult. What I am saying is simply that most of us do not know or have certain information, facts, or experience necessary to recognize and resolve the problems that are unique to these types of families.

Some people, especially men, do not think they need premarital counseling or counseling when things are not going well after marriage. However, if a wife has packed her bags or has already left him, some men agree to go to counseling. The mistake some women make is not realizing the value of marital counseling and not standing their ground. If the man loves her the way Ephesians 5 says he is supposed to love her, he will agree to go through marriage training. I have been urging pastors for more than twenty years to establish Family Training Centers in our churches to train single people in how to have sound Christian marriages. The need is even greater for those who are entering step- or blended families.

STEPFAMILIES ARE DIFFERENT FROM NUCLEAR FAMILIES

Nuclear first-marriage families begin with no children, giving the couple time to adjust and build a relationship with each other. When children are born into the nuclear family, there is a natural bonding that takes place with both parents. From the outset, both parents are involved with the development of the children. The children have genetic characteristics of both parents and are learning behavior from both.

Stepfamilies, on the other hand, are the result of broken relationships. Such families are established out of loss. Such marriages begin with disappointments from the past and high expectations to make up for the loss. These marriages can be made up of people who did not marry former lovers who produced a child, of divorced people from failed marriages, or of those who were rejected and deserted by a former spouse. Those who lost a good spouse by death will naturally be looking for the same successful marriage with a totally different person. The children involved in stepfamilies are separated from one of their natural parents either most of the time or totally.

Although stepfamilies face more challenges than other families from the very start, with the help of the Lord and good training, these families can honor and glorify God.

SOME OF THE TOUGH ISSUES STEPFAMILIES FACE

A blended family will face a number of tough issues. For example, Who will give leadership to the new household? We have two different households coming together that have operated under distinctive headships. Adjustments will have to be made by all involved. In addition, one or both of the spouses may have some of the following unrealistic expectations:

- The new marriage will make up for their being a victim
- The stepparent will solve all the problems of the stepchildren
- The new spouse will ease the burden the single parent has carried
- The stepchildren will accept the authority and discipline of the stepparent
- The stepchildren will automatically love and respect the stepparent
- The stepchildren will automatically love and get along with each other
- Because of the marriage, stepsisters and stepbrothers are now sisters and brothers so they can sleep in the same bed without a chance of sexual involvement regardless of their ages

Other issues that must be faced include:

- Living with the arrangements of children's visitation rights of former spouses and lovers without being insecure and jealous

- Trying to bring the children up in a Christian home while they are being influenced by the unsaved parent, who may be antagonistic toward Christianity
- Burdensome financial support of children from a previous relationship that affects the finances of the new household
- Putting children in a position to be loyal or disloyal to their parents

I deal with some of these issues below, and at the end of the chapter I give a list of books and other resources that will be helpful in dealing with these issues.

WHAT SHOULD SINGLE PEOPLE DO IN PREPARATION FOR BLENDED FAMILIES?

Many single people who get married, especially those who marry later in life, will be a partner in a blended family. For many years an increasing number of children in our communities have been born out of wedlock, and today that number constitutes a majority. The first year that this trend changed for the better was 1999; however, America still leads the world in teenage births. Therefore, blended families will be the composition of the majority of our families in the future.

First of all, when the relationship becomes serious and there is a possibility of a future marriage for those who already have children, the children should be courted also. It is a great mistake to have children or teenagers living with you and the only relationship these siblings have is the one that starts after the marriage. They have to adjust to this "intruder" who has turned their world upside down. At some point in the relationship, before a decision has been made to marry, the potential stepparent should intentionally build relationships with the children. Some great relationships have been developed this way before marriage, but in some cases the potential stepparent and the children will not like, let alone love, each other. For whatever reason, some adults and some children do not blend. It is better to discover this before rather than after marriage. In other words, if your intended doesn't get along with your children, there should be no marriage. It is a terrible thing for a parent to have to choose between the children and the spouse as to who must exit the household. Moreover, the majority of divorces in stepfamilies are over issues dealing with the children.

Secondly, no single person should marry anyone without premarital counseling or marriage training. In my previous book, *Reclaiming the*

Urban Family (1996), I shared that premarital counseling is so effective in the church I pastor that we have had only one divorce in the last twenty-five years of those singles who submitted to our singles courtship training and premarital counseling. Included in premarital counseling are the issues of blended families that should be worked through.

Thirdly, if it has not already been done, you need to get legal custody of your children. The custodial parent is usually the one the child lives with, and the other parent may or may not have visitation rights, depending on the circumstances. The noncustodial parent usually pays child support. Over the years, I have seen the courts make some bad decisions because they do not personally know the people that stand before them in the courtroom.

From my observation over the years, the person who files first for child custody usually is favored. And of course the person who has a lawyer has an advantage. Do not go into a courtroom without a lawyer, whether you are there for custody or for child support. It is judicial suicide. By getting custody, you stand a better chance of protecting your children spiritually and physically from wrong influences of their unsaved parent, if this is the case. We tell all single parents in our church to get legal custody of their children. Not all of them, however, will listen to wise counsel.

It is common for teenagers to rebel whether they are in a nuclear family or a stepfamily. Some of these teenagers who are being brought up under Christian rules of behavior will opt to live with their unsaved parent because they believe they will get more freedom to do what they want. Sometimes this is true. Over the years, some of our Christian stepfamilies who were experiencing the hardships of a rebellious teenager felt they were forced, and thought it would be best, that the child live with the unsaved parent for the sake of peace. In most cases, it was disastrous. For example, the teenagers often became pregnant or fathered children out of wedlock, became drug addicts or drug pushers, or were introduced to a life of crime.

THE GOAL OF ONENESS IN BLENDED FAMILIES

God is the one who created marriage and the family. Humans and the devil have come up with adultery, fornication, babies out of wedlock, divorce, and couples living together without being married. But God through his love and grace knows that we will sin and make mistakes, so the Lord has provided salvation, deliverance, and other provisions of grace.

The husband and wife in all Christian marriages must submit to God's biblical principles for the family. A basic commitment is the priority of developing oneness between the husband and wife. With the challenges stepfamilies face — problems with loving someone else's children and building a relationship with them — the unity of spouses must be unquestioned. This is not easy when you realize that it is complicated by the fact that you have to adapt to and bond with children as you try to build oneness with each other. The children may be manipulative and destructive to the couple's relationship.

Oneness is based on the fact that God's will is that people who marry should be suited for each other. For example, "The LORD God said, 'It is not good for the man to be alone. I will make a helper suitable for him'" (Genesis 2:18).

Through the single selection process, courtship, and premarital counseling, a person should have made a good choice in selecting someone who is compatible. Included in being suitable is the commitment to making a blended family work.

The oneness of God's will for married couples is powerful and mysterious. In the passage in Genesis, "the man said, 'This is now bone of my bones and flesh of my flesh; she shall be called "woman," for she was taken out of man.' For this reason a man will leave his father and mother and be united to his wife, and they will become one flesh" (Genesis 2:23–24).

As we include Christ in our marriages, it is powerful because his supernatural participation in maturing us in oneness becomes apparent. His character of selflessness, self-sacrificing, and unconditional love manifests itself in us as married couples. It is mysterious because oneness includes spiritual oneness, sexual oneness, and emotional oneness. As each year passes, couples who are committed to oneness experience deeper love and the netting of emotions and sexual relations becomes a taste of heaven because of the work of God the Holy Spirit.

To maintain this oneness, couples must have weekly talks alone to discuss issues, share God's Word, and pray together.

KEEPING PAST BAD EXPERIENCES AND PAIN FROM INFLUENCING THE NEW FAMILY

One of the problems that commonly arises in stepfamilies is that of entering marriage with unresolved conflict and unhealed internal wounds. When families are dissolved, whether because of divorce, breakup of unmarried couples living together, or desertion, there are disappointments. The children sometimes still have hope that Mom and Dad will get back together.

Some new spouses carry with them memories of painful and abusive incidents. Something has happened that perhaps has divided the family that is now attempting to blend with another person or another broken family. Often the destructive baggage is brought into the marriage unintentionally.

Premarital counseling is a good vehicle for bringing such unresolved issues to the surface. The couple must deal with negative fears and memories left over from another marriage or intimate relationship. If they were abused, they may think this will happen in the new marriage, and even a slightly raised voice may bring terror to the person who was abused. A person who has been rejected and deserted may be so insecure that each absence from home of the new spouse could be a time of uncertainty until the person physically is present again. It is unfair to burden a new partner with the sins of a former relationship. What happened in the past should be shared for understanding, empathy, and sympathy with the new partner. We are all products of past life experiences, both good and bad.

Pratt (1995) gives the following list of indicators that counseling may be needed after marriage:

1. Physically hurting ourselves or others
   a. Violence and abuse
   b. Emotional, spiritual abuse
   c. Substance abuse
2. Severe, prolonged depression
3. Inability to feel pain or react to it
4. Refusal to accept responsibility
5. Accepting total blame and condemnation
6. Behavior that is destructive to relationships
7. Loss of ability to function at school or work
8. Deterioration of peer relationships
9. Withdrawal emotionally or physically
10. Compulsive behavior
11. Panic attacks, unreasonable fears
12. Sense of reality loss
13. Manipulation of others
14. Loss of sexual interest or unusual obsession with sex (p. 5)

After facing and dealing with the past, couples and individuals must submit to the biblical admonishment: "But one thing I do: Forgetting what is behind and straining toward what is ahead, I press on . . ." (Philippians 3:13–14).

I mentioned earlier that Christ must be included in the marriage because "he heals the brokenhearted and binds up their wounds" (Psalm 147:3). God can release us from anxiety and give us joy. "When anxiety was great within me, your consolation brought joy to my soul" (Psalm 94:19). Forgiveness of past offenders is a must for future healing.

CONSIDER THE PLIGHT OF THE CHILDREN IN A NEW MARRIAGE

The first thing we need to take into consideration is what the children are experiencing because of the new marriage. One of the major mistakes that parents and stepparents make in beginning the new family is not taking into consideration what the children are thinking and feeling. When married people decide to separate and live independently of one another, children are hoping and praying that Mom and Dad will get back together. Even if the separated couple finally decides to get a divorce, the children sometimes are still set on their reconciliation. Their hopes are shattered only when the new spouse intrudes into their life and is introduced as "your new mother (or father)." The immediate changes to the children can be devastating and traumatic.

Overnight, an only child can find herself with an older brother and two younger sisters. A child who has had Mom or Dad to himself now has to share him or her with a bunch of strangers that he is now living with. Perhaps the child is living in a new, strange house in a new neighborhood. The child suddenly finds herself in a new school, snatched away from her familiar friends; and she had no choice in the matter. At night his mother now shares her bedroom with a strange man and is told they cannot be disturbed. The child may be sharing a room with a new sibling who has some very strange ways — and perhaps this child never had to share anything with anybody.

Given these issues, parents and stepparents must be sympathetic to the plight of the new stepchildren.

OBSERVATIONS THAT MAY BE HELPFUL TO PARENTS

Not only have I been ministering to stepfamilies for the last thirty years, but both my wife and I come from stepfamilies. To submit to the discipline of a stepparent is the most difficult adjustment for children, especially teenagers. Sometimes it is impossible to discipline somebody else's teenager. I will say more about discipline later.

The time it takes to blend a family with children who are infants to twelve years old is a year and a half to two years. With adolescents and older siblings, it takes years to integrate. Bird (1990) found that the blending process takes three to five years. Moore (2000) of the Sacramento Counseling Center, states that these stages on average take five to seven years to move through. Young adults from stepfamilies leave home at a younger age than their peers. In other words, there must be patience and a commitment that stepfamily development will take time.

Children who have contact with their noncustodial parent adjust better to stepparents. Families who have weekly family prayer meetings led by the fathers seem to bond better and have better communications, not to mention the fact that those who are actively involved in their church seem to be influenced by the Spirit of Christ.

HOW TO BE A STEPPARENT TO A BLENDED FAMILY

Here are eight recommendations that can assist in blending a family:

1. Initially, try to simply be a friend to the children. Make sure it is clear to all involved, including yourself, that you are not trying to be the child's biological parent. This creates unnecessary problems of mistrust, disappointment on the adult's part, and pain for both parent and child.

2. Get to know the children. Spend one-on-one time together. As stated earlier, the relationship with the children should have started before the marriage. Some children do not respond one on one, but do not be discouraged. Be a patient, understanding friend rather than an authoritative parent.

3. Open the lines of communication. Allow the children to express their sense of loss. Do not take it personally if they seem to be blaming you, but be willing to grieve with them and share their disappointment and pain. Be a friend in a time of need.

4. Do not try to discipline the children at the start of the relationship. You are a stranger who has not earned the loving right to discipline. You should learn from your mate what discipline has gone on before the marriage and how he or she feels about your disciplining the children and whether there will be any problems with the children's other biological parent if you administer discipline. Some of the most violent fights have taken place between the new married couple or between the biological parent and the stepparent because there was no prior communication on this issue.

The custodial parent should be the sole disciplinarian until a loving relationship has developed between the stepparent and the children. Sometimes, if the marriage began with teenagers, it may never be wise for the stepparent to discipline, but always rely on the natural parent to carry out the duty of discipline. This gives some stepfathers problems because biblically they are the head or the leader of the Christian home (1 Corinthians 11:3; Ephesians 5:23). Remember, I began this chapter by pointing out that stepfamilies are different. These seemingly unusual adjustments are necessary for blending a family.

5. Because you are not the biological parent, recognize that your role has its limits. You must accept this. It is not always wise to instruct the children to call the stepparents Mom or Dad. This depends on the age of the children and their relationship with their biological parent. The same wisdom and caution must be exercised in the decision to adopt the children and change their last name. I am not advising against it, but with some families this causes more trouble than blending.

Learn to be yourself with the children. Be enthusiastic in having a good relationship with the children even when it does not seem to be reciprocated. Remember, whether children or teenagers, they are immature and you are the mature adult.

6. Be honest about your uncertainties and apprehensions with the children. Ask for help in building a relationship with the children, letting them know you don't know what you are doing. This will help the children to open up and talk with you.

7. Make a commitment to love your stepchildren no matter what. It takes time to build a relationship with someone you did not choose to have a relationship with but was brought into your life through circumstances. The Lord commands us to love our enemies because he enables us (Matthew 5:44). That is, if we have been born again of the Spirit of God, we have the love of God in us. As a stepparent, let God's *agape* love flow from your heart to the new children God has brought into your life.

8. Try to serve and edify the children. Be sure to keep all your promises.

THE IMPACT OF PAST RELATIONSHIPS ON BLENDED FAMILIES

Four areas may need attention in a blended family:

1. Anger and resentment between parents creates interference of a parent's access and visitation of children. Let's look at some facts. Ahrons and Miller (1993), observing another study, stated: "Feelings of anger toward their former spouses hindered effective involvement on the part of the fathers; angry custodial mothers would sometimes sabotage father's efforts to visit their children" (p. 442).

Seltzer (1991) has indicated that "when both divorced parents share the social and economic responsibilities of child care, children appear to adapt better to their changed living arrangements than when mothers bear these responsibilities alone" (p. 79).

2. Possible fracturing of the oneness by the ex-spouse. One recurring problem is when a man wants to continue his relationship with his children who live with his former wife or girlfriend. Some new wives are insecure and jealous. It is difficult for a wife to spend time with her grandchildren at her adult child's home when she knows the former husband will be present and has no hesitation about making it clear that he still loves her. "After all, you divorced me," he says. "I did not divorce you." Christian biological parents should have a relationship with their children, especially if the other parent is not a Christian. However, this issue should be discussed before marriage and resolved to the new spouse's satisfaction.

Remember, the goal in marriage is oneness. If possible, both husband and wife should be involved with the children that do not live with them. If they cannot participate together because of hard feelings on someone's part, the priority relationship is the husband and wife relationship. ("For this reason a man will leave his father and mother and be united to his wife, and they will become one flesh" — Genesis 2:24.) Adults should be able to work these kinds of situations out to everyone's satisfaction, but sometimes this is not possible when some of the people involved are not committed to the things of God or are selfish or immoral. Some parents cannot have a relationship with their children who do not live with them.

3. Financial burdens from the past. It is very important that single people discuss finances before marriage. It is critical to know if there are any child support obligations. It can have quite an impact on the new family if a man has several children from a former marriage or relationships that he has to support financially. This can determine how many children, if any, the new marriage can bear and support.

4. Incest or rape from the past. Sometimes a woman is ashamed and fearful to tell her new husband that her former husband or live-in boyfriend had an incestuous relationship with her children. However, the results will manifest themselves in the behavior of the wife and the children. Such incidents must be shared with the spouse.

The former husband or lover might have been sexually abusive and at times forced sexual relations, thus having a profound effect on her emotionally and sexually. Again, keeping this a secret can be detrimental to the present relationship.

WORKING WITH THE OTHER PARENT FOR THE CHILD'S SAKE

One of the worst experiences for children is to be caught in a tug-of-war between two feuding parents. The ideal arrangement is for those children to experience love, support, and ongoing relationship with both of the parents. Here are some suggestions for accomplishing this:

1. **Forgive your ex-spouse.** Is there any resentment or an unforgiving attitude toward your ex? Jesus instructs us to pray "Forgive us our debts, as we also have forgiven our debtors" (Matthew 6:12). The Lord also adds, "For if you forgive men when they sin against you, your heavenly Father will also forgive you. But if you do not forgive men their sins, your Father will not forgive your sins" (Matthew 6:14–15).

2. **Commit to helping your children build a relationship with the other parent.** Although you and your ex have a broken relationship that can never be the same again, his or her relationship with the children should remain the same. Every child should have a loving relationship with both parents, if possible. Your goal should be to do all you can to see that this happens. The only exception to this is if the other parent is dangerous, criminal, totally uninterested, or incapacitated in some way.

3. **Set up a meeting with your ex to discuss the arrangements.** Your spouse should be present for support rather than as an active participant in the discussions. Make up an agenda before time. This helps people to stick with the issues and not get too emotional.

4. **Reach clear decisions regarding visitation.** Some of the items that may need to be discussed (if all the details have not been settled in court) are where, when, and how often the noncustodial parent will see the children.

5. **If possible, have similar rules for both homes.** It is best when the rules are consistent for bedtimes, curfews, what is allowed to be watched on television, homework, friendships, discipline, dating, and so forth.

6. **Discuss in advance special arrangements for holidays and birthdays.** This can save everybody hardships and avoid disappointment for the children. Help them to remember the other parent's birthday, Father's Day, and/or Mother's Day with a greeting card or gift.

7. Be careful not to place the children in a situation where they have to be disloyal to either parent. Parents should never question the children about what goes on in the other house; that is none of their business. Children should not be questioned as to which parent they enjoy being with the most.

8. Treat the other parent with honor and respect. The custodial parent should keep the other parent informed about graduations, special sports events, and recitals in which the children are participating.

CONCLUSION

Stepfamilies are growing in numbers in our communities, yet they are failing at a higher rate than other types of families. We must commit ourselves to helping make them successful. Although stepfamilies face more challenges than nuclear families, they can be good, fulfilling Christian families. The Lord Jesus Christ must be included.

RESOURCES

Einstein, E., and L. Albert. 1986. *Strengthening your step family.* Circle Pines, Minn.: American Guidance Service.

Frydenger, T., and A. Frydenger. 1984. *The blended family.* Grand Rapids: Baker.

_____. 1984. *Resolving conflict in the blended family.* Grand Rapids: Baker.

Glassman, B. 1988. *Everything you need to know about step-families.* New York: Rosen Publishing Group.

Leman, K. 1994. *Living in a step-family without getting stepped on.* Nashville: Thomas Nelson.

Richardson, W. 1996. *Reclaiming the urban family.* Grand Rapids: Zondervan.

Walters, L. S. 1993. *There's a new family in my house!* Wheaton, Ill.: Harold Shaw.

REFERENCES

Ahrons, C. R., and R. B. Miller. 1993. The effects of the post-divorce relationship on paternal involvement: A longitudinal analysis. *American Journal of Orthopsychiatry* 63: 441–50.

Bird, J. 1990. *Nine steps towards a healthy step-family.* Ogden, Utah: Department of Child and Family Studies, Weber State University.

Moore, D. 2000. *Some step family statistics.* Sacramento, Calif.: Sacramento Counseling.

Pratt, L. C. 1995. *Making two halves a whole.* Chicago: David C. Cook.

Richardson, W. 1996. *Reclaiming the urban family.* Grand Rapids: Zondervan.

Seltzer, J. A. 1991. Relationships between fathers and children who live apart: The father's role after separation. *Journal of Marriage and the Family* 53: 79–101.

Whitehead, B. D. 1993. Dan Quayle was right. *Atlantic Monthly* 271: 47–84.

Part 3
Confronting Issues of Mental Health

Julius Brooks

Chapter 9

Depression and Bipolar Disorder

Julius Brooks is a clinical staff physician at the Virtua West Jersey Health System Family Health Centers in Camden, New Jersey. He graduated from Temple University School of Medicine in Philadelphia. Dr. Brooks also attended residency training in the West Jersey Health System. He is a member of the South Jersey Medical Association, is certified with the American Board of Family Practice and the National Board of Medical Examiners, and holds a professional license in the states of New Jersey and Pennsylvania. He has more than fifteen years' experience as an attending, staff, and house physician. This includes work as an attending physician in the substance abuse drug and alcohol program ALCOVE. Dr Brooks has also held the positions of medical director for the West Jersey Primary Care Clinic and Southern Jersey Family Medical Centers Inc.

In keeping with the theme of this book, "confronting tough issues," the topic of mood disorders and specifically the extremes of depressed mood (depression) and enhanced mood (mania), is one of the most challenging and, I daresay, misunderstood areas facing the biblical counselor. Hundreds of chapters have been written over the years attempting to guide counselors in their effort to minister to individuals suffering from these debilitating disorders. Unfortunately, a diversity of biblical, educational, and philosophical influences has at times lessened the effectiveness of counselors' efforts to accurately diagnose and treat the counselee.

Using the clinical terms *diagnose* and *treat* serves as an appropriate segue to my contention that disorders of mood at their extremes are neither totally symptomatic of a spiritual problem nor totally indicative of the marginally understood biological processes. These disparate schools of thought, however, underscore some of the controversy lurking in biblically counseling people with mood disorders. Is there a role or place for medical science in this process? In many cases the obvious answer is yes. One challenge lies in the counselor's ability to recognize the client's need for medical evaluation. An example of this may be when symptoms such as insomnia, indecisiveness, or poor concentration impedes the client's ability to receive the Word of God in the management of the problem. Some may argue that these symptoms represent purely spiritual problems and speak to the client's inability to trust the Lord. Imagine the guilt the sincere believer experiences in second-guessing his or her own faith in God while considering whether to seek medical treatment to assist with sleep or relaxation. Ultimately, this guilt may serve to worsen the target condition (depression). As we shall see later, feelings of guilt is one of several symptoms often experienced by patients with depression.

The goal of this chapter is to provide the biblical counselor with a source of help in understanding the medical approach to the management of mood disorders with a concentration on major depression and bipolar disorder. We will consider aspects of the epidemiology (i.e., factors related to the frequency and distribution of these disorders in the community), diagnosis, and treatment of these problems. We'll also take a brief look at how mood disorders uniquely affect certain segments of the population: women, the elderly, and African Americans. Secondly, we will review the topic from a biblical perspective while addressing some of the controversy that still exists when one attempts to bring these two worlds together. Finally, it is hoped that these pages will enable the biblical counselor to attain a degree of comfort in ministering to clients who may be concurrently receiving or in need of medications. Remember that the desired outcome must always be the restoration and maintenance of spiritual, mental, and emotional wholeness and not rigid dedication to certain philosophies or paradigms.

THE CURRENT STATUS OF MOOD DISORDERS: DEPRESSION AND BIPOLAR DISORDER

Before considering the current status of the problem of mood disorders, it is appropriate that we define a few key terms:

- Mood — the sustained internal emotional state of a person
- Affect — the external expression of present emotional content
- Mania — having extremely enhanced mood
- Depression — having depressed mood

- Bipolar — having depressed episodes interspersed with episodes of mania

Note that depression is at times referred to as *unipolar* depression (hence the term *bipolar* denoting the presence of depression and mania in the same disorder). There are three major categories of mood disorders recognized in the field of psychiatry, although several other categories and subcategories exist. They are:

- Bipolar disorder (may be subdivided into bipolar I and bipolar II disorders)
- Dysthymic disorder or dysthymia
- Depression/major depressive disorder

Our concentration will primarily focus on bipolar disorder and depression.

DEPRESSION

Most of us experience times when, in response to disappointment or other unfavorable circumstances, we become downhearted or "depressed." This is as physiologically normal as the enhanced mood or elation we feel when we experience a positive outcome concerning something (or someone) we've invested our time and/or passions into. It is when these extremes of mood become prolonged to the point of dysfunction that we depart from the realm of normality and into the realm of disordered mood. Types of mood deviation that may be regarded by some as normal include *dysphoria* (a down, disquieted, or restless state) as seen in some premenstrual or premenopausal states. In addition, an adjustment disorder with depressed mood may occur when the bereavement related to the loss of a close loved one lasts no longer than six months. Most of us, given adequate time for healing, have the ability to bounce back and go on with our lives. However, some individuals may go on to develop a major depressive episode.

Major depression describes a pervasive, prolonged, and disabling exaggeration of depressed mood and affect associated with several dysfunctional areas such as:

- Behavioral
- Cognitive
- Psychomotor
- Neurochemical
- Spiritual

While secular organizations like the American Psychiatric Association do not take into account the spiritual aspects of individuals, several Christian authors attribute much of these disorders of mood to spiritual dysfunction. Since the biblical counselor assumes that his or her client is born again, addressing this area of dysfunction is essential. We will revisit this important aspect of the problem subsequently.

The Diagnostic and Statistical Manual of Mental Disorders, 4th Edition (1994), known as the DSM-IV, has established criteria for diagnosing a major depressive episode. The criteria are the presence of five or more of the following symptoms during the same two-week period and representing a change from a previous level of functioning:

- Depressed mood most of the day nearly every day
- Markedly diminished interest or pleasure in all activities most of the day nearly every day
- Significant change in weight or in appetite nearly every day
- Insomnia or hypersomnia nearly every day
- Change in psychomotor activity nearly every day (observable by others, not just feeling restless or sluggish)
- Fatigue or loss of energy nearly every day
- Feelings of worthlessness or guilt nearly every day
- Decreased ability to concentrate or think, or indecisiveness
- Recurrent thoughts of death or suicide or suicide attempt

These symptoms cause significant distress or impairment in social, occupational, and other important areas of functioning; are not a result of substance use or a general medical condition; are not accounted for by bereavement; and do not meet the criteria for a mixed disorder (manic and depressive symptoms).

Other noted health organizations, such as the *World Health Organization's International Classification of Diseases,* 10th edition (1993) and the National Institute of Mental Health (1993), have published similar criteria for major depressive episodes. Earlier, distinguished biblical counselor LaHaye (1974) listed the most common symptoms of depression as:

- Erratic sleeping pattern
- Apathy
- Loss of appetite
- Loss of sex drive
- Unkempt appearance
- Many physical ailments

With a few exceptions, the similarities in these lists are apparent. The point is that these are widely recognized manifestations of depression.

Epidemiology of Depression

Considering the scope of the problem, depression is among the most under-diagnosed, underrecognized, and undertreated of all medical illnesses (Amsterdam et al. 2000). Although depression occurs in 5 to 8 percent of the population, it has been estimated that only 15 percent receive adequate treatment. Of these, while 60 to 70 percent respond to some degree, only 25 to 30 percent experience remission. Thus, the majority of depressed people appear to be resistant to treatment (Amsterdam et. al. 2000). As a result, the life of the depressed individual is marred by significant pain and suffering. Issues such as family and interpersonal relationships, the workplace, and resultant personal financial problems may contribute to this devastating downward spiraling. Concomitant medical problems, hospitalization, and suicide are all common results of this problem.

As a primary care physician, I have had the opportunity to diagnose, treat, and/or refer numbers of patients suffering from depression. It is well documented that mood and depressive disorders are highly prevalent in primary care settings. Some investigators report depressive symptoms in 12 to 25 percent of medical outpatients, which is similar to the prevalence reported for upper respiratory infections (colds) and hypertension (high blood pressure) (Feldman 2000). Its economic impacts include decline in job performance, the cost of medical and psychiatric care, and costs resulting from depression-related suicides, which is estimated to surpass $43 billion per year in the United States. This impact has been found to be similar to other chronic health conditions such as diabetes mellitus, coronary heart disease, chronic back disorders, and hypertension (Feldman 2000).

Who is at risk for developing a major depressive episode? While by no means representing an exhaustive listing, some of the more important risk factors are family history, female gender, older age, and spiritual carnality.

Family history. Like several other medical conditions (e.g., Type 2 diabetes), mood disorders have been found to result from a yet-to-be-fully-understood interaction between genetic predisposition and environmental factors. The genetic tendency toward mood disorder seems highly variable: individuals with high genetic predisposition may develop mood disorder with relatively minor inciting events; while those with lower genetic vulnerability may develop these disorders with more serious and/or repeated environmental stressors (Isselbacher et al. 1994).

The evidence of genetic factors is more compelling in bipolar disorders. Adoption studies have shown that biological children of bipolar parents maintain increased risk of developing bipolar disease even when reared in nonaffected adoptive families living in nonprovocative environments. Twin studies have also shown a high propensity to develop bipolar disorder as well as major depressive disorder (Kaplan and Sadock 1998). A more in-depth consideration of bipolar disorder follows later in this chapter.

Female gender. When considering major depression, studies consistently find that the prevalence of these disorders in women nearly doubles that in men. Gender-related rates of depression in children appear to be equal until approximately age 10. The shift to favor women subsequently takes place, then persists until midlife. Thereafter, the rate in women declines to closely match that of men into older age (Kornstein and McEneny 2000). Interestingly, these rates have been consistently demonstrated across cultures and research study techniques.

Biological, psychosocial, and environmental factors have been hypothesized as influencing this apparent trend. Biological factors such as difference in brain structure and function, genetic factors, and hormonal changes during the reproductive cycle have all been suggested to play a role explaining the higher rates in women (Kornstein and McEneny 2000). Specific depressive syndromes are well documented during the premenstrual phase of the reproductive cycle (e.g., PMS). Depression during pregnancy, the postpartum period, and perimenopause is also known to be quite common. Moreover, studies have reported that women with premenstrual and postpartum depressive histories are more likely to have depressive symptoms during the perimenopausal period. This suggests that there may be a subset of women particularly prone to disturbance of mood during times of hormonal variation (Kornstein and McEneny 2000). It is believed that fluctuating levels of the hormone estrogen plays an important role in these observed trends, especially during the perimenopausal period. The limbic system, a portion of the brain known to be involved in the expression of mood and emotion, is rich in estrogen receptors (sites where the hormone triggers its biological activity). As menopause approaches, declining levels of estrogen give rise to the mood instability experienced by some women. These women are often able to re-attain some semblance of levity when they are given estrogen supplements. Yet as was noted in the preceding section on family history, biological factors only partially explain why some women become depressed while others do not.

Psychosocial and environmental factors are also believed to play a significant role in determining a woman's inclination to become depressed. For example, economic dependence, lower educational accomplishment, poverty, and domestic isolation have all been shown to contribute to depressive tendencies in women. Poor women are more likely to live in neighborhoods with low-quality housing and to experience problems in parenting and child care (Ustun 2000). This is particularly true in African American communities. Staley (1991) pointed out that the inner-city Black, single-parent, female-headed household sees a despairing situation in which women experience loneliness, isolation, and depression. In many cases, continuing cycles of poverty and alienation lead to paralyzing feelings of hopelessness.

Older age. Problems that face the elderly (generally age 65 and older) leave them particularly prone to developing depression. Despite this reality, depression in the elderly continues to be underdiagnosed. This is often because those in a position of familiarity with older individuals may attribute depressive symptoms to coexisting illnesses or just to "getting older." What factors lead to depression in the elderly? First of all, older age signals a time of physical decline. Decreased vision, hearing, and mobility problems secondary to debilitating arthritis are common in aging adults. These handicaps cause balance and coordination problems often leading to falls and other injuries. This ultimately costs the aging individual significant independence and may lead to depression in predisposed individuals. Several other medical illnesses that may be accompanied or complicated by depression are cancer, heart disease, Alzheimer's disease, stroke, Cushing's disease, and erectile dysfunction in men. Several prescription medications and over-the-counter drugs have also been associated with depression.

Second, there are psychosocial factors that may lead to depression in the elderly. These include bereavement, failed relationships in the form of divorce or separation, retirement, and relocation (Turnbull 1998). Other factors include longer hospitalization and nursing home placement. The fact that late-life depression is often underdiagnosed warrants concern since the elderly are especially prone to suffer the most devastating complication of depression — suicide. Although comprising only 13 percent of the general population, people age 65 and older make up about 23 percent of all suicides (Turnbull 1998). In the United States more than 8,000 people over age 60 commit suicide each year (Almy 2000). Moreover, studies have shown that in aged individuals, depression may be a factor in 50 to 70 percent of completed suicides (Turnbull 1998).

It is likely that these numbers include the Christian community as well as unbelievers. This data underscores the extreme importance that primary care medical practitioners, as well as biblical counselors, be well versed in the recognition of suicidal risk factors in the depressed elderly. For example, significant illness, illness of significant others, and death of a spouse are among the most common stressors leading to suicide in older adults. In addition, determining the person's perception regarding his or her medical condition ("I'm tired of being sick," or "I'm such a burden on everyone") may be indirect signals that a person may be contemplating suicide. Noncompliance with treatment plans, self-neglect, giving away of personal property, hoarding of medications, and purchasing of firearms may also be symptoms of impending suicide attempts (Bair 2000). In addition, concurrent recreational drug and alcohol use may complicate depression and significantly increase the risk of suicide (Turnbull 1998).

Some biblical counselors and authors believe that the depressed person who has decompensated to the extent of contemplating suicide is operating at the extremes of "self-pity" and self-centeredness. And while it may be true that the professed Christian finding him- or herself in this state could not possibly be "filled with the Spirit," the need for prompt medical intervention is essential. Timely medical attention may be lifesaving! Every established biblical counseling center should have specific protocol geared toward entering the suicidal individual into the care of qualified psychiatric emergency personnel. Once treated and stabilized, such people may be taught to evaluate their circumstances through God's perspective using sound biblical counseling.

Spiritual carnality. Christians are commanded to "be not drunk with wine ... but be filled with the Spirit" (Ephesians 5:18 KJV). We are also instructed to "walk in the Spirit and ... not fulfill the lust of the flesh" (Galatians 5:16 KJV). We are subsequently told in Galatians 5:22–23 that the "fruit of the Spirit is love, joy, peace, patience, kindness, goodness, faithfulness, gentleness and self-control." Clearly, it would be difficult if not impossible for a depressed person to also manifest the fruit of the Spirit. Failure to live a Spirit-filled life on a consistent basis, I would venture to say, is at the foundation of every struggle that we face as believers. There are some who teach that sin and carnality are wholly responsible for depression and mood disorders. Another view, expressed by Almy (2000), is that depression falls under the category of the suffering that we all should expect and accept as part of the believer's walk here on earth. Almy assails explanations of depression having biological contributing factors as baseless, seeing no role for medical science in the treatment of this debilitating disorder. This type of interpretation is difficult, and I believe it may in its own way be responsible for some of the guilt that forces a believer more deeply into depression.

This brings to mind a patient in my practice who presented with complaints of insomnia. After a careful history and physical exam, I became suspicious that depression might be the cause of this person's problem. A depression survey/questionnaire further supported my clinical impression. Tearfulness resulted upon my presenting my thoughts to the patient, who cried, "I thought I might be depressed, but I hoped you would find something else wrong." Rejecting any mention of treatment, the patient exclaimed, "I trust in Jesus Christ as Lord of my life — being treated for depression would suggest that I don't have faith in him." This person was undoubtedly overwhelmed by life circumstances, which included several psychosocial stressors. Her family history of depression made her vulnerable to develop the condition herself. Yet improper orientation toward the diagnosis and treatment of depression as a medical entity interfered with her ability to receive sound biblical counsel and spiritual restoration.

Is sickness and disease found only from the neck down? A definite relationship exists between anatomical structures (brain) and function (thoughts, mood, emotions). In other words, abnormal levels of brain neurotransmitters may directly or indirectly translate into the believer's inability to relate properly to his or her circumstances and thus becoming depressed.

Consider the undernourished, sleep-deprived, distraught, and guilt-ridden believer who has lost the ability to concentrate. This person, undoubtedly unable to effectively pray or study the Scriptures, deserves a medical evaluation and perhaps treatment with medication. In her book *Depression to Wholeness: The Anatomy of Healing*, Thurman (2000) said it best: "It can be like trying to run a program on a computer that's infected with a virus. You know what it is you should do; you just can't make it happen sometimes. With many forms of depression, it just isn't possible. That's when you need help." Thurman, a Christian woman, described doing all the "right things" — prayer, Bible study, pastoral and biblical counsel. Yet she made consistent progress in her battle with depression only when she added medication to her treatment arsenal.

Depression in African Americans

Because of manifold economic, family, and social problems, African Americans are also at high risk for depression. Yet taking age, gender, and income into account, depression rates are considered to be equal to that of Whites. Some feel that this misrepresents reality because Blacks may express depressive symptoms in ways not easily measured by standard diagnostic instruments (see Callahan and Wolinsky 1994). Differences in access to care and care-seeking behaviors also contribute to this underestimation. Thus, it may be concluded that the depression rate in African Americans equals, if not exceeds, that of Whites.

As is the case with many other health problems, the factors mentioned above may also translate into poorer outcomes for those suffering from depression. For example, a recent study suggested that Blacks receiving Medicaid are more likely to be treated with the older, more poorly tolerated tricyclic antidepressants than with the newer, better-tolerated drugs (Sclar et al. 1998). This obviously is more likely to lead to discontinuation of treatment and a less favorable outcome.

Treatment of Depression

The discovery of effective treatment for depression and other mood disorders remains an elusive piece to the puzzle of restoration of wholeness in affected individuals. Statistics related to treatment failure were mentioned earlier in this chapter. It is quite conceivable that unresolved spiritual issues play a role in this. Tim LaHaye (1974) pointed out that regardless of the type of treatment implemented, unless changes in the environment surrounding the depression takes place, different forms of counseling, therapies, medications, and other forms of treatment offer only a transient remedy. In this context, "environment" would include issues and thought processes affecting spiritual growth. Clearly, many Christians experience continual peaks and valleys in their ability to live Spirit-filled lives. Thus, those who are prone to develop major depression may find themselves in need of lifelong courses of treatment with medications intermittently. This is likened to the treatment of Type 2 diabetes mellitus, which, like depression, is most often initiated during early-to-mid-adulthood in predisposed persons. Once diagnosed, one usually uses medications to reestablish normal blood sugar levels. The person is then counseled to undergo lifestyle changes that include a nutritionally sound diet plan and exercise to facilitate weight loss. Individuals who are diligent in carrying out this plan in some cases can have their disease controlled without medication. Most, however, require the use of some medication on a lifelong basis. Likewise, a believer who is diligently "pressing on" may successfully manage depression without medication, whereas others may require treatment despite their effort.

Antidepressant Medications

There has been a recent barrage of newer antidepressant medication in an attempt to improve the treatment of this devastating disorder. While an exhaustive discussion of medications for the treatment of depression is beyond the scope of this chapter, some important points need to be made:

1. The neurochemical basis for antidepressant treatment is fairly well established. Several models involving the neurotransmitters serotonin, norepinephrine, and dopamine help explain brain dysfunction and contribute to plausible theories underlying antidepressant treatment.
2. Much effort and research is going into the study of treatment-resistant depression. Besides the unresolved spiritual and psychosocial factors cited above, antidepressant medication treatment often fails due to:

- Unpleasant side effects
- Delayed efficacy or onset of action
- Failure to match medication strengths to patient's problem areas
- Failure to increase or titrate the medication to its most effective dosage

Because of the onslaught of newer antidepressant agents, many physicians lack the experience to confidently treat depressed patients. This often necessitates referral to a psychiatrist who specializes in the use of these medications.

An example illustrating a treatment-related problem might involve a woman whose depression is felt to stem from a soured marriage relationship. A central item of contention between the spouses is an apparent sexual incompatibility in which the husband's insatiable sexual appetite is matched against the depressed woman's sexual indifference. Her doctor chooses the medication paroxetine, a commonly used first-line medication for depression to begin her treatment, mainly because of its favorable track record and his degree of comfort with this agent. Unfortunately, the patient's problem worsens because the physician lacked insight into this important psychosocial stressor in her life. Paroxetine and other agents in the SSRI classification are commonly known to cause sexual side effects including decreased libido. This is therefore clearly a poor choice of treatment.

Commonly Prescribed Antidepressant Medications

Monoamine Oxidase Inhibitors (MAOs) and Tricyclic Antidepressants (TCAs) represent older classes of medications whose usage has been limited by unpleasant side effects. MAOs are generally not used unless prescribed by a psychiatrist. These drugs are known for potentially harmful drug interactions. Formerly first-line agents, TCA have been largely supplanted by newer drugs having at least equal efficacy but with more favorable side-effect profiles.

The largest group of newer antidepressant medications is classified as Selective Serotonin Uptake Inhibitors (SSRIs). Commonly used SSRIs include: fluoxitine (Prozac), paroxetine (Paxil), sertraline (Zoloft), and citalopram (Celexa). Favorable features of these drugs include their safety and convenient dosing (usually once daily). Unfavorable side effects include insomnia, anxiousness, sexual dysfunction, gastrointestinal disturbances, and weight fluctuations.

Other newer antidepressants that deserve mention include nefazodone (Serzone), mirtazapine (Remeron), bupropion (Wellbutrin), and venlafaxine (Effexor). These medications possess a variety of features that enable the tailoring of drugs to match predominant symptoms of depression.

Hypercium (St. John's Wort) is an herbal treatment for depression gaining popularity in the United States. It has some effectiveness in treating mild to moderate depression, according to some studies. A lack of positive comparative studies against conventional antidepressants limits its general acceptance, however. At this point, its use is not recommended unless prescribed by a physician. Also the casual consumer should exercise caution since its use is not under quality control in the United States. Thus, the quantity of active ingredients on market shelves may vary (Feldman 2000).

BIPOLAR DISORDER

Bipolar disorder, also known as manic-depressive disorder, is characterized by periodic changes in extremes of mood. The phase noted by extremes of enhanced mood is referred to as mania, while depressed mood in this disorder is generally indistinguishable from major depression as described above. Varying degrees of this disorder have been classified and are referred to by the DSM-IV as bipolar I or bipolar II disorders.

In bipolar I, the person's mood is persistently elevated, expansive, or irritable. Manic people may become extremely disorganized and impulsive, exhibit poor judgment, or become psychotic (i.e., unable to accurately perceive reality, having bizarre delusions and/or hallucinations). This mood enhancement, which often develops rapidly, lasts at least one week and often constitutes a medical emergency.

Manic episodes are known to cause extreme occupational and social impairment, necessitating hospitalization to prevent harm to self or others. In contrast, bipolar II patients cycle between episodes of major depression and hypomania in which manic individuals continue with normal or enhanced function but without obvious lapses in judgment or impulse. They are usually diagnosed in the depressed phase, subsequently becoming hypomanic after being treated with certain antidepressant medications. In the majority of cases of bipolar disorder, the depressive phase occurs much more frequently than the manic phase. Cycling does not occur in any recognizable pattern. Cases of mania, however, have been known to result from significant psychosocial stressors. A small percentage of bipolar patients exhibit rapid cycling, in which manic and depressive phases alternate an average of four times per year but in some cases more frequently.

Epidemiologic Features of Bipolar Disorder

Bipolar disorder occurs in approximately 1 percent of the population over their lifetime, and unlike major depression, it affects both sexes equally (although women are three times as likely to exhibit rapid cycling). There appears to be some family-related predisposition as noted in genetic and chromosomal studies. Although research in this area has been somewhat inconsistent, there is clearly an increased incidence in the offspring of bipolar individuals. One study (Griswold and Pessar 2000) showed a 13 percent increased risk among bipolar offspring. The average age of onset is late adolescence and early adulthood.

Criteria for a Manic Episode

In addition to the description above, three or more of the following persist (four with only irritable mood).

- Inflated self-esteem or grandiosity
- Decreased need for sleep (e.g., feels rested after only three hours of sleep)
- More talkative than usual or pressure to keep talking
- Flight of ideas or subjective experience that thoughts are racing
- Distractibility (i.e., attention too easily drawn to unimportant or irrelevant external stimuli)
- Increase in goal-directed activity (either socially, at work or school, or sexually) or psychomotor agitation
- Excessive involvement in pleasurable activities that have a high potential for painful consequences (DSM-IV 1994, pp. 327, 332)

Disinhibition, often marked by compulsive gambling, unwise investment, excessive spending, immodest attire, and promiscuity commonly labels the bipolar person. It is extremely important that these people be accurately diagnosed because similarities to schizophrenia may be indistinguishable to the untrained eye. This has important treatment implications. Psychotic features may include preoccupation with political, religious, and paranoid ideation and delusions. Also, large proportions of bipolar people are substance abusers (60 to 70 percent by some accounts).

Undiagnosed manic children may be noted only by their tendency to be irritable and hyperactive and to have temper tantrums. Adolescents demonstrate risk-taking behaviors typical of this stage of life but exhibit a constellation of antisocial behaviors such as substance abuse, school problems, psychotic episodes, and sometimes suicide attempts. Again, misdiagnosis as schizophrenia is common.

Unfortunately, bipolar disorder tends to be chronic and recurrent, posing a significant burden on family and loved ones. Because of the outlandish tendencies of bipolar people, it is not unusual to have problems with the police and legal system complicate matters. Successful management of this disorder is extremely difficult and requires a coordinated effort on the part of the patient, his/her family, and medical personnel, including the psychiatrist and/or family physician and the biblical counselor. Once stabilized, one of the more imposing tasks is that of convincing these patients to stay in treatment.

Medication is the key to the bipolar person's stabilization. Yet because of taboos, misconceptions regarding "mental disorders," and unpleasant side effects, these people are unlikely to take their medications faithfully. This is a place where the biblical counselor can make a significant impact. Equipped with a solid knowledge base concerning this disorder, the counselor helps to strengthen him or her spiritually through the Scriptures. And part of the message should be one of stewardship. Once educated concerning the disorder, "wellness" is maintained by caring for one's "temple" (1 Corinthians 6:19). This, again employing the diabetes analogy, involves continuing in the plan of care. We should all be good stewards of our temples as unto the Lord.

Treatment of Bipolar Disorder

Again, medication is the key to the successful treatment and stabilization in bipolar disorder. Remember that a person showing signs of an acute manic attack should be referred urgently to a healthcare provider. If previously diagnosed, it is helpful to have a record of the bipolar person's psychiatrist and/or family doctor. If the patient's behavior suggests significant risk to self or others, the police may need to be notified under the proper legal protocols.

Medications used in bipolar disorder are referred to as "mood stabilizers." They include Lithium, Depakote, and Tegretol and newer atypical drugs. "Atypical drugs" are antipsychotic medications commonly used to treat schizophrenia. These agents have broader neurotransmitter activity than "typical" antipsychotic medications and have thus shown themselves capable of improving mood symptoms.

Remember that the use of TCA antidepressants has been associated with a switch to the manic cycle in bipolar patients. Also, in certain cases combinations of these drugs, along with antipsychotic, SSRI antidepressants, and sedative medications may be indicated. Although this is beyond the scope of this chapter, it is important that the treating physician stabilize these patients in a way that addresses their primary symptomatology while minimizing side effects and harmful medication interactions.

In addition to the role the biblical counselor may play as above, he or she may also intervene in important family and psychosocial issues that may help keep bipolar individuals in treatment.

CONCLUSION

The approach to the management of mood disorders remains both difficult and controversial. As a Christian and a physician, I see an excellent opportunity to minister to sisters and brothers stricken by these disorders in a way that has been unrealized in the past. For the biblical counselor, truly confronting this tough issue should mean increasing one's knowledge concerning these disorders and allowing for the use of all that God has blessed us with to learn both spiritually and scientifically. Intermittent depressed mood or dysphoria is not major depression; this distinction must be made.

This is a difficult issue, since many still reject the idea of a "disease model" and feel that the use of medications in treatment of these individuals is more a hindrance than help. The key word here is *help* since drugs can't begin to address the multitude of issues that factor into both the development and proliferation of these disorders. Yet in many cases the reestablishment of neurochemical balance in the brains of depressed people may allow them to more effectively receive biblical counsel.

This being said, we must not lose sight of the fact that the use of chemical agents is far from perfected. While the body of medical literature on treatment-resistant depression continues to grow, I have no doubt that effective biblical counseling in settings that don't illegitimize the medical aspect of the problem will lead to improved outcomes.

REFERENCES

Almy, G. L. 2000. *How Christian is Christian counseling?* Wheaton, Ill.: Crossway.

Amsterdam, J. D., J. F. Greden, A. A. Nierenberg, and M. E. Thase. 2000. Treatment resistant depression. (Depression Insight Series). *Journal of Clinical Psychiatry-Intercom* (August 2000): 1–12.

Bair, B. D. 2000. Presentation and recognition of common psychiatric disorders in the elderly. *Clinical Geriatrics* 8 (February 2000): 26–48.

Callahan, C. M., and F. D. Wolinsky. 1994. The effect of gender and race on the measurement properties of the CES-D in older adults. *Medical Care* 32: 341–56.

Diagnostic and statistical manual of mental disorders, 4th edition. DSM-IV. 1994. Washington, D.C.: American Psychiatric Association.

Feldman, M. 2000. Managing psychiatric disorders in primary care: 1. Depression. *Hospital Practice* 35: 75–90.

Griswold, K., and L. F. Pessar. 2000. Management of bi-polar disorder. *American Family Physician* 62: 1343–53.

Isselbacher, K. J., et al., eds. 1994. *Harrison's principles of internal medicine,* 13th edition. New York: McGraw-Hill.

Kaplan, H. I., and B. J. Sadock. 1998. *Synopsis of psychiatry,* 8th edition. Baltimore: Williams and Wilkins.

Kornstein, S., and G. McEneny. 2000. Enhancing pharmacologic effects in the treatment of depression in women. *Journal of Clinical Psychiatry* 61 (suppl. 11): 18–27.

LaHaye, T. 1974. *How to win over depression.* Grand Rapids: Zondervan.

Sclar, D. A., L. M. Robison, T. L. Skaer, W. M. Dickson, C. M. Kozma, and C. E. Reeder. 1998. Antidepressant prescribing patterns: A comparison of Blacks and Whites in a Medicaid population. *Clinical Drug Investigation* 16: 135–40.

Staley, S. 1991. Single female parenting. In *The Black family: Past, present, and future,* edited by L. N. June. Grand Rapids: Zondervan.

Thurman, D. 2000. *From depression to wholeness: The anatomy of healing.* Monroe, Va.: Cedar House.

Turnbull, J. M. 1998. Depression and suicide in the elderly. *Family Practice Recertification* 20, no. 7 (July): 27–40.

Ustun, T. B. 2000. Cross national epidemiology of depression and gender. *Journal of Gender-Specific Medicine* 3 (March/April): 57.

World Health Organization's international classification of diseases, 10th edition. 1993. Geneva: World Health Organization.

Michael R. Lyles

Chapter 10

Schizophrenia:
A Psychiatric Perspective

Michael R. Lyles graduated from the University of Michigan's six-year Accelerated Premedical-Medical Program in 1979. His categorical internship (psychiatry/pediatrics) and his psychiatry residency took place at Duke University Medical Center. In 1983 he was named Assistant Professor of Psychiatry and Associate Director of Outpatient Services at the University of Kentucky College of Medicine and continued this appointment for the next three years. Dr. Lyles is licensed by the North Carolina, Kentucky, and Georgia state boards of medical examiners. He is certified with the American Board of Psychiatry and Neurology. His professional interests lie in mood/anxiety disorders, psychopharmacology, and attention deficit hyperactivity disorders.

Dr. Lyles opened his private practice in 1986. He has published a wide range of works, including "Spontaneous Abortion and Emotional Conflict" in *U.S. Navy Medicine*, "Treating Psychiatric Problems in Medical Students" in the *American Journal of Psychiatry*, "Psychiatric Aspects of Addiction" in *Christian Counseling Today*, and "Interracial Pastoral Counseling with Black Males" in the *Journal of Pastoral Care*, among others. Michael Lyles resides in Atlanta, Georgia, with his wife and three children.

Schizophrenia is a psychiatric disorder that affects approximately one half to one percent of the population. It is the most common cause of psychotic symptoms and is a major cause of involuntary psychiatric hospitalization. It is characterized by odd behavior, bizarre thought patterns, withdrawn social behavior, and lack of interest or pleasure in work, fun, or social interactions. Persons with this disorder can demonstrate an apparent loss of reality as evidenced by hallucinations, delusions, or paranoia. Their problems are then made worse by their inability to appreciate the inappropriateness of their thoughts or behaviors, leading to social isolation and refusal to accept appropriate medical care. They tend to be very lonely people who seldom marry or are able to support themselves financially. Their bizarre behaviors tend to frighten and intimidate people, thus further isolating them from social contact. Consider the following case example:

> Donald was a 28-year-old single male who lived with his parents. He constantly complained of hearing voices that talked about him from just outside of his window. The voices would call him names and accuse him of being gay. He became paranoid as he worried about the neighbors' hearing these voices and believing their accusations. He began to avoid going to the supermarket because he felt that everyone was talking about him and could read his mind. He stayed in his home and lifted weights — his only hobby. He stopped listening to the radio or watching television, feeling that the voices were speaking to him from the radio or television. He had not been able to hold a job because of paranoia about co-workers. Donald only dated briefly and seldom attended church with his family, usually getting very anxious and awkward in social situations. Were it not for his family, Donald would be living on the streets.

THE SYMPTOMS

The symptoms of schizophrenia are divided descriptively into "positive" and "negative" categories. The "positive" symptoms are the most obvious. They include psychotic symptoms and symptoms relating to disorganization of thoughts and behavior. "Negative" symptoms reflect more on the progressive decline of normal personality and interpersonal functions that occur over time with this disease. The positive symptoms seem to flare up at times and become less prevalent as the person ages. The negative symptoms seem to remain constant, causing significant impairment throughout the person's life. Thus, the negative symptoms are in fact more problematic and disabling than the positive symptoms over the life of the individual.

Positive psychotic symptoms include hallucinations and delusions. *Hallucinations* are represented by abnormalities in sensory perception so that a person hears (auditory), sees (visual), smells (olfactory), feels (tactile), or tastes (gustatory) something that is not there. The most common hallucination by far is the auditory, where the person hears voices talking about himself or others outside of his head. It is not the person's own voice daydreaming in his mind. It also occurs while the person is fully awake and not under the influence of drugs or alcohol. It should be noted, however, that auditory hallucinations can also be seen in bipolar mania (manic depressive or bipolar disorder) and severe cases of psychotic depression. The other kinds of hallucinations (visual, tactile, etc.) are highly associated with a variety of medical and neurological conditions, thus necessitating the need for medical evaluation. For example, hallucinations can occur apart from schizophrenia when someone is falling asleep (hypnagogic hallucinations) or when someone is waking up (hypnopompic hallucinations).

Delusions are erroneous beliefs that are strongly held, despite evidence to the contrary. *Paranoid delusions* involve fear that someone is trying to cause harm to the individual. Ideas of reference involve thoughts that someone is trying to send the individual a message through secret messages referring specifically to them on television, radio, or in print. With thought broadcasting, the individual becomes certain that others can hear his thoughts, as if they were being broadcast to others. *Somatic delusions* revolve around fears of having some bizarre bodily ailment, such as fearing that a skin rash is indicative of having cancer. *Delusions of control* revolve around fears that someone or something is controlling one's thoughts or behavior, often by using some type of odd technology such as implanted chips or satellite tracking systems. Delusions can be religious in nature, such as the delusion of the patient who told me she was the Virgin Mary and was pregnant with the new baby Jesus. Sometimes delusions are not so bizarre and can be difficult to evaluate because they represent a distortion of a possible reality. Consider the following case:

> Nick was a 30-year-old Black male who lived in a predominantly White community. He was very aware of stares that he would get when out in the community. He became convinced that his neighbors had hired the police to follow and harass him so that he would move out. He was adamant in his belief that many of his neighbors were racially uncomfortable with him. Several members of his family agreed with his assessment. However, over time he began to think that a device had been planted in his vehicle so that he could be "tracked." He was certain that chemicals had been placed in his home to allow the White police to monitor him. Every time he read something about racial conflict in the newspaper, he asserted that it confirmed his perceptions. In his mind, anyone that disagreed with him was an Uncle Tom, naïve, or crazy.

Schizophrenic *disorganization* can affect patterns of thinking and behavior. Thinking and speech patterns can become poorly organized to the point of being hard to follow in mild cases and totally nonsensical in severe cases. The person may ramble in such a disconnected fashion that his speech appears to be a word salad. Behavior can become so disorganized that the individual has trouble taking care of personal hygiene, dress, and grooming. They can become easily agitated and frustrated with minor tasks of everyday living. Their disorganized behavior can become very unnerving to someone who does not appreciate the implications of the situation. Consider the following example:

> Roy was a 48-year-old man who was diagnosed with schizophrenia in his twenties. He no longer had major problems with hallucinations or delusions; however, it was very difficult to talk with him. He would begin a conversation talking intensely about his favorite sports team, the New York Yankees, and then abruptly switch to discussing whether it was going to rain. Then he would switch mid-sentence to asking for a cigarette and then ramble for what seemed to be an eternity about former presidents of the United States. All of this would occur without giving the listener an opportunity to respond — even to the request for a cigarette. It was as though he was talking to himself.

Negative symptoms of schizophrenia refer to the enduring effects of this disease on the personality and interactive abilities of the individuals. They seem to lose the ability to express emotions normally. Their emotions are either blunted, as if they did not have any, or inappropriate to the situation (e.g., laughing at a funeral). They progressively lose the ability to initiate social or work activities, instead becoming loners who speak only when spoken to. They can develop odd habits and mannerisms, such as sitting on the edge of a chair grimacing all the time, that draw negative attention. They simply tend to act, think, and speak in strange manners. These symptoms tend to worsen and outlast the positive symptoms as the person ages. Negative symptoms cause more problems with family and friends than the positive symptoms since they persist as the background static against which the hallucinations and delusions flare from time to time.

The symptoms of schizophrenia tend to cluster into groupings called subtypes. "Disorganized Type" is characterized by silly or blunted emotional expressions and incoherent, highly disorganized speech or thought patterns. Hallucinations and delusions are not prominent here. "Catatonic Type" features a kind of physical and emotional "stuck in the mud" presentation. They can be physically rigid, assume odd positions from which they resist being moved, or be mute or in a stupor. In rare cases, they can switch from this rigid stance and become wildly excited and agitated. "Paranoid Type" is the most common and is characterized by the classic hallucinations and delusions. "Undifferentiated Type" refers to individuals with a mixture of symptoms. "Residual Type" refers to someone who no longer has positive symptoms but does suffer with negative symptoms.

MAKING THE DIAGNOSIS

The presence of occasional hallucinations or delusions does not mean that someone is schizophrenic. The positive and/or negative symptoms must persist for more than six months, with at least one month of active psychotic symptoms. These symptoms must cause a gradual impairment in work, school, and relationships or hinder the ability of the individual to care for himself. The symptoms must not be due to other psychiatric or medical conditions that can have delusions and hallucinations as prominent symptoms. The following chart samples some of the medical disorders that can present with schizophrenic-like symptoms.

MEDICAL DISORDERS PRESENTING WITH PSYCHOSIS

Huntington' Chorea	Temporal Lobe Epilepsy
Frontal/Temporal Lobe Tumors	Cerebral Vascular Accidents (strokes)
Multiple Scherosis	Porphyria
Thyroid Disease	Systemic Lupus Erthematosis
Parathyroid Disease	Wilson's Disease of the Liver
Drug/Alcohol Intoxication	Drug/Alcohol Withdrawal
Narcolepsy	Steroid Toxicity

Consider the following case of a misdiagnosis:

Lydia presented to the emergency room barefoot, in a dirty wedding dress, at three A.M. She proceeded to talk incoherently about having special powers, and she actively talked to the walls, commanding them to "shut up." She had aluminum foil in her ears to keep people from reading her thoughts. I diagnosed her with possible bipolar disorder or schizophrenia, only to be told by her internist that I was totally wrong. She was a dialysis patient who had to take steroids when her kidney disease would flare. Every time she took high-dose steroids, she became psychotic. When not on steroids, she was the mother of three who taught Sunday school.

Hallucinations and delusions can also be seen in a variety of psychiatric disorders. Depressed patients can become psychotic when severely depressed for long periods of time. Bipolar (manic depressive) patients can become so psychotic when manic that they become indistinguishable from someone who is schizophrenic. In fact, psychiatric textbooks are loaded with stories of people who were diagnosed with schizophrenia and locked up in state hospitals for years only later to be found to have Bipolar Disorder. This is an important differentiation because Bipolar Disorder is much easier to treat and has a much more positive prognosis. Individuals with paranoid disorder can present with just the chronic paranoid symptoms. Young adults with autism can mimic the negative symptoms of schizophrenia very well. Psychotic symptoms can occur for very brief periods of time, meriting psychiatric diagnoses such as schizophreniform disorder or brief reactive psychosis. The point here is that a careful diagnostic assessment needs to be made before labeling someone with a chronic disease such as schizophrenia. Consider the following example:

> Mark was 25 years old when he was initially diagnosed with schizophrenia. He had been on disability all of his adult life and lived with his parents. He moved to another part of the country and consulted a different psychiatrist. After several months of careful consideration, the diagnosis of schizophrenia was changed to Bipolar Disorder (manic depressive disorder). His medication was also changed from tranquilizers to lithium. He began to demonstrate dramatic improvement. He became employed and returned to school. He recently graduated with an engineering degree and became engaged to marry a fellow student. He has been symptom-free for more than four years. The initial diagnosis of schizophrenia was made based on a fifteen minute interview without any information from the family or consideration of his past history of mood swings and depression.

DIAGNOSTIC ISSUES AND THE CHRISTIAN

A different kind of diagnostic concern arises in the Christian community regarding individuals with schizophrenia. Many assume that these individuals must be demon possessed or oppressed because of the bizarre nature of their symptoms. Some assume that the voices that they are hearing are the voices of oppressive demons. Others draw a parallel with the demon-possessed man from Gerasenes (Mark 5:1–20). As a Christian first and a psychiatrist second, I truly wish that it were this simple for the individuals and families with this disorder. I wish that we could reliably and consistently employ spiritual answers to totally heal patients with other degenerative brain disorders such as Parkinson's disease and Alzheimer's disease too. However, a brief review of the kinds of phenomena usually associated with this kind of activity is not as relevant to most schizophrenics as many would assume. Most have never been involved with occult activity prior to the onset of symptoms. In fact, many of the patients that I have treated would identify themselves as evangelical Christians. When I worked in a state hospital, it was not uncommon to find the Bible as the only book that many of these patients read. Unlike the Gerasene man, they do not demonstrate unusual strength and are seldom prone to violence. (By the way, it is not clear that the Gerasene was hallucinating or delusional. In fact, he was quite clear in his perceptions of Jesus and the implications of his coming.) The voices that schizophrenics hear are usually self-condemning and accusatory, not blasphemous or sacrilegious. If the voices are from demons, why do they often diminish or stop as the person gets older? If the voices are from demons, why would medications quiet the voices dramatically — without sedating the patient?

Schizophrenics have many spiritual needs — probably more than most people because of the tremendous impact of their disease. However, they do not need the spiritual stigma and rejection that too often comes with the quick, premature assessment that all their problems are demon related. Consider the following case example:

> Jackie was a 20-year-old college junior who was recently hospitalized and diagnosed with schizophrenia after experiencing a psychotic break. When she came home to recuperate, her mother scheduled a counseling session with her pastor. Upon learning the nature of her symptoms (hearing voices), he pronounced her demon possessed and took her to several deliverance services. He asked her to stop taking her medications as a demonstration of her faith. After several more deliverance services, she became psychotic again and was re-hospitalized. At this point, her pastor declared her void of faith and said that there was nothing that he could do for her. She became depressed and contemplated suicide, only then venting anger at God.

WHAT HAPPENS TO PEOPLE WITH SCHIZOPHRENIA?

Most patients have their first psychotic episode in the mid to late twenties. Prior to this they may be overly shy, awkward in relationships, and socially withdrawn: 60–70 percent do not marry or have significant relationships; 25–50 percent develop depression; 10 percent become suicidal. They have a shorter life expectancy and are at risk for developing drug, alcohol, or nicotine dependency. The positive symptoms tend to go away with aging, but the negative symptoms do not. Thus, most of these individuals do not get totally healthy. They tend to have job and school problems due to a loss of interest or motivation. Hygiene and grooming can become progressively more challenging as they age. Many are noncompliant with their medications and can become so impaired that they become homeless. Others have a much better prognosis. This prognosis is associated with an onset after age thirty, absence of family history of schizophrenia, good functioning before the onset of symptoms, and the presence of a precipitating event for the episode.

THE CAUSES OF SCHIZOPHRENIA

What causes schizophrenia? The short answer is that we don't know completely. We do know that genetics are involved in some fashion. For example, rates of schizophrenia are ten times higher in close relatives of schizophrenic patients than in the general population. There are much higher rates in identical twins of schizophrenics than in fraternal (nonidentical) twins. These higher rates persist even if the twin or close relative is adopted out of the family.

Brain scanning research has identified structural differences in the brains of large numbers of schizophrenic patients. There is enlargement of two fluid-containing portions of the brain, the lateral and third ventricles. Atrophy (shrinkage) has been observed in areas of the limbic lobe of the brain associated with mood, initiative, pleasure drives, and learned emotional memory (the amygdaloid and hippocampal regions). Finally, there is decreased volume in areas of the frontal lobe, perhaps accounting for some of the negative symptoms.

Abnormalities in the functioning of brain tissue have long been described in this illness. Dopamine is a protein in the brain that functions as a phone system that helps parts of the brain to coordinate emotional, cognitive, and muscular activity. There are several different dopamine pathways in the brain. Excessive activity of dopamine in certain areas of the brain's dopamine (mesolimbic) pathways is associated with hallucinations and delusions. That is why tumors and other neurological diseases that affect these brain structures can reproduce the symptoms of schizophrenia.

WHAT ABOUT THOSE DRUGS?

The medical treatment of schizophrenia is rooted in the hypothesis that excessive dopamine activity in the mesolimbic pathways accounts for a majority of the positive symptoms. Thus, medications have been developed that block these pathways and lead to resolution of hallucinations and delusions. These medications fall into two categories: typical and atypical "neuroleptics." Typical neuroleptics focus on decreasing dopamine activity and decreasing positive symptoms. Examples include chlorpromazine (Thorazine), thioridazine (Mellaril), haloperidol (Haldol), thiothixene (Navane), fluphenazine (Prolixin), trifluoperazine (Stelazine), perphenazine (Trilafon) and loxapine (Loxitane). They were not particularly helpful with negative symptoms and caused a number of side effects, including muscle spasms, excessive drooling, shaking of the extremities, slow/rigid walking, sedation, decreases in blood pressure, and long-term side effects with muscle spasms and twitches.

Atypical neuroleptics were developed to decrease these side effects, address positive symptoms, and reduce negative symptoms. They include clozapine (Clozaril), olanzapine (Zyprexa), risperidone (Risperdal), quetiapine (Seroquel), and ziprasidone (Geodon). Some of these drugs have shown potential as antidepressants and mood stabilizers. They each have their own side-effect issues, but on the whole they have represented a major advance in treatment. The latest concerns about these medications revolve around the issue of weight management and blood sugar control. Schizophrenics as a group have a higher incidence of diabetes mellitus, especially adult onset. Some of these medications can increase appetite and lead to a weight gain that increases the risk of blood sugar problems.

WHAT YOU CAN DO TO HELP

I cannot overemphasize the lonely experience of schizophrenic patients *and their families.* Many times the family feels the stigma of the disease more than the patient, who is unaware of the inappropriate nature of his behavior. It is the family who is aware of the stares at the market and at church. It is the family who argues to the point of frustration with the patient about the need to take her medication. It is the family that obsesses about what further can be done for the patient. It is the family that takes financial responsibility for the needs of the patient with limited ability to earn income. It is the family that worries about their loved one ending up on the street, homeless and on drugs or alcohol.

Schizophrenics and their families need support and practical help. They need someone to vent their fears and frustrations to. They need the grace of God in human form to help them work through their self-imposed guilt about whether they did something to cause this situation. The families need help in finding work and social opportunities for their loved one. They need an objective ear to give appropriate wisdom about avoiding over-involvement in the person's life.

Schizophrenics need help in developing social confidence and lessening awkwardness around people. They need to feel hope because many of them have lost a sense of having any kind of future. They need to have a relationship with our Lord, perhaps even more than most, due to the emptiness of their lives. They need what we all need — to know that they are loved and accepted by a God who will never leave, forsake, or make fun of them — as if they really do matter.

CONCLUSION

Schizophrenia is a degenerative neurological condition that causes behavioral symptoms that alienate and frighten others. They tend to live lonely, unproductive lives — too often in a very private fantasy world. Great advances have been made in the biological understanding of this disease state, with better treatments evolving at a rapid pace. However, the greatest need for individuals with schizophrenia is for a friend, a mentor, and a spiritual tutor. They need a human touch that is not afraid or ambivalent. Their families need support, education, and an opportunity to vent at times. Support groups such as National Alliance for the Mentally Ill (NAMI) and the National Mental Health Association (NMHA) provide a greatly needed resource for advocating for their needs. However, the relationship between the patient and his or her physician remains core to the process. There needs to be enough communication and trust that the patient and his or her family have a sense of participation and ownership in the treatment. Concerns about the treatment process need an arena for review so that the patient is less likely to "act out" his frustrations by the premature interruption of treatment. Since patients are already at risk for becoming paranoid, it is important that they feel safe and informed medically, socially, and spiritually.

REFERENCES

For Further Study

Kaplan, H. I., and B. J. Sadock. 1995. Schizophrenia. In *Comprehensive textbook of psychiatry,* 6th edition, 889–1018. Baltimore: Williams and Wilkins.

Stahl, S. 2000. Psychosis and schizophrenia. In *Essential psychopharmacology,* 365–458. Cambridge, U.K.: Cambridge University Press.

Resources

National Alliance for the Mentally Ill (NAMI)
200 North Glebe Road, Suite 1015
Arlington, VA 22201
www.nami.org

National Mental Health Association (NMHA)
1021 Prince Street
Alexandria, VA 22314–2971
www.nmha.org

National Alliance for Research on Schizophrenia and Depression
(NARSAD)
60 Cutter Mill Road, Suite 404
Great Neck, New York 11021
www.mhsource.com

Michael R. Lyles

Chapter 11

Attention Deficit Hyperactivity Disorder: The Disease of the Shadows

Michael R. Lyles graduated from the University of Michigan's six-year Accelerated Premedical-Medical Program in 1979. His categorical internship (psychiatry/pediatrics) and his psychiatry residency took place at Duke University Medical Center. In 1983 he was named Assistant Professor of Psychiatry and Associate Director of Outpatient Services at the University of Kentucky College of Medicine and continued this appointment for the next three years. Dr. Lyles is licensed by the North Carolina, Kentucky, and Georgia state boards of medical examiners. He is certified with the American Board of Psychiatry and Neurology. His professional interests lie in mood/anxiety disorders, psychopharmacology, and attention deficit hyperactivity disorders.

Dr. Lyles opened his private practice in 1986. He has published a wide range of works, including "Spontaneous Abortion and Emotional Conflict" in *U.S. Navy Medicine,* "Treating Psychiatric Problems in Medical Students" in the *American Journal of Psychiatry,* "Psychiatric Aspects of Addiction" in *Christian Counseling Today,* and "Interracial Pastoral Counseling with Black Males" in the *Journal of Pastoral Care,* among others. Michael Lyles resides in Atlanta, Georgia, with his wife and three children.

The understanding and treatment of mental disorders has changed greatly over the last twenty years. Advances in technology have allowed us to describe the normal biological workings of the brain well enough to explain disease states that were previously hard to understand or treat. Detailed chemical and hormonal models of the brain have ushered in a host of medical treatments that are superior to those available when I became a psychiatrist in the early 1980s. For example, problems with depression and anxiety that were previously confusing and disabling are now treatable 75 to 85 percent of the time. This has been particularly significant as we learn more about the negative impact of conditions such as depression and anxiety on other medical conditions such as hypertension, heart disease, diabetes, and stroke. In a very real way, the advances in treatment options have paralleled our understanding of the lethal nature of many of these disorders when left untreated.

However, these advances have failed to make an impact on the African American community to the fullest degree. We have historically tended to underutilize secular mental health professionals and have held quite negative attitudes toward these disciplines. This would be expected when one considers the historical relationship between psychiatry and the African American community. Prior to the late sixties, the only source of treatment available to us was segregated state hospitals, where the standard of care and facilities were less than those for our Caucasian counterparts. Involuntary commitment was the means of entry to these facilities, where psychotic and violent patients were overrepresented. Thus, going to see the psychiatrist meant that the police showed up unannounced at your home and took you away in handcuffs, in front of staring neighbors, to a place that was potentially unsafe and where help was not expected or forthcoming. Persons would be held in locked facilities for years in some cases. The similarities between this "treatment" and jail were all too obvious. We did not have a history of therapists or outpatient facilities where friends and family members received help in a positive manner.

The mental health center movement of the early 1970s brought an end to services being delivered in these state hospitals. Care was shifted to community-based clinics, staffed predominantly by therapists with little connection to Afrocentric culture. Racial bias and cultural ignorance were reflected in professional articles that questioned the mental capability of "Negroes" to suffer from the psychological problems that Caucasians experienced. Fears of igniting "Black Rage" lead some therapists to keep counseling superficial or avoid patients of color because they were too "difficult." Until the past decade, many training programs in psychiatry did not discuss the influence of race on the therapy process. Thus, mental health resources were still viewed by African Americans with well-earned suspicion, fear, and a consequent lack of information about disease states and treatment alternatives.

History documents that the Black church filled the void created for years by the bias and neglect of the secular mental health care system. Many works have discussed the role of pastors as providers of therapy to their flocks. However, the pastor in the Black church was the therapist/healer/psychiatrist/psychologist/social worker/financialcounselor/lawyer/job counselor and also preacher/teacher/administrator. In many cases this was expected of the pastor without any formal training in these areas. Thus, it became easy for the pastor to share the lack of information about disease states and treatment alternatives that the "flock" already embraced. This is tragic with obvious disease states such as depression, anxiety, or psychosis. However, it is almost unspeakable with a disorder that lives in the shadow of other problems and disorders: Attention Deficit Hyperactivity Disorder (ADHD).

THE IMPACT OF ADHD

People still argue over whether ADHD exists, despite scientific evidence that supports that it does. The impact of this disorder on African Americans is largely unknown because we have not been represented in the research on this issue. The impact of ADHD on Christians is also poorly documented. We are, however, learning enough to assert that this "disease of the shadows" is having more of an impact on children and adults than we had ever thought.

> **Case Example.** James was a 17-year-old African American male who was referred for a psychiatric evaluation by his pastor due to failing grades and fighting at school. He had a long history of disruptive behavior at school, such as talking in class and getting out of his seat. He was characterized as being a restless child, who underachieved in elementary school. He tended to daydream a great deal and seemed bored in class. His teachers in elementary school called him lazy. He continued to have academic difficulties in middle school, along with a growing sense of frustration over his inability to concentrate on his studies. He became the class clown to distract attention away from his problems — especially with reading comprehension and math. His teachers began to think of him as being stupid and lacking regard for authority. He began to associate with other kids who were poor students. Through these associations, he began to use alcohol and marijuana. His grades declined further and he developed temper problems as he passed through puberty. His parents blamed each other for his problems and subsequently divorced.

James was doing increasingly poorly in school and was temporarily suspended from school for fighting. During this time, he and his mother visited a local church with friends and had "born again" experiences. James became very motivated to "get my act together" but nearly got into a fight in his Sunday school class while debating a point of Scripture. His grades were now failing. The teachers had labeled him as a rebellious Black male and distanced themselves from him. His pastor suspected that James may have ADHD and referred him for a psychiatric opinion. The diagnosis was confirmed and James went from flunking to making the honor roll for two semesters and excelling in sports. He then discontinued treatment because, he said, "I don't believe in that stuff."

Six months later he became drunk at a party and assaulted his girlfriend for allegedly flirting with another young man. He left in his car and was arrested for simple assault, driving under the influence, and resisting arrest. He remained incarcerated for several weeks and lost a potential athletic scholarship to a small college.

ADHD: AN OVERVIEW

There are few psychiatric diagnoses that conjure up more fear, anger, and confusion than Attention Deficit Hyperactivity Disorder (ADHD). It is estimated to occur in 6 to 9 percent of school-age children. Approximately 70 percent of these children will show persistence of symptoms into the teen years. About 10 to 50 percent of these teens will experience symptoms that persist into adult life. About 2 percent of adults are estimated to have ADHD.

Experts debate as to whether ADHD is overdiagnosed. Talk shows present it as a cultural excuse for any problem a person may have. A class action lawsuit is entering the courts challenging whether this diagnosis even exists. The suit claims the diagnosis is a ploy of doctors and drug companies to convince patients to spend money on medical services. Thus many people have mixed feelings about this diagnosis. Even the name has been controversial, changing over the years from Minimal Brain Dysfunction to Hyperactivity Disorder of Childhood to Attention Deficit Disorder (ADD) to the current name of Attention Deficit Hyperactivity Disorder (ADHD). It is no wonder that James and his teachers and family never considered this possibility earlier. We as a profession have had trouble knowing even what to call it.

The mental health community has had changing definitions of what comprised the diagnosis. Initially the focus was solely on hyperactive physical or motor behavior as the main symptom of this disorder. As we have learned more about ADHD, however, the symptoms have expanded to include problems with inattentiveness (inability to sustain attention, disorganization of behavior, and easy distractibility) and impulsivity. In fact, the current name, Attention Deficit Hyperactivity Disorder, seeks to better reflect the diversity of symptoms seen in this disorder. The hyperactivity is characterized by squirming, fidgeting, inability to stay seated, excessive running or climbing, and difficulty playing quietly. Examples of impulse control problems include blurting out answers, interrupting, and difficulty waiting. Inattentiveness is seen in careless mistakes, not listening, poor follow-through, poor organization of tasks, losing things, being easily distracted, forgetfulness, and inability to sustain attention. Most patients have combinations of these symptoms as illustrated below.

Case Example. Mary was 17 years old and a high school dropout when she was referred for psychiatric evaluation. She was promiscuous and was using marijuana daily. She had begun using alcohol and marijuana at 12 years of age in order to calm down. She was very frustrated in school because she had to read her materials over and over again before she could remember what she had read. She constantly procrastinated with her homework, waiting until the last minute and "pulling an all-nighter." She was chronically late to everything—if she could remember that she was supposed to be there. She had the reputation of being an "airhead" because her mind would wander so much. Her forgetfulness and absentmindedness was legend. She was banned from a local gas station due to pulling out on several occasions with the pump nozzle still attached to her car. She considered herself to be stupid.

Five years later, she has responded marvelously to treatment for ADHD. She had stated that she always knew that there was something wrong with her, but she couldn't put her finger on it. Now she knew what the it was and had learned how to address the problem. She had completed her GED and was a junior in college. She had been promoted four times in her part-time job and was encouraged about her future career prospects.

THE BIG UMBRELLA: SYMPTOMS OF ADHD

The larger spectrum of symptoms has made more people eligible for the diagnosis. Most of the research on ADHD has been on boys because they exhibit more of the hyperactive/impulsive symptoms than do girls. Young girls tend more toward the inattentive symptoms. Thus, with the more expanded symptom format, more girls are being diagnosed. Furthermore, it was customary to say that ADHD was just an illness of youth. Adults could not have it; kids would grow out of it. This was indeed true of the hyperactive symptoms, which do tend to improve as the child gets older and matures neurologically. However, the impulse control, distractibility, inattention, and disorganization of behavior do not often improve with aging. Thus, we began to identify adults with these kinds of symptoms of ADHD that have persisted into adult life.

> **Case Example.** Bill was a 55-year-old husband and church deacon with three children by three different women. He had a reputation of being a wild man all of his life. "Nobody could ever do anything with Bill. He was go for bad and would fight you over nothing," his friends would say. He was so distractible as a child that his teachers made him sit in the front row and wear cardboard flaps on the side of his glasses so that he would "pay attention." He had trouble sitting still and was forever getting into trouble for talking and getting out of his seat. He joined a gang in high school and barely finished high school, despite appearing to be very bright.
>
> He worked 32 different jobs before the age of 30 and stayed in financial trouble from writing bad checks and overusing credit cards. He was constantly involved in extramarital affairs, often getting involved impulsively with women that he barely knew. He was "quick to anger" at home, assaulting his wife on several occasions. He became a "numbers runner" later in his life, as he was drawn to the thrill and danger of it. His wife and son referred him for psychiatric evaluation when she threatened divorce. He was diagnosed with ADHD but refused treatment. He was soon thereafter found to be experimenting with cocaine. He stated that it helped him to "mellow out." His pastor was aware of the domestic abuse but not of the drugs. He never confronted Bill, because Bill was a large contributor to the church's building fund. Bill died of a heart attack while snorting a line of cocaine.

The symptoms of ADHD can cause many problems in a person's life, especially when it is not diagnosed until adulthood. These individuals have usually had lives that have been characterized by failures and disappointments. They have lost jobs, relationships, and self-respect as a result of their illness. They struggle with anger, shame, guilt, and embarrassment over their past. They have much grieving to do over lost opportunities. Their inability to listen, show empathy, or control their temper usually has caused the breakup of marriages and relationships.

Reading difficulties, problems handling paperwork, and easy distractibility usually leads to job and school problems. My average patient with ADHD has lost or quit nearly ten jobs before the age of 30. Most of my patients with the symptom of distractibility have stacks of projects lying around their offices or homes that they are working on but haven't completed. One of my patients had so many stacks of papers on the floor of his office that his friends called it the "maze." All the other symptoms, plus impulsive spending habits, usually lead to significant financial problems. The following case examples illustrate the impact of ADHD on these areas of a person's life.

ADHD AND MARRIAGE

Case Example. Herman was brought in by his wife. They had been married for twenty years, and she couldn't take it anymore. He had lost fourteen jobs through their marriage, usually for tardiness or getting into arguments due to his quick temper. He also had a long history of spending their money so impulsively — seemingly without thought — which had brought them near bankruptcy and eviction from their home. He would write checks and forget to write them in the check register, leading to hundreds of dollars of returned check fees per year. He charged several credit cards up to the limit and then "forgot" when the payments were due.

His wife was tired of covering for him, since she was always the one trying to talk to the creditors and the employers. She was tired of playing the game and wanted a divorce. However, he was a deacon, and she was the superintendent of the Sunday school. Thus, they were both concerned about their testimony. She thought that he was just "sorry and lazy — trying to live so big!"

ADHD AND FINANCES

Case Example. John appeared to be a successful physician. However, he presented for evaluation due to his inability to pass his medical board recertification exams. He could not study for the exams without his mind wandering. He also had trouble sitting still long enough to read and study. At the office, he never had a chance to sit still due to his schedule. However, he faced losing his hospital privileges if he did not pass his boards. He was very anxious and depressed. He had encountered similar difficulties when he was in college and medical school, but had drank up to twenty cups of coffee per day in order to stimulate his mind enough to study. He now had high blood pressure and couldn't do that anymore.

John was making a mess of his finances, despite a six-figure income. Quite simply, he forgot to deposit his paychecks for weeks at a time and actually lost a number of checks in his bedroom (which looked like a disaster scene). He was bouncing checks due to his failure to deposit his paychecks.

With treatment for his ADHD, he cleaned his bedroom and found over $50,000 of uncashed payroll checks, which had been "lost" in his bedroom.

ADHD AND CAREER

Case Example. Mary was a wonderful real estate agent — to a point. She was full of energy and seemed to be able to anticipate just what her customers needed in a home. She described herself as having the "gift of knowledge" in regard to her customers. However, she was losing the customers that she had worked so hard to get. She was so forgetful that she would fail to show up for appointments to show houses to people. She would forget specifics that her customers had told her about the houses unless she wrote them down. She made so many mistakes in her paperwork that several closings had to be rescheduled in order to allow her the time to get the paperwork done properly. She was working hard with little to show for it. She was working twice the hours of her co-workers and getting home to an unhappy husband on a regular basis.

ADHD AND SCHOOL

Case Example. Jean was a rising sophomore at a local college. She had a scholarship that required a B average in order to get funded for the next year. She had a B-, despite studying so much that she never had any social life at all. She was concerned that if she was having this kind of trouble with freshman courses, she would flunk out her sophomore year. She simply couldn't "focus" easily when she would study. She couldn't follow the lecturers without getting distracted by the other students in her 200-student lecture hall. She camped out in a study carrel at the library until it closed every day of the week to get her B-.

During the summer between her freshman and sophomore years, Jean was diagnosed and treated for ADHD. She called me in October to report that she was making all As. However, that was not the highlight of the call. She was more excited over having a social life. She went on and on about attending her school's football games, for she had attended none during her first year of college.

ADHD AND SELF-ESTEEM

Case Example. Phillip was a 14-year-old who was making all failing grades when his Sunday school teacher talked his mother into referring him for an evaluation for ADHD. His teachers at his school had written him off as being a troublemaker because of his talking too much in class. He couldn't play sports because of his grades, and he had not even considered going to college. He described himself as being "slow."

Phillip was subsequently diagnosed and treated for ADHD. His first report card was all A's and one B. When I saw him, he had the nerve to "have an attitude" about the B. "I'm not making nothing but A's now. Everybody thought I was dumb. I thought that I was just another dumb Black guy. Now I've got a chip on my shoulder academically. I've got something to prove!"

ADHD AND SOCIAL RELATIONSHIPS

Case Example. Adam was an 11-year-old boy with ADHD, which had been diagnosed by three other doctors before me. He was hyperactive to the point of squirming around in his chair the whole time. His parents had refused to let anyone treat him because they didn't "believe in that stuff."

He was becoming very unpopular with his peers at this time. He played first base in baseball and had tremendous trouble paying attention to the game. He would start daydreaming during the game, only to be roused to alertness by the incoming throw from the third baseman — who had a very strong arm, according to my patient. You can imagine what the teammates had to say. They moved him to the outfield and stationed his father behind the fence to yell at him if a ball was hit in his direction.

THE DISEASE OF THE SHADOWS

ADHD is a very "sticky" disorder when untreated because it tends to develop into a number of other psychiatric disorders. Depression occurs in 15 to 75 percent of cases. Significant problems with anxiety are present in 25 percent of cases. Of elementary school-age children, 66 percent have at least one other emotional problem besides ADHD. A variety of learning disabilities occur in 25 to 30 percent of cases. Addiction to a variety of substances such as alcohol, marijuana, caffeine, anti-anxiety drugs, and narcotic pain drugs can also occur. The other problems that can accompany ADHD can be so significant that the ADHD is lost in the shuffle. It becomes the disease that lurks in the shadow of the other problems, such as depression or alcoholism. No one would ever think about ADHD in these situations because the other problem is so bad. As a psychiatrist, I force myself to consider ADHD in all patients who abuse marijuana, drink excessive amounts of caffeine, or smoke cigarettes compulsively because these behaviors can represent their attempts at self-treatment.

Brain imaging studies are starting to give us information about why ADHD is so commonly linked to other problems. These studies have identified areas of low brain activity in areas of the brain adjacent to areas that control feelings, mood, and impulse control. These "cold spots" seem to involve lowered activity of certain hormones in the brain such as dopamine, serotonin, and norepinephrine, which can lead to a variety of other psychological and medical problems. This research has also begun to explain why people with ADHD often demonstrate worse concentration with greater effort. The "cold spots" actually get larger when an ADHD individual is given a task to perform.

TREATMENT OF ADHD

The treatment of ADHD involves a number of factors. Education about the illness is important for decreasing stigma in the patient and family. Organizations such as Children and Adults with ADD (CHADD) are very helpful sources of this kind of information. Counseling is necessary to address the shame, guilt, poor self-esteem, and grief over past failures and losses. These people need practical help with time management skills, financial planning, anger control, and stress management. Spiritual counsel is needed to address the long-standing issues of anger and apathy that many of these individuals have toward God. They need counsel regarding how to listen, be empathetic, and in general develop healthy relationships and marriages. Diet and exercise changes are needed to develop a healthy lifestyle.

A variety of medications are used to help with the core symptoms of this disorder. Psychostimulants are the main class of drugs that are used. They increase dopamine and norepinephrine in the brain, especially in the areas where the "cold spots" occur, thus "warming them up." These drugs include Adderall, Ritalin, Concerta, Dexedrine, and Cylert. Side effects include decreased sleep, loss of appetite, weight loss, headache, irritability, minor increases in pulse or blood pressure, and muscle twitches (tics). These drugs have abuse potential, and other drugs are used when this is a consideration. Wellbutrin, Tofranil, Norpramine, and Zoloft are antidepressants that are used for ADHD. Potential side effects differ with each drug but would include headaches, upset stomach, difficulty sleeping, nervousness, or dry mouth. These drugs do not have abuse potential. More information about medications may be obtained from the internet at *www.CHADD.org*.

CONCLUSION: THE GIFT

ADHD is a very real disorder that can cause much havoc in the life of individuals and their loved ones. However, ADHD can also be a gift. Most people with ADHD are very creative and are able to think of possibilities that others cannot see. Many of my patients with ADHD are immensely talented but unable to focus those talents. They are like baseball pitchers who can throw a ball one hundred miles per hour — over the backstop. The goal of counseling and treatment is to help them throw it still at a hundred miles per hour but for a strike — in other words, to learn to focus and control their quick minds and boundless energies. In a very real way, I seek to help my patients to view their ADHD as a gift from God, not a curse. Then the focus shifts to learning how to use the gift appropriately. It's similar to receiving a very fast sports car as a gift. You can learn how to use it appropriately and have fun — or not use it appropriately and get killed.

Like many other issues in life, we have to take responsibility for being the best that we can in life, regardless of the circumstances, because of our stewardship to the Lord (Colossians 3:23). An old man once told me that this was called "blooming where you are planted." The nice part about ADHD is that with treatment the blooms can be outstanding and God can be glorified.

SUGGESTED READINGS

Fowler, M. C. 1999. *Maybe you know my kid: A parent's guide to identifying, understanding, and helping your child with attention deficit hyperactivity disorder.* New York: Birch Lane Press.

Hallowell, E. M., and J. J. Ratey. 1995. *Driven to distraction: Recognizing and coping with attention deficit disorder from childhood through adulthood.* New York: Pantheon Books.

Silver, L. B. 1999. *Attention-deficit hyperactivity disorder: A clinical guide to diagnosis and treatment for health and mental health professionals.* 2d edition. Washington, D.C.: American Psychiatric Press.

Chapter 12

Suicide

Cupid R. Poe is a psychiatrist and a minister. He is a graduate of Tennessee State University and Meharry Medical College in Nashville, Tennessee. In 1996 he earned a bachelor of theology degree from American Baptist College. He has been involved in working with the homeless and prison ministry over the past fourteen years. He is in private practice as a Christian psychiatrist, working primarily with a geriatric and a chronically mentally ill adult population.

Dr. Poe is former interim pastor of Spruce Street Baptist Church in Nashville and a former pastor of First Community Church, also in Nashville. Currently he serves as an assistant minister of the Fifteenth Avenue Baptist Church in Nashville. He was the coordinator and founder of the Committee for the Study of Violence and Health, Nashville, and is also the founder and coordinator of the Institute for the Study of Racism and Health to be located within the School of Allied Health at Tennessee State University. He has self-published booklets and has written several magazine articles, some with Dr. Julius Adekunle, a minister and African historian.

Dr. Poe is an adjunct professor at Tennessee State University in the Department of Psychology and is a lecturer at Meharry Medical College for the Department of Psychiatry and the Department of Obstetrics and Gynecology. He is married to Diana Kittrell, and they have a son, Courtney, and a daughter, Caron.

From a biblical perspective, suicide is in opposition to the will of God. Contrary to the thinking in some cultures, suicide is not an act of honor or courage; rather, it is often an act of despair. Suicide is an not an act of love, but it is often an act of self-rejection. It is most often a desperate attempt to escape from the pain and despair of one's present condition. Suicide may also be considered in some cases as an attempt to get one's own way with God and with others. In some cases, suicide is motivated by the wish to get even with a loved one for some real or imagined hurt or rejection. Suicide, in my view, in no way provides an escape from the pain and frustration of a soul's existence in God.

THE PREVALENCE OF SUICIDE

In 1997, according to statistics reported by the National Center for Health Statistics of the United States Department of Health and Human Services, the suicide rate for the United States was 10.4 per 100,000 people, or 30,535 people. The ten states (including the District of Columbia) with the highest suicide rates, in descending order, were Nevada, Alaska, Montana, Wyoming, New Mexico, Idaho, South Dakota, Arizona, Oregon, and Colorado. The ten states with the lowest suicide rates in descending order were Michigan, Maryland, Minnesota, Ohio, Massachusetts, Connecticut, Illinois, New York, Rhode Island, New Jersey, and the District of Columbia. Based on this same survey, a person kills him- or herself every 17.2 minutes in the United States.

When one examines the 30,535 suicides committed in 1997 by race and sex (see table below), one sees some interesting trends. The suicide rate among males in the U.S. population is very high, and the suicide rate among White males is especially high. I believe these disturbing facts deserve further examination.

SUICIDES IN 1997

	Whites	Blacks	Other non-Whites	Total
Males	22,042	1,764	686	24,492
Females	5,471	339	233	6,043
Total	27,513	2,103	919	30,535

Source: National Center for Health Statistics

Suicide is the eighth leading cause of death in the U.S. population and the third leading cause of death among young people 15 to 24 years of age after auto accidents and homicides. In 1997, 750,000 people were reported as attempting suicide, and it is estimated that out of every 25 attempts, there is one completed suicide. Based on numerous studies, females attempt suicide four times more often than males. However, males *complete* suicide three times more often than females. Males more often use lethal methods such as handguns, hanging, or jumping from high places. Females more often ingest sleeping pills.

Historically, African Americans have had a significantly lower suicide rate than other ethnic groups in the American population. There is strong scientific evidence that faith in God and involvement in the church that has characterized many African Americans since the time of slavery is the main factor responsible for the much lower suicide rate. Historically, as indicated by the statistics in the table, the White male has had the highest suicide rate; and based on statistics compiled in 1997, this rate was 20.2 per 100,000. Based on a study reported by the Centers for Disease Control, the suicide rate among Native American Indians in 1999 was slightly higher than for the Caucasian male.

FACTORS CONTRIBUTING TO SUICIDE RATES

My belief is that the very high suicide rate among Caucasian males is largely a manifestation of unconfessed self-centered lifestyles. An unconfessed self-centered lifestyle most often involves a rejection of the authority of God and therefore a rejection of what is best for oneself. Rejecting the authority of God involves an attempt to find a substitute for God in money, things, power, and status. The pleasures of having a lot of money and having influence over others becomes the number one goal in life.

Any male or female who chooses to reject the authority of God will often choose to become sexually promiscuous. I believe that the level of sexual promiscuity is high among employed, single American Caucasian males whose income level is very high. The sexually promiscuous married male of whatever racial identity is often mentally, emotionally, and physically abusive to his wife and children. Such highly unconfessed self-centered lifestyles often cause guilt and shame that eventually become unresolved despair and rage. Suicide, unfortunately, is too often a desperate attempt to undo and escape from the pain, shame, and despair that result from turning away from God, as evidenced by sexual promiscuity and the abuse of others and oneself.

Historically and currently, the African American female has the lowest suicide rate of any group in the American population: a rate of 1.9 per 100,000, according to statistics compiled in 1997. However, over the last twenty years, the suicide rate even among African Americans has more than doubled, particularly in the 15 to 19 age group. I believe that a turning away from God, often provoked and made worse by past and current racism and evidenced by alcohol and other drug abuse, sexual promiscuity, family dysfunction, or unconfessed self-centered lifestyles is the major reason.

RECENT TRENDS

In recent years, there has been a trend toward an increasing suicide rate among females, adolescents, and children. In addition, statistical evidence indicates that more widows than widowers kill themselves. One study reported that the suicide rate among U.S. high school students is between 8 and 9 percent (Carson and Butler 1992). This is a staggering figure because actual suicide attempts and completed suicide statistics must often go unreported in order to avoid the shame related to a suicidal attempt and a completed suicide and also for insurance purposes.

There is some evidence that over the last ten to twelve years the suicide rate for children from well-to-do families has rapidly increased. Among the well-to-do, suicide frequently follows an epidemic pattern. For example, in Omaha, Nebraska, in 1986, there were seven suicide attempts by high school students in a suburban school, three of whom actually took their lives. The largest increase in the suicide rate in our nation has occurred among people aged 15 to 24, and there is also some evidence that the suicide rate in this age-group has tripled since the 1950s. This dramatic increase may be related to parental neglect and drug abuse involving parents, youth, and young adults (hence related to unconfessed self-centered lifestyles).

In addition, there is reliable survey data that suicide attempts and completed suicides are a significant problem among college students in the United States. According to one survey, the suicide attempt rate and the completed suicide rate are highest in the larger universities as compared with the smaller liberal arts and community colleges (Carson and Butler 1992). It is likely that social anxiety, the impersonality of being among very large groups of people unfamiliar to oneself, the academic demands, and a high level of emotional immaturity in college students as compared to young adults not in college may be significant factors contributing to a high suicide attempt and completion rate among U.S. college students. According to one survey, approximately 10,000 college students in the United States attempt suicide each year, and a little over 1,000 actually complete suicide. It is also very likely that students who go to college are more prone to leave behind their involvement in church and church-related activities in favor of attempting to integrate themselves into the social life of the university to which they have become a part.

THE CONCEPT OF A LOW SELF-ESTEEM CONDITION

Suicide is rarely an impulsive act. It is most often an act that emerges with a history behind it. That is, people who commit suicide are frequently in a prior condition that sets the stage for their ending their lives. This condition has certain identifiable and characteristic features, and I call it a *low self-esteem condition*.

A low self-esteem condition is characterized by the affected person's not having a growing relationship with God. This may also be viewed as not having God first in one's life. Another way of saying this is that those who do not have the Lord Jesus first in their lives have a low self-esteem problem whether they know it or not. Furthermore, people who have been saved and who, although saved, have since turned away from God will also be in a low self-esteem condition as long as they are in rebellion against the will of God.

People in this condition will often manifest a number of problems such as excessive anxiety, frequent depressed mood swings, rejection, hypersensitivity, and personality disorders that often involve being focused on having one's own way. These people will often take in excessive fatty foods, salt, and refined sugar and will be prone to eat large quantities of food. The incidence and prevalence of cigarette smoking and abuse of alcohol, marijuana, cocaine, or crack cocaine, Valium, Xanax, and heroin are significantly higher among people who are in a low self-esteem condition. Such people are often persistent in their pursuit of self-gratification or negative excitement, especially that which involves sexual promiscuity. If not self-employed, they often have difficulty maintaining employment and are frequently involved in no-win, destructive relationships. Their relationship to God and to the church is often ambivalent or involves a mixture of both positive and negative feelings.

CONSEQUENCES OF A LOW SELF-ESTEEM CONDITION

People in a low self-esteem condition will most often have a very negative image of themselves. This negative self-image is part of the related problems of self-rejection. Having a very negative image of themselves, they will often assume that other people also have a very negative image of them. One of the results of this false assumption is excessive fear of being observed and examined by others while performing, eating, or engaging in other activities. This persistent anxiety is called *social anxiety disorder*. Largely based on their self-rejection, negative self-image, and social anxiety, suicide attempts and completed suicides are a frequent occurrence in the life of people so affected.

There is research evidence, especially over the last twenty-five years, that people who have an active faith in God and who pray, read Scriptures, and attend church on a regular basis have a much lower incidence and prevalence of both emotional and chronic physical illnesses. In addition, some research studies involving elderly adults in the United States reveal that elderly people with an active faith in God have better-functioning immune systems, helping them fight off chronic infections, physical diseases, and depression.

Dr. Harold G. Koenig of Duke University Medical School has done a pioneering study that began in 1992 involving the relationship between religious involvement and immune system functioning as indicated by lower levels of Interlukin-6 in elderly adults who were more involved in religious activity as compared to those who had no involvement. The result of this study is reported in a book entitled *The Healing Power of Faith* (1999). I believe that Dr. Koenig's groundbreaking study highlights the need for more scientific studies looking at the relationship between non-involvement in religious activities or living a self-centered lifestyle and therefore how this condition contributes to a high incidence and prevalence of chronic physical and mental illnesses and related suicide attempts and completed suicides.

WHAT IS A SUICIDAL CONDITION?

To be in a suicidal condition is to be in a condition of despair or chronic repressed rage. Persons who are in a suicidal condition are most often focused on self-gratification and are determined to get their own way. In addition, such people most often have a very negative self-image and suffer from varying degrees of self-rejection. Frequently they suffer from clinical depression, social anxiety disorder, panic disorder, agoraphobia, and oftentimes generalized anxiety disorder. It is also true that alcohol and other drug abuse and dependence is very frequent in this group. It is very likely that the self-rejection, the very negative self-image, and the high level of anxiety strongly relate to persistent self-centered behavior, which results in spiritual and social isolation and therefore a high incidence of completed suicides.

Many people who are in a low self-esteem condition do not go on to a suicidal condition. The main reason some people do so is that they often persist in refusing to do what God has asked them to do. God asks that we repent of our sins and turn to him or turn back to him through faith, as evidenced by our obedience to the teachings and commandments of our Lord and Savior Jesus Christ. God asks that we connect with a fellowship of believers and become baptized by water and by the Holy Spirit. He asks that we try as best we can to live a life pleasing to him based on the revealed word of God as found in the Holy Bible. Persons who continue to refuse to follow the instructions of God will find themselves eventually in the condition of chronic despair or repressed rage and will therefore find themselves in a suicidal condition.

A MAJOR CAUSE OF SUICIDE

Some people who become suicidal and who go on to commit suicide have a family background of neglect, rejection, abuse, and a lack of spiritual nurture and guidance during childhood and adolescence. Others who become suicidal and who in fact commit suicide are people who, at a very early age — often beginning in preadolescence — decided to go their own way or to "do their own thing." I am convinced that there are other background factors that are not known that give rise to a low self-esteem condition followed by suicidal conditions and in many cases result in a completed suicide.

The goal in this section, however, is to identify what I consider to be one of the most frequent causal factors resulting in suicide. There are those who believe and who suggest that changes in our genes play a significant role in suicide. I must differ with this hypothesis, however, for I believe that most suicides are due to conscious decisions or choices made over time, manifesting as an unconfessed self-centered life pattern. I do not believe that for the most part we as human beings are victims of genetic changes that have no basis in highly self-centered behavior. I believe that in most cases the primary cause of the low self-esteem and suicidal condition and completed suicide is the persistent effort to get one's way with God and others. This unconfessed determination to get one's way almost always leads to persistent frustration and rage toward God, others, and oneself.

Suicide, in some cases, is, at a subconscious level, an attempt to get even with God and in some cases is a conscious attempt to get even with another person or persons because the suicidal person was unable to force God and others to give him or her one's own way. Even in situations where the overt motive in a suicide attempt or a completed suicide is to get even with a former girlfriend or boyfriend, husband or wife, often the subconscious motive is still to get even with God.

SUICIDE PREVENTION: A CHALLENGE TO THE CHURCH

As previously stated, suicide among African Americans going back to slavery times has been low compared with other ethnic groups despite years of abuse physically, emotionally, educationally, politically, financially, and sexually. However, as also noted earlier, over the last twenty-five years, we have seen a gradual rise in the suicide rate among African Americans.

The organized, committed church must respond to the challenge being posed to the religious community, to the American people, and to many nations of the world by the epidemic of suicides. Over the last twenty years, statistical evidence supports the view that many homicides and other self-destructive kinds of behaviors — especially criminal behavior, wife abuse, husband abuse, child abuse, and alcohol and other drug abuse — are often suicide equivalents or manifestations in a person who is suicidal at a subconscious level.

The high prevalence of suicide in our nation and in the Western industrialized world today is an unmistakable sign that too many people have turned away from God and that our values have become primarily physical or materialistic rather than spiritual. This turning away from God is very widespread, and if it is not challenged by the committed Christian church and by other committed people of faith in God, it will continue to escalate and will result in more widespread despair and destructive behavior, including suicide.

Committed believers in the Lord Jesus Christ have long known that God is all-powerful and that he is the answer to all questions and the solution to all problems. Committed believers have long known that there is no problem too big for God to solve. At the same time, as Christians we also know that God will not do everything. He will not make us turn to him as persons, as a nation, and as a world; but he will prepare those who are willing to be used to go out and to compel others to repent and to turn to him through faith in his only begotten Son, the Lord Jesus Christ.

CONCLUSION

I believe that the challenge of suicide prevention is being laid at the feet of the organized, committed church because God has given us the Lord Jesus Christ, his written Word, each other, and prayer, all of which are the greatly needed spiritual resources to deal with our most stubborn problems. I believe that God is more than ready to prepare those of us who are willing to be prepared to fight the blight of highly self-centered living, values, and lifestyles that often lead to the low self-esteem and suicidal condition and to completed suicides.

Several examples of suicides are reported in the Bible. Among these are Saul (1 Samuel 31:4), Saul's armor-bearer (1 Samuel 31:5), Ahithophel (2 Samuel 17:23), Zimri (1 Kings 16:18), and Judas (Matthew 27:5). Each of these individuals were highly self-centered, determined to have their own way, and therefore wanted to be equal with God. However, God will not be defeated. God cannot and will not be equaled and replaced. God cannot and will not fail in his efforts to train willing people who want to be faithful servants in his kingdom on earth and are willing to be used by him to win people to him and bring backsliders back to obedience to the commandments of our Lord and Savior Jesus Christ.

It is my hope and prayer that those who are in a low self-esteem or suicidal condition will not end their lives. Rather, my hope and prayer is that they will seek and find a growing relationship with God. With a growing relationship, one can receive forgiveness of sins and experience joy, peace, and involvement in the creative ministry of encouragement to others.

REFERENCES

Belluck, P. 1998. Black youths' rate of suicide rising sharply. *New York Times,* March 29, 1998. A: 1.

Centers for Disease Control and Prevention. 1998. DC Suicide among Black youths — United States, 1980–1995. *Journal of the American Medical Association* 18, no. 13: 193–96.

Durkheim, E. 1951. *Suicide: A study in sociology.* Translated by John A. Spaulding and George Simpson. New York: Free Press.

Freud, S. 1949. *Mourning and melancholia.* London: Hogarth.

Gibbs, J. P. 1969. *Suicide.* New York: Harper & Row.

Hayes, L. M. 1989. National study of jail suicides: seven years later. *Psychiatric Quarterly* 60: 7–29.

_____. 1995. Prison suicide: An overview and a guide to prevention. By the National Center on Institutions and Alternatives. *Prison Journal* 75: 431–56.

Koenig, H. G. 1999. *The healing power of faith: Science explores medicine's last great frontier.* New York: Simon & Schuster.

Maris, R. W. 1969. *Social forces in urban suicide.* Homewood, Ill.: Dorsey.

Myers, H. F. 1982. Stress, ethnicity, and social class: A model for research with Black populations. In *Minority mental health,* edited by E. E. Jones and S. J. Korchin. New York: Praeger.

National Center for Health Statistics. 1997. *The national vital statistics reports.* Washington, D.C.

Poussaint, A. F. 1975. Black suicide. In *Comprehensive textbook of Black-related diseases,* edited by R. A. Williams, 707–14. New York: McGraw-Hill.

Prudhomme, C. 1938. The problem of suicide in the American Negro. *Psycho-Analytic Review* 25: 372–91.

Schneidman, E. S., and N. L. Farberow, eds. 1957. *Clues to suicide.* New York: McGraw-Hill.

Stanley, E., and T. Barters. 1970. Adolescent suicidal behavior. *American Journal of Othopsychology* 40: 87–96.

U. S. Public Health Service. 1999. *The surgeon general's call to action to prevent suicide.* Washington, D.C.

Patricia Richardson

Chapter 13

Grief and Loss:
A Personal Testimony

Patricia Richardson is vice president of Christian Research and Development, Inc., in Philadelphia, Pennsylvania, which she founded with her husband, Willie Richardson. Born in Seaford, Delaware, she grew up in Philadelphia and studied at Temple University. She is a certified biblical counselor.

Patricia Richardson is the First Lady and Women's Ministry Director at Christian Stronghold Baptist Church in Philadelphia and is also a national and international speaker at Christian conferences. She has more than twenty years' experience in counseling and ministering to women and teenagers and has developed a women's discipleship training ministry called Women of Great Price. Patricia and her husband of forty years, Willie, have four children: Gregory, Garin, Gwendolyn, and Gerald.

> Yea, though I walk through the valley of the shadow of death. . . .
> (Psalm 23:4 KJV)

O h good grief" was a statement I have often heard and used. However, after experiencing the mental distress and pain caused by the death of a very close friend, I ceased to use it as much. There is nothing good about grief. Even when you know your loved one is in heaven, it still hurts.

As a pastor's wife, I have the responsibility of attending many funerals or "home goings." The sorrow and grief of people losing loved ones is real; it is up close and heartbreaking pain. The grief, however, should not last forever.

Grief is also felt when a husband, wife, or friend refuses to submit to one another in love and compassion, and when each one wants his or her own way with little regard for the other. The distance and distress caused by a loss of companionship and broken fellowship bring a deep sadness and loneliness of grief and pain.

Grief is a feeling of remorse and sadness combined with pain and heartbreak. Whether in sickness, death, or broken fellowship, grief can cause stress within the body. It can lead to depression, isolation, and wandering away from worshiping God. If grief is not mastered by self-resolve, counseling, or submission to the hope that is found in the words of God, it causes self-protection or self-centeredness. Looking only to the power of the flesh will not overcome grief.

According to the Word of God, the power of the Holy Spirit conquers grief. The name of Jesus sends the satanic attack of grief on its way. If we stand in the face of Satan and his demons in our strength alone without God's help, we are nothing.

Many people in grieving situations stay away from worship and from other Christians who are happy in Jesus because they feel sad. You must press your way to the house of praise and worship to have your spirit lifted, even filled with the Spirit of God.

The Holy Spirit heals, empowers, strengthens, revives, comforts, and keeps the people of God. That is why God left the Holy Spirit to be a comfort to those in need. Second Corinthians 1:4 states: "Who comforteth us in all our tribulation, that we may be able to comfort them which are in any trouble, by the comfort wherewith we ourselves are comforted of God" (KJV).

GRIEF AND TERMINAL ILLNESS: MY STORY

Terminal means a limit is placed on time or duration of time or a final time. Terminal means coming to the end — a hopeless situation with a limited amount of time. When a doctor tells a patient that he or she has a terminal illness, it darkens the path of life. It shocks your faith. Grief like sadness creeps in. The shadow grows bigger and more prominent. The shadow tries to shut out the joy of living. The shadow tries to dominate every thought and action.

When my oncologist gave me my diagnosis of cancer from a mammogram and a subsequent biopsy, he said, "This cancer is a killer disease." I had heard others say how bad a disease it was, and I had prayed never to get it. Sorrow and grief coupled with fear sprang into my mind. My heart tightened immediately. My thoughts turned to Jesus, my Lord and my Savior. Only Jesus can fix this. Surely, three recommended doctors and test after test were necessary, but only Jesus can heal me of this terrible disease. (My doctors were the best, and I appreciate their knowledge, work, and concern, however.)

The "valley of the shadow of death" appeared as I prayed before the nine-hour surgery, but I put it in the light of Jesus' words and promises. In 3 John 2, the Bible says, "Beloved, I wish above all that thou mayest prosper and be in health. Even thy soul prospereth" (KJV).

I had to make a very big decision in a short period of time. This cancer was a fast-growing one. One August, after a yearly mammogram, it was not there. In a rehabilitation hospital after my hip replacement in February, there it was — the size of a quarter.

I had actually made my decision six years before knowing of its presence. My friend was diagnosed with a return cancerous tumor and asked my advice. The words came back to my memory in the oncologist's office as he was speaking to me: "Get rid of the cancer, get rid of a body part, and save your life." I had desperately wanted her to live. But she had wanted to be with our Savior, and she told me so. I don't remember when I released her, but not long after, she was in the presence of our Savior.

Surgery of any type is a valley with a shadow. I had had four surgeries before this one. I have learned to lean on Jesus through it all, feeling his presence, his comfort, his healing, and his joy. Lying in a hospital bed hooked up to machines for your recovery is a valley with a shadow. You must not surrender to the adversary, who certainly stops by. You must know the Lord and Savior before this test. You must know his past record of healing to believe he can do it again. As I looked up into the face of the anesthesiologist and the surgeons, I would focus on Jesus and turn my life over to him through their minds and hands. "And this the confidence that we have in him, that, if we ask anything according to his will, he heareth us" (1 John 5:14 KJV).

Most doctors will advise you to talk to your family about terminal illnesses and corrective procedures as did mine. As patients, we can request Christian doctors and surgeons if they are available at the scheduled time. I have had the blessings of a Christian anesthesiologist to pray with me before he puts me under. My husband, as my pastor, also prayed with me before entering the operation room.

I did not want my children present until after the surgery. But afterward, my daughter became my "nurse" for more than a year. She had healing hands and nerves of steel, and she helped me through my sensitive moments. For example, treatment for cancer includes chemotherapy of various types — one of which will remove the hair from your body. Through my bald-headed days, my daughter was a strong encouragement by caring for my scalp. She said that it needed to be ready for the returning hair, which eventually returned twofold.

Chemotherapy also dims your vision. When this happened, I saw through dim eyes the valley of a shadow of death. Through prayer, my husband helped me remember what Jeremiah said in the book of Lamentations regarding suffering (see Lamentations 3:15–25).

The loss of life, the loss of body parts, the loss of hair, the loss of sight — all these certainly test our faith. But there is no other healer. Jesus Christ heals. If he chooses not to heal, he takes us home to be with him: "I go to prepare a place for you" (John 14:2 KJV).

Faith sustained me throughout. "Faith is the substance of things hoped for" (Hebrews 11:1 KJV). Faith in Jesus is dependence on someone stronger, bigger, and greater than anyone or anything we can imagine. I believe as did Enoch, Abraham, Moses, and Sarah that God can and will keep all of his promises.

Faith is belief in Jesus and his words. Mark 11:24 states, "Whatever you ask for in prayer, believe that you have received it, and it will be yours" (NIV).

THE ISSUE OF DEATH

Most people consider death, as I did, as a dark valley, permanent in its state — a skull and crossbones. Merriam-Webster (1993) describes it as "the destroyer of life represented usually as a skeleton with a scythe." Death is often depicted as a skeleton dressed in black and carrying a staff or a spade and mattock.

The apostle Paul calls it the wages of sin. But the gift of God is eternal life (Romans 6:23). For to be absent from the body is to be present with the Lord (2 Corinthians 5:8). The sting of death is sin; the power of sin is the law; but we have victory over both through Jesus Christ (1 Corinthians 15:56). When my friend walked through the valley of the shadow of death, she was not fearful. Even in the terminal state of cancer she was steadfast in her desire to be with the Lord.

The only way to survive grief and loss is placing your body, mind, and soul in the hands of Jesus. You overcome fear from Satan and the world.

Tragedies or trials will come as a test of life. Whether such events are temporary or terminal, it is wonderful to have a praying, born-again family. When your mate and your children lean on Jesus and depend on the all-sufficient God, and you see this on their faces, it brings comfort and light. If you have a praying church and friends far and near praying for you, e-mailing prayer requests from church to church, city to city, state to state, Jehovah Rapha ("Jehovah heals") hears and answers prayers. The grief is short-lived in his presence.

DEALING WITH BEING SCARRED

After surgery was over and a blood vessel broke (a side effect of breast surgery that was repaired without returning to the operating room), my plastic surgeon told me that I would have a scar that would need future surgery. My question was, "You mean be put to sleep, anesthetized and cut again, and possibly have another blood transfusion? It took days to find someone in our congregation with my rare type blood!" His surprised reaction was to try to calm me. He said, "Not now — perhaps in the future."

To beautify my body, I would need cosmetic surgery. Asking God for many blessings and healing were constant and everyday issues. Asking him to beautify me seemed vain and immature. No matter when you are cut on your body, vessels, veins, and muscles become disrupted. Cells and blood pressure and other major functions become impaired. During the procedure, I felt it necessary to reject future surgery. After surgery, there are machines hooked to your body to help you recover. You are confined to your bed and machines. You cannot move from the bed without being unplugged and assisted. I am claustrophobic and I felt freer with my room door open, as I could see people walking up and down the halls. I greeted people with a smile since it was good to be alive and hear even if I was restricted to my bed.

I knew that God had me there for healing and to be a witness. When I asked my family physician, Dr. Edward Williams, who is a born-again believer, for an oncologist (Dr. Thomas Frazier), a plastic and reconstruction surgeon (Dr. Murphy), and a hematologist (Dr. Steven Cohen), he recommended these as good men and great in their fields of medicine. I found them to be comforting, concerned, and attentive. I asked a lot of questions, and never once did they get tired or refuse to answer them. Dr. Frazier's favorite good-bye phrase was, "Keep the faith, kid."

Eventually I did have plastic surgery, and the scar was partially repaired.

DEALING WITH CHEMOTHERAPY

When my husband and I left Dr. Cohen's office after a visit preparing me for chemo, I knew all the side effects of the medication (adriamiyia), which I still cannot pronounce and which, when it is necessary that I say it, sounds like a girl's name. It can challenge your heart and stomach, remove all body hair, and cause blurred vision. The purpose is to kill any remaining cancer cells, but the choice is yours whether you want the doctor to administer it. Other side effects are nausea, headaches, and loss of strength. After signing for the treatments and realizing the side effects, we were both nervous and I wept.

I knew God was going to bring many people into my life. This gave me many opportunities to speak of God's goodness, mercy, and healing grace. These were divine appointments that I may never have again. A special surgical nurse named Barbara showed my husband how to dress my wound. Barbara, who attended seminary, was a comforter and a sister in God's family.

Our society has many medical plans; I believe my husband has the best for our family and his staff's families. I received nursing care, therapy care, doctors' care, and home care from interesting, tender, patient, and loving people. I now know this was a special blessing. As I share my story with other women who are not receiving this good care, I am saddened by their stories.

I had prayed for all Christian doctors, but this was not God's will. The doctors he provided were in his will. I requested Dr. Day, an anesthesiologist, to pray with me before putting me out. He was busy in another responsibility but was able to come and pray and then leave.

Sometimes we entertain angels unaware. At other times, we experience miracles and overlook them. Days later, I kept asking nurses for Dr. Day so that I could thank him. He was not known in the hospital. It was as if he had disappeared. Before a previous surgery I had my Bible on my chest while I was waiting for my surgery, and a red-headed young man came over and asked me why. I told him reading the Bible before surgery gave me great comfort from my Savior. He said, "Praise the Lord, my sister, can I pray with you before you go to sleep?" Again, he prayed and left. I know this is God's goodness and mercy following me all the days of my life and that I will dwell in the house of the Lord forever (Psalm 23:6).

CONCLUSION

Now I have opportunities to speak for cancer foundations. I also have the choice to speak and train women in our churches who are not educated in the statistics of this disease. I have opportunities to be transparent. I have opportunities to advise women to do their self-exams, to get mammograms for early detection. Every church should have a day of screening and obtaining information to save lives. Included in this knowledge is the importance of securing a healthier lifestyle by eating correctly and by exercising. Being overweight can lead to cancer. Eating fatty foods and holding body fat can lead to cancer. Sweets and comfort foods can lead to becoming overweight and developing cancer. Overeating starches, pastas, and other carbohydrates can lead to cancer. We must change our eating habits and walk or work out twenty to thirty minutes every other day. This, along with yearly gynecological visits, will bring early detection that leads to saving lives.

Psalm 34:7 says, "The angel of the LORD encampeth round about them that fear him, and delivereth them" (KJV). Being chosen to be a victim of a killer disease or a terminal illness was a test — to grieve and give up, or to trust God to use my life as an example of God's woman to other women, both near and far.

God had given me many other tests. I had trusted him, and he had delivered me. Surely now he can heal. God's woman, that is what I want to be, an example of God living in me.

REFERENCES AND RESOURCES

Barnhart, C. L., and R. K. Barnhart, eds. 1987. *The world book dictionary.* Chicago: World Book, Inc.

Merriam-Webster's collegiate dictionary, 10th edition. 1993. Springfield, Mass.: Merriam-Webster.

Pfeiffer, C. F., H. F. Vos, and J. Rea, eds. 1983. *Wycliffe Bible encyclopedia.* Chicago: Moody Press.

Stone, N. 1944. *Names of God.* Chicago: Moody Press.Dr. Edward Williams — Internal and general medicine.

I would like to thank the following doctors, all of Bryn Mawr Hospital in Bryn Mawr, Pennsylvania, for their work with me during my illness:

Dr. Edward Williams — Internal and general medicine
Dr. Thomas G. Frazier — Oncology and laparoscopic general surgery
Dr. Brien Murphy — Plastic and reconstruction surgery
Dr. Steven C. Cohen — Hematology and oncology

Chapter 14

Suffering for a Season: A Physician's Perspective on Grief and Loss

Pamela Turnbo, M.D., is an Assistant Professor of Medicine at the University of Medicine and Dentistry of New Jersey/Robert Wood Johnson Medical School at Camden. She is Board Certified in Internal Medicine by the American College of Physicians. She serves as a general internist in the University Medical Group at Cooper Hospital University Medical Center in Camden. Her special interests in medicine include primary care and community outreach, targeting minority communities. Since 1989, Dr. Turnbo has also been an active member of Christian Stronghold Baptist Church, Philadelphia, where she serves as one of the choir directors. Over the years she has written articles for the church newspaper, served with the medical ministry, and performed educational workshops on various health topics for the Christian and general communities in Philadelphia and the surrounding areas.

I have had to deal with my own issues of grief and loss. As a teenager, I lost my best friend to leukemia. It seemed surreal. How could a gracious God let him die at only 14 years old? For a while, thoughts of suicide overwhelmed me. Then I heard the Lord say, "It is not for you to question. I am still here." This life experience prompted me to seek Christ as my personal Savior and to find a higher calling in my life.

The irony is that my experience is common to many of us. The body of Christ needs to understand God's purpose for grief and loss, and how it can be used to edify the church.

THE STAGES OF GRIEF

There has been extensive research with regard to death and dying. Elisabeth Kübler-Ross was one of the first medical professionals to develop a systematic approach to the dying patient. Her discussion of the various stages of death and dying (or grief) in her book *On Death and Dying* should be considered in any Christian counseling arena. Though the principles were written in 1969, they are still very applicable today. We need to understand the stages that people pass through as they deal with grief and illness, so we can be instruments of change.

Kübler-Ross describes five stages of death and dying. These are:

- Denial and isolation
- Anger
- Bargaining
- Depression
- Acceptance

Denial and isolation are a natural initial response to a traumatic event in one's life. This emotional response may serve as a defense mechanism to protect the person's emotional and physical well-being. Although usually temporary, denial may actually provide an opportunity for the person to synthesize the trauma and develop a coping strategy over time. Even the strongest Christian may question the almighty God and his divine will. This is not always an accurate reflection of one's spirituality, but more likely the way that the Lord has programmed our emotional makeup.

Anger may be the response immediately after denial. Whether a person directs his or her anger toward the Lord or toward loved ones, the end result may be devastating for the person and those around him or her. Support systems may be drained, since it is difficult to help someone who is hostile, even if it is misdirected.

Once people leave the stages of denial and anger, they may start to look at the circumstances and begin to **bargain** with God for a solution. They may view good behavior as deserving a blessing from the Lord and a way out of the trial. They may think that if something is sacrificed, God will be more merciful. We know to the contrary, however, that God's mercy is independent of any efforts that we may make.

Depression may manifest itself once a person realizes that the problem or trial may be here to stay.

When the person has successfully passed through all four of those stages, the healthy end result will usually be **acceptance.**

The sequence of the stages may not be exact, and the timing will vary, but most people will progress through these stages to some degree. The Christian believer assisting a grieving person must identify these stages and then counteract the problems with scriptural hope and support.

Grief may result after the loss of a loved one; the diagnosis of a terminal or chronic illness; or the loss of a critical organ, such as the kidneys, heart, or extremities. Chronic illness may cause a person to grieve over loss of health or of independence. Reliance on others may seem to be an admission of inadequacy. Whatever the circumstances, people may respond in similar ways.

When someone is confronted with the death of a spouse or the diagnosis of a terminal illness, it is natural for that individual to go immediately into denial. Certainly the next question is, "Why me, Lord?" or "Where are you, Lord?" Worse yet, the person may say that there is no Lord at all. However, as believers we know that trials and tribulations can bring about total reliance on the Lord. Second Corinthians 1:9 says exactly that: "But this happened that we might not rely on ourselves but on God, who raises the dead."

God is quite capable of strengthening us beyond this phase of denial. In the Old Testament, for instance, Job immediately acknowledged the power of God in his circumstances and stated, "The LORD gave and the LORD has taken away; may the name of the LORD be praised." He is commended for his words: "In all this, Job did not sin by charging God with wrongdoing" (Job 1:21–22).

We should also consider conflicting emotions that may occur over the loss of a loved one. If a caregiver has sacrificed his or her time, energy, and self for a loved one, there may be a true sense of relief of the burden when the loved one dies. The caregiver may be relieved that the suffering is over. He or she may even feel relief that life is taking on a new dimension and that now he or she may need to move forward. The grief over losing someone may then be coupled with guilt. Most people never articulate this sentiment, but it is certainly a common response. It is crucial to acknowledge this as an appropriate response to the relief of the stress and to acknowledge that these feelings do not reflect a lack of love or compassion in any way.

We often have complete loss of control when we go through a trial. It is probably our carnal nature that wants to make things right immediately. Denial is a weak attempt by the person to exert control of the situation. Our human nature is geared to rebel against the will of God. Our mental, physical, and spiritual beings come under subjection to this rebellion. As a result, the anguish will take a toll on the entire person.

GRIEF AND THE MIND

Grief will manifest itself initially in psychological ways. Two of these, as we have mentioned, are depression and anger.

Depression. With depression, people may start to feel as if they are not in their "right mind." Activities of daily living such as eating, sleeping peacefully, or getting dressed may be problematic. Visual or auditory hallucinations may occur. In severe cases, thoughts may not connect properly, and the person may start to have illogical reasoning. Outwardly, the person may not seem to be adjusting to the tragedy, since the patient may seem to be acting illogically by the hallucinations and such, but in reality this is just the depression. Surprisingly, all of these symptoms should not be assumed to be pathologic. This is probably the mind's mechanism of coping with tragedy. If the symptoms persist and don't improve within a few weeks or months, then more serious interventions, such as intensive Christian counseling or even medications in extreme cases, may need to be approached.

The accepted grieving period, based on most psychiatric standards, is approximately six months. Some people may require much less time; others may require much longer. Anyone who is still in mourning years after the death of a loved one may be experiencing more than the normal grief reaction. Although the time frame for mourning may seem unrealistic, the individual's feelings should be validated, not disregarded. In this scenario, chronic depression should always be considered and the proper help sought.

Anger. Anger toward the Lord, toward the support systems such as family and friends, and toward the situation itself may make it difficult to deal with a bereaved individual. It may appear that the person doesn't want to interact with others, but in reality this may be a plea for assistance. It is very easy for others to become frustrated when all efforts seem to be thwarted. However, part of the healing process should include the person's ability to express their true feelings about the situation. The root causes of the anger, such as unresolved forgiveness and guilt, should be considered especially if there is no quick resolution of the anger. In time and with prayer, the grieving person will begin to accept that his or her feelings will not change the situation. Submission to the Lord's will is inevitable.

GRIEF AND THE BODY

The bereaved person may start experiencing new, unfounded physical symptoms. For example, a family member of a patient diagnosed with cancer may be completely healthy but may start making appointments with his or her physician for multiple complaints. Common symptoms include headaches, visual changes, insomnia, breathlessness, chest pains, palpitations, stomach pain, diarrhea, and joint pains. If the evaluation does not yield a clear diagnosis, the assumption is made that there is some psychological overlay with the person's ailments. Grieving may make people feel that they too are physically ill. Though concrete evidence for the symptoms may never be found, credence to the symptoms is crucial to identifying and treating the grief reaction. The grieving person may need to reaffirm that he or she is well, and the physician plays a critical role in that affirmation.

GRIEF AND THE SPIRIT

A grieving individual may start questioning God. Withdrawal from the usual support systems is typically an initial step. The hurt of the situation may cause a person to stop attending church and ministry activities. Ultimately, ongoing communication with the Lord through prayer and Scripture reading may cease. And when a Christian doesn't have the armor of the Word, he or she is defenseless against spiritual warfare. Isolation is a strong weapon of the enemy.

If ignored, all of these reactions will inevitably lead to depression and hopelessness. The inability to cope with the situation will be a sure start of the downward spiral of despair. In order to help someone through the grieving process, we must readily identify the early symptoms of grief. Depression may manifest itself as a sleep disturbance (with too little or too much sleep), loss of appetite, lack of interest in basic or enjoyable activities, and social isolation. In Psalm 51:10, David recognized that he needed a renewed spirit and a pure heart to deliver him from his transgressions. The key to being delivered from the depression is crying out to the Lord that there is a problem. Denial and anger should also be easy to recognize even in casual conversation.

We can facilitate the grief transition by providing the Word and by giving our personal testimonies of victory through similar situations (2 Corinthians 4:8–15).

ETERNAL HOPE

So where is the hope in grief? What is the purpose of the pain? *God is ultimately glorified when believers learn to conquer their sorrow.* Romans 5:6–11 starts off by stating that "at just the right time, when we were still powerless, Christ died for the ungodly." We don't have to worry about *our* control over the situation. Christ is the one who holds the cure to the sorrow.

The trial has nothing to do with us, but everything to do with Christ! Romans 9:16 states, "It does not, therefore, depend on man's desire or effort, but on God's mercy." His mercy lets us stand in the midst of tribulation. His mercy delivers us out of the pain. Besides, who are we to talk back to God? It makes sense that the created one should not challenge the Creator, but yet we still do (Romans 9:20–24).

Through our self-inflicted alienation from God, we need to learn how to pray even when we don't have the words to pray (Romans 8:26). The Holy Spirit intercedes for us when we can't visualize an end to the pain. In fact, God understands our sorrow in that he had to sacrifice his only Son to die for us so that we may have eternal life (John 3:16). The separation of God the Father from his Son is the ultimate example of suffering and pain. God loved us that much to give us eternal life with him, despite the separation. How can we even fathom that kind of love?

We can also have the confidence that "in all things God works for the good of those who love him, who have been called according to his purpose" (Romans 8:28). It is natural for someone to mourn the loss of a loved one. Love is an emotion that sets us apart from the rest of the creatures on the earth. However, in the passing of another, we can learn to extract the good from the situation. The example of another's life may draw one to Christ. Through the building of our own faith, we will be able to help the faithless. Ultimately, we are reassured that we as believers will see each other again in heaven. The time we have on earth should be cherished, for life is but a vapor (James 4:14).

We have an assurance that suffering is only for a while, so we shouldn't lose heart (2 Corinthians 4:16–18). Our momentary grief will eventually be replaced with peace and resolution. Praise God that we are made perfect through no efforts of our own, but through the blood of Jesus Christ. This is why the Word says, "Cast all your anxiety [or cares] on him because he cares for you" (1 Peter 5:7). We have an advocate in Christ; we don't have to carry the pain and grief alone.

CONCLUSION

Finally, when we grieve or go through a trial, we are blessed and we will receive the crown of life (James 1:12). It may be difficult to see clearly at the outset of a trial. However, as the bereaved individual progresses through various phases of grief, the healing process will begin. Once reality comes into view, the struggle should be given back to our awesome and omnipotent Lord. We will grow to understand God's mercy in each situation. Unreserved surrender to his divine power will bring perspective to the situation. Romans 5:3–4 states that "we also rejoice in our sufferings, because we know that suffering produces perseverance; perseverance, character; and character, hope." It is the suffering that strengthens our faith in God. When there seems to be endless pain, there is comfort in knowing that the suffering is always for a season (Ecclesiastes 3:4).

REFERENCES

Kübler-Ross, E. 1969. *On death and dying.* New York: Macmillan.

Part 4

Confronting Other Critical Issues

Chapter 15

Conflicts

Willie L. Davis Jr. and his wife, Brenda, are the founders of Hilkiah Family Ministries, Inc. This ministry centers on the prevention of family violence via counseling, advocacy, education, training, and material development. Willie and Brenda, who have been married for thirty-three years, have ministered to married couples for more than twenty years. Residing in Croton-on-Hudson, New York, they have five children: Willie III, Martina, Krystalyn, Nathaniel, and Shayna.

Davis attended Cheyney State University, Rowan College, and Wilmington College and is currently working on his dissertation for a Ph.D. in biblical counseling at Trinity Theological Seminary, Newburgh, Indiana. He was pastor for two years at Calvary Baptist Church in Ossining, New York. He has also served as the Associate Pastor of Pastoral Care and Counseling and as the Director of Community Resources for Alpha Baptist Church and its Joshua Counseling Center near Wimington, Delaware.

> "Blessed are the peacemakers, for they shall be called
> the children of God." (Matthew 5:9 KJV)*

Conflicts are inevitable in life. Conflict may be defined as a strife that threatens the relationship between two parties or causes inner turmoil. Conflicts began with the very first couple we read about in Scripture: Adam and Eve. Genesis 3 tells of Adam's disobedience to God's commandments and authority. This conflict led to shame, guilt, hiding, exposure, lying, family discord, violence, death, judgment, and indeed, all of humankind inheriting Adam's sin nature.

---

*Scripture quotations in this chapter are from the *King James Version* (KJV) unless otherwise noted.

People tend to respond to conflict in two ways. They are either proactors or reactors. Proactors anticipate conflict and prepare to control it and lessen its effects and stress. Experience and knowledge help prevent negative responses to conflict. Proactors use knowledge from past victories to solve current problems by dividing the problem into manageable small parts (Taylor 1991).

Reactors do not anticipate or prepare for conflict. They tend to act on emotions, lack insight, exhibit poor decision-making skills, and poor planning skills and have no sense of control over the strife.

Many people are lulled into believing conflicts will never happen to them. The proactors know from experience that conflict can occur at anytime, anywhere, over anything, and in almost any situation. The chances of a conflict occurring even in an established long-term relationship are raised considerably based on the quality of the investment (time and emotion) one has made toward that relationship.

TYPES AND OUTCOMES OF CONFLICT

Conflicts can be intrapersonal (internal) or interpersonal (external). Intrapersonal conflicts create internal stress through struggle with personal issues or problems or decisions. Interpersonal conflicts, by contrast, are those where there are struggles with issues, problems, or are the result of disagreements with another person.

The outcomes of conflict can take many directions. Here are a few of them, though by no means all:

- Property destruction
- Yelling
- Anger
- Fights
- Distrust
- Lying
- Abuse
- Separation
- Divorce or other broken relationships
- Hurt
- Bitterness
- Resentment
- Manipulation

It is important to remember that the person who best presents his or her side may emerge satisfied and victorious, but the desirable end of conflict is reconciliation, not victory. Scriptrue enables us to see the ultimate example of reconciliation in God's plan of salvation for sinful humankind. "God . . . hath reconciled us to himself by Jesus Christ" (2 Corinthians 5:18). "But God commendeth his love toward us, in that while we were yet sinners, Christ died for us" (Romans 5:8). God desires to bring sinners, in thought and deed, face to face with the need for a conversion experience. That experience will turn the person around, bringing with it right thinking and right acting (Spurgeon 1948).

Yet, not every conflict has a favorable solution. I can say that with confidence based on my experience as a professional counselor. No style of response can guarantee a hundred percent satisfactory resolution every time. Many deep-rooted issues take time, skill, and patience to resolve. Moreover, some people sense a gain from unresolved conflicts and seek to perpetuate them.

We must also recognize that conflict has a positive side. There are at least five potential benefits arising from conflict:

- New methods and procedures for handling conflict emerge
- Renewed and stronger relationships emerge
- People are more in tune with issues and preventive measures
- Relationships are protected from future threats
- Personal goals are protected from future threats

USING SKILLS AND SETTING THE TONE

Conflicts manifest themselves anytime and anywhere, even with the most simple of events such as what program to watch on television. People with more serious issues such as marital problems, alcoholism, stress, anger, adultery, or violence often seek counseling. Counselors are to help people work through issues of conflict toward reconciliation, resolution, and restoration of the relationship. Good counseling skills can also help equip the people to deal with future conflicts more effectively.

Effective counseling means having a keen sense of one's role as a facilitator, thinking clearly, discerning what is fair and right, acting rather than reacting, encouraging open communication, and making good decisions as well as organizing goals and plans. It means having foresight, insight, and hindsight, remaining calm, and staying in control. Effective counselors will confront those who are self-centered and use lies for their own good and forsake mercy. They will confront the person who is bent on spiritual, emotional, physical, and relational destruction. This wickedness must be confronted and challenged so as to set one's eyes upon God, to obey his Word, to live to his glory, and in this to confess and experience that "salvation is of the LORD" (MacArthur and Mack 1994).

Effective counselors are not to be weak or overbearing. Weak counselors leave people confused and without direction or hope. An effective counselor is proactive, works to resolve issues, and has viable goals to discuss. The counselor must anticipate future problems based on discussions in the session. Counselors deal with each conflict on its own merit.

Counselors know that many people will question every decision made or direction taken with them. When this happens, don't take offense. In this field it is important to anticipate questions that may be asked, even if the person is antagonistic. As an authority on conflict, demonstrate your competency for handling problem issues.

A secure counselor will consider a person's suggestion and even allow the person the chance to try it out. A nonviable course will reveal itself in time. By contrast, don't be offended when a counselee's insight, intellect, or suggestion works and bears fruit. Instead, rejoice.

Good counselors understand their position and authority during sessions and don't misuse them. They partner with their clients. Keep a humble profile. Be fair. The counselor, with the aid of the Holy Spirit, controls the counseling environment. Do not hinder matters that are moving favorably. We need to understand that many people cannot resolve conflicts without help. So we need to teach them — by demonstration — how to show grace and overcome pride when a decisive conflict has been won. Give reverence to God and respect to others.

If there are any interpersonal issues between the counselee and the counselor, they will dissipate as the Holy Spirit is allowed to control the session. A watchful counselor knows when issues are being concealed. Quickly confront the person, because hidden areas only prolong conflicts.

STYLES OF CONFLICT MANAGEMENT

There are several basic styles or strategies for conflict management, including win/win, compromise/accommodation, win/lose, avoidance, and lose/lose. Many factors determine which style is most appropriate for a given situation, including the kind of relationship, the level of desire for reconciliation, and the values, emotions, and spirituality entailed.

Win/Win

The goals of win/win are open discussions, mutual priority, and consideration of all parties in conflict, including their personal needs and goals. Open communication includes clearly defined facts, mutual agreement on goals, a reasonable time frame for goal achievement, and maintaining the relationship. Haviland (1989) noted that

> One of the really important things to emerge from anthropological study is the realization of just how fundamental cooperation is to human survival.... Stemming from the parent-child bond and the interdependency of men and women, the family has traditionally been the starting point for people to collaborate in handling problems faced by all human groups. (p. 198)

Communication must be open, sincere, clear, accurate, and honest. Listen attentively. Incorporate pertinent facts. Evaluate all important issues. Plan. Recognize and accept others' contributions as important. Maintain mutual respect regardless of another's difference. Let the Holy Spirit control your temperament and use godly wisdom when exercising power and authority.

Compromise/Accommodation

The goals of compromise/accommodation are to negotiate with parties to work on solutions mutual to both sides. Outcomes are often not desirable per se but are acceptable. Sacrifices are required of all parties in conflict to bring about a settlement. This style maintains and keeps the relationship intact as issues are worked out. The sincerity of one party may be called into question if it appears the person is more interested in merely resolving the conflict rather than seeking to improve the relationship. That means the relationship becomes secondary to the person's real goal.

Use the compromise/accommodation style when taking the following into consideration:

- You are trying to stay close to original plans and goals
- A surrender of personal goals is not required immediately
- Negotiations may stifle the relationship for a period of time
- Commitment to promises can enhance the relationship

Use this style especially when all can negotiate on their own strength and not jeopardize the relationship but improve it.

The compromise/accommodation style is often used with substantive matters such as values, goals, budgets, and schedules. Each party relinquishes something for the sake of resolution, starting with the least important goal first.

Win/Lose

The name clearly defines the goal here: manipulate so "I win and you lose." The goal is the "god," and the "god" is the goal. In win/lose, people manipulate a situation so that they can exploit their knowledge of the other person to obtain an advantage they normally would not have (Brams and Alan 1999). The "god-elevated goal" will cause people, aggressive or not, to manipulate any relationship to achieve what they want. Reducing intrapersonal conflict (guilt), personality changes, and control enhances a person's chances of reaching his or her goal. Therefore he or she seeks to win at all cost.

Many people have a "prioritized fighting instinct." They are easily aroused to hostility, not the least because of the sin nature, pride, and desire for personal gain. This instinct is, in fact, probably the ultimate cause of many social conflicts. One significant thing that separates human beings from the animal kingdom is that our conflicts usually come as a means to personal goals rather than from instinctual reactions. Thus conflict becomes a strategy in innumerable social contexts: marriage, school, work, play, politics, and religion (Turner, Beeghley, Powers 1989).

Avoidance

In adopting an avoidance style, people have decided that they want no involvement with the conflict. Their personal goals, views, and relationships with the other person are of little concern to them. It may be they have decided that some conflicts can be resolved without their intervention or that the conflict is not within their range or that there are no answers for the conflict.

Lose/Lose

With the lose/lose style, no one cares about the conflict, the relationships, personal goals, or the positive side of the outcome, should the conflict be resolved. Each person has an "I don't care, I give up" attitude. No one sees a valid reason to invest in the marriage, family, business, or whatever. This style emerges from repeated fears, frustration, and attempts that did not work. Each party senses defeat when efforts were made in the past. In marriages, separation and divorce often result. The entire family loses, no matter how you look at it. There are no winners.

HELPING YOUR STYLE DELIVER RESULTS

All five styles for conflict management are useful and have value. The conflict most often determines the style to use. How effectively a style is used affects the outcome of the conflict. Many conflicts may call for people to change or modify their approach, since people do change their minds and feelings about issues.

Knowing where to begin is crucial. Jay Adams (1970) has well stated,

> The counselees learn how to use scripture . . . to solve problems. Counselors are to help clients solve . . . several representative problems from a list which the clients themselves have prepared . . . and to initiate the regular, daily process of problem-solving communication. In the very process of agreeing upon areas of conflict, both parties begin to work together. (p. 194)

Yet there are two reasons why there are no guaranteed results. First, some destructive conflicts and personalities exceed our ability to handle. Frustration sets in when we have a heart's desire to resolve an issue and can't. No one person can successfully resolve every conflict. In the helping process, be sincere and patient and know your limits. Second, time is important, so don't waste it. As time passes and issues remain unresolved, frustration, doubt, and fear will set in.

Investigating Alternatives

Knowing when to change styles is crucial. According to Rapp (1998),

> A strategy that fails to produce the needed resources means either that new sources of resources need to be considered or that new strategies need to be developed. The learning that occurred during the unsuccessful effort often can be used to formulate a revised plan. (p. 145)

It is imperative for counselors to help people review all the options to their dilemma. To alleviate stress, the causative issue or root problem has to be identified. Other options may replace what has already been considered a viable goal. As we said earlier, if a counselee rejects your suggestion and has one of his or her own, don't reject it out of hand; give it strong consideration. Accepting that person's suggestion for resolving conflict doesn't mean you aren't giving acceptable help. It doesn't reflect on your ability to give acceptable help. Keep in mind that the goal is to resolve conflict as a means toward reconciliation.

Many alternatives are too threatening to people who don't want to let go of their beliefs. In some cases the parties will refuse to come to what Adams (1970) calls "the conference table" — the place of resolution.

Preventive Maintenance

People often want their counselors to be "miracle workers" who can fix problems immediately even though these problems may have developed over months and even years. Very few problems are resolved in a few sessions, while others may never be resolved, no matter what. A counselee must therefore understand several factors.

First, a person should never wait to seek help. Passing time only complicates issues, increases the potential damage to relationshops, and makes satisfactory solutions more difficult to reach.

Second, progressive counseling sessions allows counselors to intervene with techniques to offset "destructive conflict." People need to give relationships regular maintenance in the same way that mechanics need to perform regular maintenance to keep cars running smoothly. Give the relationship what it needs on a daily basis to maintain it.

Preventive maintenance includes investing time, energy, patience, effort, and sincere commitment to forestalling problems. Use wisdom, knowledge, and your understanding of conflict management styles to prevent volatile situations (Taylor 1991).

Effective Communication

Communication is essential to all relationships. As Saleebey (1997) states, "Humans can only come into being through a creative and emergent relationship with others. . . . In dialogue, we confirm the importance of others and begin to heal the rift between self, other, and institution" (p. 10).

God desires for all relationships to be loving and enhanced by communication. When communication is used only to obtain information and not enhance a relationship, problems begin. Family members should be able to "appropriately" verbalize concerns without threat. Freedom of speech "without seasoning" leads to conflict. The Bible instructs us on the importance of good communication:

> Let no corrupt communication proceed out of your mouth, but that which is good to the use of edifying, that it may minister grace unto the hearers. And grieve not the holy Spirit of God, whereby ye are sealed unto the day of redemption. Let all bitterness, wrath, and anger, and clamor, and evil

speaking, be put away from you, with all malice: And be ye kind one to another, tenderhearted, forgiving one another, even as God for Christ's sake hath forgiven you. (Ephesians 4:29–32)

Sending, receiving, and interpreting messages are all part of communication. Unfortunately, most communication is focused on sending. Communication incorporates language, meaning, and understanding (Thass-Thienemann 1973). It also takes place through body language, gesturing, facial expressions, and tone of voice. The meaning of language involves interpretation. Understanding is knowing what was said and acting accordingly.

Clear and concise information prevents conflicts in several ways. First, when information is correct, factual, and timely, the receiver can see the message's value. Say what needs to be said; people are not mind readers. Rogers (1961) stated that

> Real communication occurs when the evaluative tendency is avoided, when we listen with understanding. . . . It means to see the expressed idea and attitude from the other person's point of view, to sense how it feels to him, to achieve his frame of reference in regards to the thing he is talking about. (pp. 331–32)

Second, receiving the message is just as important as sending it. Listen carefully to what is said and to what is not said. Be alert and receptive to pending conflict. Listen with your ears, mind, eyes, and heart.

Use caution and spiritual discernment to communicate. The information given first is not always the real reason for the conflict. Good listening skills get to the core of the problem.

Communication must continue if a resolution is to be reached. Use words of edification, not corrupt words, to resolve conflict. Keep the minor things minor and don't make them major.

MANAGING ANGER

When conflicts become manageable, it will be when anger is under control. Anger is the fuel that keeps conflicts burning. The Bible has much to say about anger.

> Let not the sun go down upon your wrath (Ephesians 4:26)
> Wrath is cruel, and anger is outrageous (Proverbs 27:4)
> Anger resteth in the bosom of fools (Ecclesiastes 7:9)

Unger's Bible Dictionary (Unger 1985) describes anger this way:

> Anger, the emotion of displeasure, indignation, arising from the felling of
> injury done or intended, or from the discovery of an offense against the
> law.... Anger is sinful when: it rises without reflection; when injury occurs;
> if it is disproportionate to the offense; when the innocent are hit by it; when
> it is too long protracted and becomes revengeful. (p. 53)

Scriptures are often misquoted or misrepresented to indicate that
Christians are not to get angry, that it's sinful, and should not be a part of
one's life. Yet other people get angry, so why not Christians? What is over-
looked is that anger is normal for all people. When conflicts erupt, no one
is immune from anger — but it should be kept under control at all times.
The murder of Abel by his brother Cain (Genesis 4:8) is a clear example
of anger out of control. Cain's anger led him to kill his brother out of rejection and jealousy. God warned Cain: "Sin is crouching at your door; it
desires to have you, but you must master it" (v. 7 NIV). God's warning is our
admonition to change and not sin in the midst of anger.

But, you say, didn't Jesus express anger? Yes, he showed anger during his
time on earth. He was angry toward the sin and injustices committed
against him and others. We cannot deny him this aspect of his humanity.
John 2:13–16 describes one of Jesus' moments of anger, of righteous indig-
nation. He flogged the money changers at the temple, loudly denouncing
the desecration of his Father's house.

The following three principles show how anger works in the context of
conflict.

> First, anger can inflate a conflict. Expressing yourself in a negative
>   manner during a conflict is an anger reaction.
> Second, once initiated, conflict is fueled as long as anger and self-
>   justification continue.
> Third, anger may remain even after resolution and thereby possibly
>   re-ignite the conflict. There is no "best time" to express anger.

Expressing Anger

So if anger is a normal human response to circumstances, how should it be
expressed?

First, counselors should examine how best to help people identify the
origin of their anger. Some anger arises from situations or events of years

gone by simply because they have been avoided or dealt with ineffectively. Never mix old and new anger; resolve each separately.

Second, express anger appropriately. Generally, anger is internalized first before there is external evidence. Externalized anger can be released like an explosion or a puff of smoke — it's then over and done with. Internalized, or suppressed, anger may cause illness or injury, can lead to poor health, will stifle relationships, and will hinder spiritual growth. The proper expression of anger calls for patience, creativity, maturity, sensitivity, and courage. Anger is to be without retribution; as the Bible says, "Be ye angry, and sin not" (Ephesians 4:26).

Third, do not live with anger. Anger closes the door to forgiveness. Use prayer, fellowship, Bible study, family ties, counseling, and healthy relationships to work through anger.

DEVELOPING CONFLICT AWARENESS

Conflict awareness is the knowledge of a conflict, not the denial of it. Understanding how continual conflicts disrupts one's peace of mind and relationships can quickly resolve it. Unity, strength, the elimination of stress, and the resurgence of hope are all born from this. When people involved in a contention finally realize they are unable to solve the problem on their own, they may then seek help. The counselor must use what I refer to as the "I-reasoning," whereby a counselee centers on his or her contributing behavior and not on another's. Each comment the person makes should begin with "I," not "you." I-reasoning keeps the person involved in the discussions and taking responsibility for what he or she will do to bring about resolution. This eliminates insensitivity and shifting blame.

The potential for violence is prevalent every time the parties in conflict come for counseling. You as the counselor must ask questions that expose and quench this possibility. If your client has had a history of violence and was in counseling before, collaborate with the other therapist via signed consent forms. You will want to be able to assess the history of violence by knowing how long this person has been acting in an impulsive, unpredictable, or assaultive way; how often he or she acts like this; and how recently he or she was involved in a violent situation. From this the counselor needs to determine how severe the violence was, whether a weapon was used, and whether it resulted in personal injury (Lukas 1993).

ADDITIONAL SPIRITUAL ASPECTS OF DEALING WITH CONFLICT
Biblical Direction
Frey (1994) presents five steps in what he calls Biblical Directionism for the process of conflict management. The five steps are

- Profiling — Gathering historical data on the counselee
- Silhouetting — Employing data to contrast the counselee's current state against what the Bible has to say
- Confrontation — Showing the counselee how his or her life is not in line with God's standards and how future problems can arise
- Commitment — Helping the counselee face the need to commit to change so his or her life is in line with biblical directives
- Conditioning — Helping the counselee make practical use of biblical principles so that help and healing can begin

The Place of Prayer
Prayer helps in resolving conflicts (although a counseling session should not become a prayer meeting). A counselee gains strength and comfort from it. And God does answer prayer. Discern when prayer should be offered. Help the person develop the following:

- A committed daily prayer life
- A sense that God is near and knows the conflict
- An awareness that God offers guidance and comfort to our lives
- Being in touch with people who care

The Place of Forgiveness
Forgiveness during conflict paves the way for reconciliation. God's forgiveness is entailed in our salvation. Jesus obligated us to a life of forgiveness: "Forgive us our sins; for we also forgive everyone that is indebted to us" (Luke 11:4). Christians should be ready to forgive. Wise (1956) noted that

> Reconciliation requires facing all realities, which may be very painful and difficult. It is on this . . . that much attempted forgiveness fails. . . . The Christian relationship of forgiveness is not an easy . . . matter. It represents the achievement of a high level of spiritual maturity and the sacrifice of all of the inner attitudes and feelings that create barriers toward others. (p. 88)

CONCLUSION

In conclusion, we can say that, yes, conflicts are inevitable, but we can see God's love, virtue, wisdom, and holiness through them. Scripture assures us that we "can do all things through Christ" who strengthens us (Philippians 4:13), enabling us to "be holy and without blame before him in love" (Ephesians 1:4). In our daily walk God gives us an "oughtness," a sense of right and wrong. Even when we don't want to do right, we have the knowledge of what is the right thing to do (White 1987).

REFERENCES

Adams, J. E. 1970. *Competent to counsel*. Grand Rapids: Baker/Presbyterian and Reformed Publishing.

Brams, S. J., and A. D. Taylor. 1999. *The win-win solution: Guaranteeing fair shares to everybody*. New York: W. W. Norton.

Frey, D. B. 1994. *The biblical basis for counseling: Biblical directionism, a biblical approach to counseling methodology*. Newburgh, Ind.: Trinity Theological Seminary. Unpublished manuscript.

Haviland, W. 1987. *Cultural anthropology*. 5th edition. New York: Holt, Rinehart, & Winston.

Lukas, S. 1993. *Where to start and what to ask: An assessment handbook*. New York: W. W. Norton.

MacArthur Jr., J. F., and W. A. Mack. 1994. *Introduction to biblical counseling: A basic guide to the principles and practices of counseling*. Dallas: Word Publishing.

Meir, P. D., F. B. Minirth, F.B. Wichern, and D. E. Ratcliff. 1997. *Introduction to psychology and counseling*. Grand Rapids: Baker.

Pearson, P. 1997. *When she was bad: Violent women and the myth of innocence*. New York: Viking Penguin.

Rapp, C. A. 1998. *The strengths model: Case management with people suffering from severe and persistent mental illness*. New York: Oxford University Press.

Rogers, C. R. 1961. *On becoming a person*. Boston: Houghton Mifflin.

Saleebey, D. 1997. *The strength perspectives in the social work practice*. 2d edition. New York: Longman Publishers.

Spurgeon, C. H. 1948. *The soul winner*. Grand Rapids: Zondervan.

Taylor, A. 1991. *Managing conflict*. Newburgh, Ind.: Christian Education Enterprise.

Thass-Thienemann, T. 1973. *The understanding of language*. Volume 2: Understanding the unconscious meaning of language. New York: Jason Aronson Publishers.

Turner, J. H., L. Beeghley, and C. H. Powers. 1989. *The emergence of sociological theory*. 2d edition. Belmont, Calif.: Wadsworth Publishing.

Unger, M. F. 1985. *Unger's Bible dictionary*. Chicago: Moody Press.

White, J. 1987. *Putting the soul back in psychology: When secular values ignore spiritual realities*. Downers Grove, Ill.: InterVarsity Press.

Wise, C. A. 1956. *Mental health and the Bible*. New York: Harper & Row.

Joan A. Watson Ganns

Chapter 16

In Search of a Healthy and Authentic Faith

Joan A. Watson Ganns is a therapist in the area of West Palm Beach, Florida. Prior to her counseling career, she was an elementary and secondary school teacher. She has a bachelor of science degree from Eastern Illinois University, a master of science degree in education from the University of Illinois, and a master of arts in psychology from Trinity Evangelical Divinity School in Deerfield, Illinois. She grew up in Chicago. She and her late husband, Joseph Ganns, have one son, Lawrence; two daughters, Kimberly and Karin; and five grandchildren. She resides in Wellington, Florida, with her mother, LeJeun Watson.

The purpose of this chapter is to discuss an area in our Christian life that is rarely discussed — that of a healthy versus an unhealthy faith. It is, however, an area that will need increasing attention as the numbers and variations of belief systems escalate.

WHAT IS FAITH?

One of the definitions of *faith* in *Webster's Third International Dictionary* (1976) is "a system of religious beliefs." As such, faith may consist of fundament tenets, cherished values, beliefs, and ideals of an individual, group, or people. In this chapter, however, I define faith as knowing God and knowing Jesus Christ, whom God has sent.

Knowing God does not come through a program or a method. It is a relationship with a Person. It is an intimate love relationship. Through this relationship, God reveals his will to us and invites us to partner with him in establishing his kingdom on earth. We will want to worship him for choosing us to work wherever he is working. When we obey God, he accomplishes through us something only he can do. Then we begin to experience an intimate relationship with a real God, who is sufficient for the realities of life. When we become hungry and thirsty for God, we are promised fulfillment.

I am suggesting that this passion and determination of believers (the Bride) searching for her Bridegroom (Jesus Christ) is the ultimate in a healthy faith. Notice how Psalm 42:1 portrays the relationship: "As the deer pants for the water brooks, so my soul pants for You, O God" (NKJV).*

MY OWN SEARCH FOR AN AUTHENTIC FAITH

I come from a rich heritage of at least four known generations of bishops, pastors, ministers, missionaries, evangelists, deacons, Christian educators, and faithful followers of Jesus Christ. Both sets of grandparents, although only laypeople, were pioneers in churches that seventy years later still exist. However, at the age of 12, I realized that God had no grandchildren, so I gave my life to Christ.

After the death of my husband, Joe, I became more dependent on my Eternal Husband (Jesus Christ), and my hunger for his presence increased. Six years later my father died. This was difficult. As his only child, I felt that I was the apple of his eye. However, in time I came to see that nothing of God had died. God tenderly moved into my life and began to fill up the empty places of my grief with his presence. In my vulnerability, I became even more hungry for God. I began to seek assurance of the promise of his presence. I was exhilarated to find and experience it! ("And the LORD said, 'Here is a place by Me ...'" [Exodus 33:21].)

Recently, while reading Tommy Tenney's *God Chaser* books (1998, 2000) on worship, I was thrown into an Isaiah 6 experience of seeing my "undoneness."

> In the year that King Uzziah died, I saw the Lord sitting on a throne, high and lifted up, and the train of His robe filled the temple. Above it stood seraphim; each one had six wings: with two he covered his face, with two he covered his feet, and with two he flew. And one cried and another said,

---

*Scripture quotations in this chapter are from the *New King James Version* (NKJV) unless otherwise indicated.

"Holy, holy, holy is the LORD of hosts; the whole earth is full of His glory!" And the posts of the door were shaken by the voice of him who cried out, and the house was filled with smoke. Then I said: "Woe is me, for I am *undone!* Because I am a man of unclean lips, and I dwell in the midst of a people of unclean lips; for my eyes have seen the King, the LORD of hosts." (Isaiah 6:1–5)

As in Isaiah's life, death of a loved one brought me face to face with my dependence and the reality that God alone is worthy of my worship. As I saw the glory and majesty of God anew, I felt exposed, but I was hungry for more and more of his presence. I was ready to yield my passions, dreams, ambitions, desires, and attachments to have more of him. I was now in search not just of the hand (blessings) or the visitation (emotional experiences) of God, but rather the face and the habitation (manifested presence) of God. Like Isaiah, I became aware of being undone, ruined! Religion and church as usual had no appeal for me anymore. I became a desperate woman, being pursued by and in hot pursuit of the One who loved me first and chose me to be his very own. This feeling and experience are expressed in the following verses.

No, dear brothers, I am still not all I should be, but I am focusing all my energies on this one thing: Forgetting the past and looking forward to what lies ahead, I strain to reach the end of the race and receive the prize for which God, through Christ Jesus, is calling us up to heaven. (Philippians 3:13–14 NLT)

WHAT IS RELIGION?

Webster defines *religion* as "a body of institutionalized expressions of sacred worship, observances, and social practices found within a given cultural context." Rites and rules, however, are often practiced with rigidity, resulting in legalism. Customs may be repeated often enough that although unwritten, they may be placed on the level of law. These legalistic codes of behavior keep followers in line and serve to identify those of a particular group.

Arterburn and Felton (1999) write that many get caught up in religious activity to avoid pain, working hard and running fast "to stay one step ahead of the hurt" (p. 160). Further, they write, "Busyness becomes the goal, and religious compulsivity provides a false presence of God" (p. 160) — thus an inauthentic faith.

Ellul's work (cited in Baker 1999) states that "religion goes up and revelation comes down." These two arrows capture this contrast.

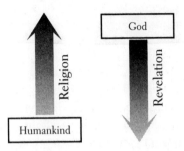

In this system the law of merit rules, not the law of grace. Grace does not fare well in a religious system. God in his grace wants to pour out riches and favor, and the religionist wants to earn it by pulling up on his own religious bootstraps. A fundamental assumption of religion is that as humans we must take the initiative and through our actions attempt to move God to action. However, at the heart of authentic faith is the revelation that in God's graciousness, he took the initiative and came down to us.

THE GOD OF RELIGION

Those dedicated to keeping religion alive foster an angry God, demanding good deeds and punishing our misdeeds. Consequently, condemnation may be experienced for any infraction of the rules. One may wear guilt like a continual hangover. From this vantage point, God is seen as a distant and authoritative "bad" father waiting to do us in. Rather than love for God, there is an unnatural fear of him. Cultural and historical factors may have contributed to the perpetuation of legalism. For those who have had slavery as a part of their historical past and others who have suffered from negative backgrounds, this very punitive "God" serves as a type of slave master. Such people know this Scripture in Hebrews 13:17 all too well: "Obey those who rule over you." A better translation is "those who lead you." The Bible does not encourage control freaks. God himself, while in control, does not seek to control. Rather, he draws us to himself with mercy and lovingkindness.

HARRIED RELIGIOUS ACTIVITIES

There is often a lot of feverish activity in practicing religion. Many functions are raised to a level of religion because of their sincerity, sacrifice, and fervor. There is the bringing together of people, forming organizations to achieve good causes and sustain certain shared values. Six areas that may take on the form of religion and be counter to an authentic faith are civil rights, social services, religious training, parachurch groups, education, and church work.

Civil rights. Many clergy and nonclergy leaders use the jargon of religion to bring social salvation to the poor, the dispossessed, and the imprisoned. Many wrongs have been made right, and some significant gains have been made for social justice. But as important as it is to be a drum major for social justice, this kind of activity may not result in one's finding an authentic faith.

Social services. Many men and women give their lives to serving humanity in countless positive ways. There are those who seek to protect others by serving in the military or other protective forces. Many go to foreign fields, serve the needy, feed the homeless, keep foster children, or adopt children. Others serve in soup kitchens and teach in "deprived" areas of the world. Volunteerism is an American way of life. Our hearts may bleed, and we may join forces to alleviate pain and suffering in countries other than our own. As sacrificial as these acts might be, however, they may not lead either the participants or the receivers to a healthy and authentic faith.

Religious training. Many students attend parochial schools and dedicate themselves to religious professions. Some choose to go into the ministry. Others go to graduate schools of religion or to seminaries. I was one of those. I attended a very solid and conservative seminary in the Chicago area. There I repeatedly witnessed students who sacrificed not only their family life but also their relationship with God. Sometimes it was easier to give priority to emulating the "heavyweight" professors and mastering Greek and Hebrew. In my own case, my personal time with God was all too often shifted as I instead gave ever-increasing time to studying my assignments, desiring to make impressive grades. Yes, one can lose one's intimacy with Christ while studying about him, even in seminary. One can study to know God and yet be very far from experiencing him.

Parachurch groups. During the latter half of the twentieth century, a number of very influential parachurch groups were raised up to support the church in this country and around the world. The work they have done has been phenomenal, and thousands have been led to Christ and perhaps to an authentic faith. Promise Keepers and T. D. Jakes's Man Power conferences have energized the Christian men's movement like no other. There are a number of national and international conferences on a range of topics such as prayer, spiritual warfare, and restoration that one can attend and receive spiritual help. Likewise, multitudes attend the Joyce Meyers conferences and T. D. Jakes's Women Thou Art Loosed conferences. Many attendees find spiritual and emotional healing. However, some folks are just conference "junkies." They get a "high" while present, but once the conference is over, they fail to live up to the challenges given.

Sometimes one is not hungry enough! I received an excellent spiritual foundation as a Chicago teen by participating in a wonderful Youth for Christ group. Then, as a collegian, I was a part of InterVarsity and the African American arm of Navigators. Our children also participated in Youth for Christ, and my husband and I were sponsors. Our family also participated in Harambee, an African American branch of Campus Crusade for Christ. I've attended and participated in a number of conferences, workshops, and seminars. And yet today, in my reflective years, I still hunger for the Living God! One doesn't take a drink from the spiritual fountain of God and never thirst again, but the continual thirsting and hungering after God will be fulfilled.

Education. Many of us have been blessed to receive an education. What a wonderful privilege we were given — a gift that many who were perhaps even more gifted than ourselves did not have. However, we, the "educated," must watch that we do not get so involved in the exchanging of ideologies and in philosophical debate that we forget our God. Solomon, one whose life request was to find true value in life, says this:

> The words of the wise are like goads, and the words of scholars are like well-driven nails, given by one Shepherd. And further, my son, be admonished. . . . Of making many books there is no end, and much study is wearisome to the flesh. Let us hear the conclusion of the whole matter: Fear God and keep His commandments, for this is man's all. For God will bring every work into judgment, including every secret thing, whether it is good or evil. (Ecclesiastes 12:11–14)

So the acquisition of information and worldly knowledge has its value, but one would do well not to forget to seek him who is true wisdom.

Church work. The African American church early on became a place where the disenfranchised could find a place. Churches were often seen as a place of refuge, but they were also sites where many would find a "place to become." Many used their talents and gifts for the service of the Lord. Music and musicians have always played a large part in the church, albeit, often a problematic part. Leaders often struggled to placate the temperaments of the young, not-so-young, gifted, and Black as they sought to find a place in this bastion of hope.

The church kitchen has been a mainstay of garnering finances, and only very recently have some churches refused to "sell dinners" as their main source of revenue. Some churches were so successful in their cooking and selling that they closed their doors to services and became restaurants. In the church where my late father pastored, cooking dinners was always a big part of our church life. Some of the cooks only came to fix their culinary specialties. When my father passed away, I asked what would happen if a new pastor came and shut down the kitchen. Two ladies said they would go somewhere and start their own. One of them is now deceased, and I do not know if she ever received Christ as her Savior. That is quite a tragedy and is a result of what I believe are misplaced values.

I have heard many say, "Well, people need something to do." One only has so much energy. If it is used up in the kitchen, will there be energy to spend on one's knees? Isn't it important to obey God by paying the tithes and offerings and trust him to provide for his church? Let's elevate the saints to bringing in the glory of God in his house, rather than majoring in gorging on gourmet dishes.

CONCLUSION: JESUS AND RELATIONSHIP, NOT RELIGION

Jesus always valued relationships over rules. He modeled how he wants us to connect with each other in the way he related to his twelve disciples, the inner circle of three (Peter, James, and John), John the beloved friend, and the multitudes. Jesus was up close and personal in the expression of his love, and he expects the same from us, his church. This expectation is captured in the following verses:

> "A new command I give you: Love one another. As I have loved you, so you must love one another. By this all . . . will know that you are my disciples, if you love one another." (John 13:34–35 NIV)

Love is so very dynamic in its power. It will always find a way to communicate the love of Jesus. This is why Joyner (1999) says, "Satan wants to attack the church in this area. If we can stay focused on our activities and ourselves, we won't focus on loving each other" (p. 136). He further states that one of the tactics of the enemy "comes in the form of a religious spirit, which is the counterfeit of true love for God and true worship"; a religious spirit is "an evil spirit that seeks to substitute religious activity for the power of the Holy Spirit in the believer's life" (p. 136).

However, we can praise God that we do not need a substitute. Why have a form of godliness while denying its power? An authentic faith works by love: love for God and love for one another. Paul writes, "For in Christ Jesus neither circumcision nor uncircumcision has any value. The only thing that counts is faith expressing itself through love" (Galatians 5:6 NIV).

REFERENCES

Arterburn, S., and J. Felton. 2000. *More Jesus, less religion: Moving from rules to relationship.* Colorado Springs: Waterbrook Press.

Baker, M. 1999. *Religion no more: Building communities of grace and freedom.* Downers Grove, Ill.: InterVarsity Press.

Blackaby, H. T., and C. V. King. 1990. *Experiencing God.* Nashville: Lifeway Press.

Joyner, R. 1999. *A prophetic vision for the twenty-first century.* Nashville: Thomas Nelson.

Tenney, T. 1998. *The God chasers.* Shippensburg, Pa.: Destiny Image Publishers.

_____. 2000. *The God chasers: Experiencing the manifest presence of God.* Nashville: Thomas Nelson.

Webster's third international dictionary. 1976. Springfield, Mass.: G. and C. Merriam.

Darrell V. Freeman Sr.

Chapter 17

Demonology: A Pastoral Perspective

Darrell **V. Freeman Sr.** is the Senior Pastor of the Alpha Baptist Church, President and Founder of Truth Bible Institute, the Joshua Counseling Center, People Impacting People (PIP—Community Development Corporation), and Little Miracles Child Development Center in Belvidere and Newport, Delaware. He holds a bachelor of science degree from West Chester State University and a master of arts degree from Moody Graduate School and graduated from the Philadelphia College of the Bible. He is a Ph.D. candidate at Trinity Theological Seminary, Newburgh, Indiana. He is the author of two books, *Investing in Our African American Youth (Can You Handle It?)* and *A Handbook for Youth Leadership: For Youth Leaders on the Move.* He also wrote the article "Why Men Run from Counseling" for *Excellence Magazine.*

Freeman is in demand nationally as a preacher, teacher, plenary speaker, and workshop instructor for churches, seminars, camps, and retreats. He is a single parent and resides in Middletown, Delaware, with his four children, Darrell Jr., Patrice, Phylicia, and Darren.

The primary goals of this chapter are to focus on counseling people who have been demonized; to aid those interested in working with people who have symptoms indicative of demonology; and to introduce readers to this complex topic in the hope that they will explore these issues further.

Biblical counselors, pastors, therapists, and others can no longer afford to ignore the spirit world because doing so closes the door on our ability to enter the total world of our clients.

Entering the world of the demonized may arouse fears. While these fears are understandable, they also limit many churches, counseling centers, and mental health institutions from dealing with the whole person (spirit, soul, mind, and body).

SOME GENERAL QUESTIONS TO CONSIDER

If one is to counsel in the area of demonology, several general questions need to be considered and addressed, among them:

- Is it possible for a person to be both demonized and mentally ill?
- Are Christians and churches in a position to help?
- Is there any training being offered in this specific area of spiritual/mental health?
- Is a deliverance ministry the answer or even necessary today?
- Is demon possession or oppression the kind of thing that makes someone talk like a mentally ill person, or does a mentally ill person have all the symptoms of a demonized person?
- What is the difference between mental illness and demon possession?

POSSIBLE SYMPTOMS AND QUESTIONS RELEVANT TO DEMON POSSESSION

There are some symptoms and questions any good biblical counselor must ask if the matter of demonology is to be adequately addressed and the counselee is to be free of bondage. In working with people who are demonized, we must address *all* the issues: spiritual (spirit), mental (mind), volitional (will), physical (body), emotional, and medical. Ignoring any of these areas could inhibit the counselor from knowing which demonic domain to confront. Since demons play games in an effort to hinder the freeing process, the counselor must stay focused. Not staying focused can leave the counselor vulnerable and defenseless.

The critical symptoms and questions relating to these issues are as follows.

Spirit

In the matter of the spirit, one must ask:

- Can the clients do things with their minds (E.S.P. or telekinesis)?
- Do they have a friend or spirit guide?

- Do they think that there is something special about them?
- What tends to happen at night while they are sleeping (types of dreams, fears)?
- Is there or has there been any involvement with the occult?

Mind

With regard to the mind, the following must be considered:

- When the Scriptures are being read or the Word of God is being preached, are they able to concentrate?
- Is there an ongoing battle with doubting the Word of God?
- Are their thoughts out of control (that is, can't stop fantasizing about sex, violence, cursing, or have a bizarre or "deviant" imagination)?
- Is there verbal interference and possibly hallucinations?
- Is it hard to pray?
- Do they black out at any time, anywhere, and then become forgetful?
- Are they confused and just can't get their thoughts together?

Will

Regarding the will, one should consider:

- Has there been a change in their personality (lashing out through avenues such as anger, fear, strife, and sexual behaviors)?
- Is there rebellion against authority?
- Is there a refusal to submit to the Lord Jesus Christ?
- Is there a refusal to confess and repent of known sin?
- Does the person respond to different voices that encourage negative behavior?

Emotions

On the issue of emotions, one must consider:

- Does the person unwillingly struggle to forgive?
- Is there the presence of some serious guilt and feelings of unworthiness?
- Does the person have a legitimate reason to be depressed, or is he or she even aware?
- Does he or she have many phobias?

- Does this person sometimes act different or unusual (for example, crying for no reason, laughing for no reason, directing disdain at the counselor for no reason, etc.)?
- Does the thought of suicide cross his or her mind?

Body

One must consider these questions with regard to the body:

- Is the person's body cold one minute and then hot the next?
- Does he or she experience shortness of breath while you are interviewing them concerning spiritual warfare? Do they say to you as a counselor things like "They told me not to come"?
- Are there signs of extreme fatigue?
- Does the person appear to be getting dizzy and experience headaches?
- Are there any signs of nervousness when you talk about Jesus, ask them to look at a Scripture, begin to pray, or ask them to pray?
- Can this person look you directly in the eye, or does it seem as though he or she is trying to avoid making eye contact? Have you asked the person to look at you, but he or she can't?
- Is his/her body consistently aching?
- Does he or she speak in unknown languages?
- Does this person act worried about something and just can't be still?
- While preaching or teaching is occurring, is it hard for him or her to stay seated, or do loud outbursts occur at the most inappropriate times?
- Has he or she ever tried to hurt, cut, or destroy one's own body in anger?

Medical Issues

In terms of medical issues, one must be sensitive to the following:

- Does the person experience buzzing in the ears, an inability to talk or hear, increased loudness, supersensitivity to touch, a dry mouth, or body numbness?
- How often does he or she have seizures, and how long do they last?
- Are there continuous medical problems, sickness, and illness?

For a more detailed treatment and consideration of these issues, see Anderson (2000).

SIMILARITIES BETWEEN DEMONOLOGY AND OTHER ISSUES

Symptoms of demonology may mimic or show similarities to other problems, particularly schizophrenia. In both of these, for example, the person may report or experience hearing voices; experience controlling thoughts or behaviors; experience fearfulness, hallucinations, or delusions; have thoughts of suicide; and have areas of severe and unhealed psychological wounds.

Additionally, the person may report or experience feelings of "generational bondage" (see Exodus 20:5) to certain sins; feel compelled to do certain acts of violence; have recurring and disturbing dreams regarding demons and other frightening events that involve terror; seek to withdraw from others; experience depression; engage in substance abuse; and have a starry, glassy, or strange look about and in the eyes.

Because Schizophrenia and demonization are very different but can have similarities, accurate testing and a clear diagnosis are essential.

TREATING DEMONIC OPPRESSION AS A LEGITIMATE AREA OF COUNSELING

I reiterate that psychological problems in and of themselves do not imply the presence of demons. In my graduate school class at the Moody Bible Institute in Chicago called "Counseling: Spirit Oppression," we were taught by Dr. C. Fred Dickason, a theologian, and Dr. Daniel Rumberge, a psychologist, not to "look for demons behind every bush but recognize bushes and that the sin nature provides the toehold for satanic activity." Demonic activity can lead to spiritual, psychological (worry and ulcers), emotional, and physical problems (Luke 13:10–17). Thus, the flesh, the world, and demons can overlap.

Given the reality and influences of demons, it is critical that one recognize that biblical counseling is legitimate. Dr. Ed Murphy states in his book *The Handbook for Spiritual Warfare* (1992) that

> No one who has never suffered the agony and confusion of the intrusion of foreign thoughts, or voices into their mind, can fully understand the living hell this represents to a human being. Whether it be the internal voices of demons, alter personalities or related internal voice disorders, or the external voices of schizophrenia or related brain disorders, to live in such a condition is to live in a madhouse. (p. 284)

There is no doubt that whatever the case or facts may be for an individual experiencing these conditions, a biblical therapist, biblical counselor, or mental health worker should bring any information and personnel to the counseling table to assist in the healing of the counselee.

MY STORY

I grew up a very frightened child. I would not sleep in the bed alone but always with my older brother. I, like many of you, was afraid of the dark and of going to the bathroom by myself. I was afraid of all of the vampire movies and would close my eyes for fear that I might see something. No one knew about my childhood fears because I kept them all to myself. Even after I became an adult, I maintained them — until one day I was delivered and released from spiritual bondage. I refer to this as spiritual bondage because, before I was delivered, I began to think that there were really people in the room and I was afraid to lift up my eyes to see. I thought that being older would result in their going away, but this did not happen until I rededicated my life to Jesus, which started my journey to freedom.

I later learned that my fear started when I woke up one morning and heard my mother shouting at the top of her lungs because my uncle was lying dead at the bottom of the steps. I went into some kind of shock, but no one knew about it but me. When I was eleven years old, my father died. I just stared at him in the coffin and did not cry until two weeks later. Years later I walked in on my godmother, who was found dead in our house from her illness after leaving the hospital. It wasn't until adulthood that I began to face my fears because I knew I had held onto this secret long enough. Becoming a dedicated Christian worked for me because now I had someone to trust, my Lord and Savior, Jesus Christ.

Then I was called to the pastorate, and my work has included dealing with Satan and his demonic world. It was then that my unresolved childhood issues revisited me! Preaching, teaching, administration, loving people, and counseling people were all things I could handle. But Satan, the devil, demons — "spooky" and scary stuff, I could not handle.

One day some members of our church were struggling with some issues that I believed to be satanic, and I knew then that I needed help. A couple of pastor friends of mine told me about an annual pastors' conference at the Moody Bible Institute in Chicago. I attended the next one and heard about a master's degree program they were just starting. Needless to say, I enrolled, and the first course that caught my eye was "Spirit Oppression." This was a most informative and influential course. I learned about my fears, my past, and about what Satan's plan is for the church and the people of God. During the course I got so excited that I asked Dr. Dickason, "How can I help my church and my members?" There was no way that I could get all of this help, truth, and information about spiritual warfare from the Bible, a theologian, and psychologist and not use it right away. Dr. Dickason suggested that I purchase *The Bondage Breaker* by Neil T. Anderson, read it, teach it, and apply the principles in my church. I did this and received a major blessing, and because of his material, I also got delivered from my own fears and Satan. I was loosed from bondage, and I received a freedom that felt so good.

However, there remained one problem. That problem was that helping the members of my congregation meant dealing with Satan and his demons all over again. As a committed and caring under-shepherd, I had to take that next step. As a result, the Spirit of God now moves in our congregation, and we are all reaping the benefits.

A RADICAL CONSIDERATION

As a result of sin, self, Satan, and societal woes, the church needs the mental health community, and the mental health community needs the church. For too long the two have been at odds. I believe that once both address their fears, complete healing can take place for the person in need.

However, where is the partnership? Where is the marriage? Where is the respect and appreciation for both the biblical community and the mental health community? Simply put, professional biblical counselors and biblical therapists have just as much to offer, if not more, than the non-biblical clinical counselors and therapists. Biblical counselors and therapists are able to discern some things that non-Christians are not allowed to see or understand (see 1 Corinthians 2:9–16). Isn't it the goal of both professions that individuals (church members, clients, etc.) be whole and healed? To minimize the effects of good secular therapy is to ignore the full effect that sin has had on the human mind, heart, soul, and body. The church at best is able to be lead and to get help, wisdom, and guidance directly from the Lord through the instrumentality of the Scriptures and the power of the Holy Spirit. The mental health community as well as the church community must understand that in order to be effective in counseling demonized clients, it must be approached biblically.

Christians are believers who according to their position in Christ (Ephesians 1:3–14) are blessed to be in right standing before God the Father. But in their condition, they still need all the help the Lord has made available (see Romans 3; 6; 7:14–25). Proverbs 11:14 tells us, "Where no counsel is, the people fall; but in the multitude of counselors there is safety" (KJV).

No one system of secular beliefs or disciplines has all of the answers; it is this island mentality that has countless numbers of people still hurting and in need of further assistance. There are professional biblical counselors and therapists who would tell you that there is a lot of biblical teaching out there wrapped up in secular clothes; and if you are unfamiliar with the Bible, you may get lost in the masquerade due to a lack of knowledge and discernment. This partnership is not about the church joining up with the world and placing spiritual and biblical truth on the altar. Instead, it is about eating the meat and throwing the bones away. This world has not seen counseling at its best until they see a well-trained and Spirit-led biblical counselor, or biblical therapist in action. This is truly when the member/client gets the best of both worlds. I see, hear, and experience it happening every day at our counseling center.

A LOOK AT GOD AND HIS POWER TO HEAL

What we know about God can help us to understand how much we need his help in treating demonized clients. For instance, when we look at God's attributes and names, we realize that his person, works, knowledge, wisdom, intellect, and understanding far exceeds that of humans and the spirit world. For the counselor or therapist who is interacting with the demonic, these are the kinds of things that need to be understood and to serve as reminders for effective treatment.

God's Attributes and Names

When working in the area of demonology, it is extremely important to fully understand, appreciate, and draw upon God's attributes and the power inherent in his names and his Word. Since a detailed treatment of God's names and attributes is beyond the scope of this chapter, one should consult books such as those by Dean (1963), Enns (1989), Ryrie (1986), and Stone (1944).

CONCERNING THERAPISTS WHO ARE CHRISTIAN

As Christians, when we use psychological principles, we must also submit to biblical authority — God's Word — and place Scripture over opinion.

Additionally, we must make it a priority to integrate psychology with Christianity and not Christianity with psychology. Finally, we must allow conflict or differences of opinion to yield to biblical resolution.

CONCERNING TREATMENT OF DEMONIC OPPRESSION

The following must be kept in mind when treating demonic oppression:

- Counseling in the matter of demonology is a legitimate role of counseling because of the attention Christ gave to it as he met needs.
- The Bible has not ignored its reality. Today we have things like occultism, psychic hotlines, the New Age movement, spiritists, and witches — all of which are indicative of demonology.
- Missionaries are afraid to tell all that they know, learned, and experienced upon their return from the field because dealing with demonization is too often left to church history and charismatic churches.

Several truths bring reality to demonology and underscore the need for counselors to be well versed and specifically equipped in this area:

- There are two worldviews: the natural and the spiritual (see 1 Samuel 16:13, 14; Job 1; 2 Corinthians 4:4, 17; James 5:16).
- There are two kinds of angels — fallen and unfallen — and both are organized to follow their leader (see Dickason 1995).
  - Fallen angels are Satan's emissaries and seek to destroy the works of God and his people. Unfallen angels are those who follow God and him only and do his bidding.

- There are two opposing systems: God's truth and Satan's lies.
- There is a psychological perspective on spiritual warfare. That is,
  - Demons can affect physical, mental, and physiological status.
  - Demons are able to intensify sexual pleasure. They can help you to turn it on or up.

- There is a process known as spiritual warfare counseling, which must be organized and systematic so that it can achieve the goal of delivering people from bondage. Thus we must remember that:
  - Demonization is a present-day term to become familiar with
  - Just as with psychological problems, there are signs, symptoms, and testing that need to be done for effective assessment and diagnosis.

— One must organize a ministry or counseling practice to be able to handle spirit oppression cases and also know when to refer to an outside agency.
— The goal is to get people freed up. Deliverance is one thing; freedom is another.

PREPARING FOR SPIRITUAL WARFARE

To be equipped for spiritual warfare, one must memorize as many Scriptures as possible that have to do with the topic; find a prayer partner; and secure an accountability partner.

CONCLUSION

Today there are all kinds of deliverance ministries. However, an effective deliverance ministry has as its central goal freedom from bondage, since demons, as we know them from the Scriptures, can return stronger than they were before they left (see, for example, Matthew 12:43–45). When confrontation with the demonic is unavoidable, it must be undertaken with the aid and power of the Holy Spirit and with the biblical knowledge that God has provided. Therefore a true and effective biblical counselor working with the demonic will commit to prayer, preparation, practicing biblical principles and relying on the power of God.

In working with demonic situations, it can be helpful to have the assistance of a biblical counselor who is trained and experienced in the areas of spiritual warfare and spiritual conflicts. Such a person would be mindful of the extreme importance of history (personal, family, church, and secular involvements that have spiritual overtones); the purpose and timing of prayer; God's sovereignty and authority; our biblical authority as believers; the importance of the blood of Jesus Christ and the power of God; the need for confession of one's personal and sometimes family sins; how we as biblical counselors must live consecrated and Spirit-filled lives in order to be successful in counseling; the value of the counselee's permission and truthfulness; the commands of Christ and the necessity of demons to obey when biblically told to do so; the duty, activity, and destiny of Satan and his demons; and the victory promised to every believer.

There is no doubt in my mind that counseling the demonic is important and much needed today. When we are treating the demonic, the Word of God *must* be used to control a session, since we are dealing with spiritual beings taking residence in or demonizing a person. In the event that there is uncertainty, the therapist should consult a psychiatrist, and vice versa, to achieve successful healing results. Keep in mind that a biblically oriented psychologist, counselor, or social worker is able to bring to a session the best of both worlds: spiritual insight as well as mental health. When a person well equipped in both worlds is not available, the biblical counselor would do well to have a psychologist available for mental health advice or consultation.

As noted earlier, this chapter is intended to serve as an introduction to the issue of counseling with the demonic. For more details, readers are encouraged to consult the references cited in the chapter. For those interested in an outline for spiritual warfare/conflict counseling, see the section on the topic in Neil Anderson's *Steps to Freedom in Christ* (2000) and its *Leader's Guide* (1993).

REFERENCES

Anderson, N. T. 2000. *The bondage breaker.* Eugene, Ore.: Harvest House.

_____. 1993. *Steps to freedom in Christ.* La Habra, Calif.: Freedom in Christ.

_____. 1993. *Steps to freedom in Christ: Leader's guide.* La Habra, Calif.: Freedom in Christ.

Dean, W. A. 1963. *The names of God.* Philadelphia: Philadelphia College of the Bible.

Dickason, C. F. 1995. *Angels elect and evil.* Chicago: Moody Press.

Enns, P. 1989. *The Moody handbook of theology.* Chicago: Moody Press.

Murphy, E. 1992. *Handbook for spiritual warfare.* Nashville: Thomas Nelson.

Ryrie, C. C. 1986. *Basic theology.* Wheaton, Ill.: Basic Books.

Stone, N. 1944. *Names of God.* Chicago: Moody Press.

Chapter 18

Unemployment

Artis **Fletcher** is a member of the Christian Community Development Association, the NAACP, and the National Black Evangelical Association (NBEA). He received his biblical education from the Southern Bible Training School in Dallas, Texas; Washington Bible College in Washington, D.C.; and Los Angeles Baptist College and Theological Seminary in Los Angeles, California. He received the Civic Circle Award as outstanding citizen of the year in 1984 for his numerous efforts toward community service and cooperative development in the southern states.

Rev. Fletcher is the senior pastor of Mendenhall Bible Church in Mendenhall, Mississippi, where he resides with his wife, Carolyn, and three daughters, Cynthia, Aimee, and Janice.

Blanche **Womack-Ross** is a member of the Christian Community Development Association, the National Association of Female Executives, the NAACP, and local organizations. She graduated from Mendenhall High School in Mendenhall and attended Alcorn State University in Lorman and Draugham's Business College in Jackson, all in Mississippi. She received her biblical education through various discipleship classes. Womack-Ross is the Director of Development and in her twentieth year at the Mendenhall Ministries in Mendenhall, where she resides with her husband, Benny Sr.; two sons, Gromico and Benny Jr.; and four grandchildren, Gromico Jr., Kierra, Kendra, and Jacquille.

Work should be viewed as a spiritual matter. We, and God's entire universe, are to work as a unit, supporting one another to his glory. God has designed humans in such a way that they must work in order to be healthy physically, emotionally, and spiritually. Unemployment does not fit the way we are designed. A person who is unemployed can soon begin to feel a lack of self-worth, which affects his self-image. That person can begin to feel a sense of being unsatisfied or unfulfilled, which can lead to feeling down and depressed to the point of not caring. When this happens, he or she is emotionally and spiritually incapable of evaluating negative thoughts or suggestions. This downward spiral leads to hopelessness.

Sometimes we encounter people who are unemployed because of some deeper root problems. It is not that they cannot get a job, but they do not seem able to keep a job for any length of time, so they spend much of their time unemployed. Some of these root problems are selfishness, pride, impatience, self-pity, greed, malice, envy, deceit, laziness, and jealousy.

Something else to consider as we counsel those who are unemployed is whether or not they have discovered what their gifts are. When we are born into this world, God gives us one or more gifts (talents). Some refer to these as "gifts of grace" because they are given to each person at birth. Career guidance resource material, such as the book entitled *Finding the Career That Fits You* (Burkett and Ellis 1994), can often help people to determine what their talents or gifts of grace are.* Afterward, they can find work in an area in which they are gifted. By doing so, they will find more satisfaction, fulfillment, and longevity in their jobs. The person who is gifted with numbers would be drawn to jobs related to using mathematics. Learning other languages would fascinate a person whose talent is in the area of language. For example, since Artis is mechanically gifted by God, he finds fulfillment and a release of tension and stress by fixing things.

When we work in the area in which we are talented, it is a fit for us — like placing a round peg in a round hole. When work is honoring to God and a part of his plan for us, the fulfillment we receive is the same as when we had discovered our spiritual gifts. We are using them in the body of Christ to bless the body and bring glory to God.

There are several Scripture passages that demonstrate that work is viewed positively by God:

- Work is a partnership with God (Genesis 1:28–31; John 5:1–18; John 14:8–14)
- Christ has lordship over work (Ephesians 1:22–23; Philippians 3:12–21; Colossians 1:15–23; 3:12–17)
- Work helps us to provide for the poor (Proverbs 31:17–20; Luke 4:18–19; Galatians 2:9–10; Ephesians 4:28)

*This book is a major resource for this chapter and is also used extensively in our work with clients.

- God designed work to provide for us and our families (1 Thessalonians 2:9; 3:11–12; Proverbs 6:6–11; 31:21; Isaiah 65:17–25; Proverbs 12:11; 2 Thessalonians 3:6–12)

THE JOB SEARCH

An unemployed person should begin by putting the ball in God's court. Many years ago, the rules for girls' basketball were different from the rules for the boys. The boys could dribble the ball as much as they wanted to, but the girls could only dribble three times. Two of the girls had to stay in their home court, and three of them could travel full court. The girls who could travel full court would work hard at defensive tactics to retrieve the ball and get it back to their end of the court for an opportunity to score. In this same way, with job searching, we need to put the ball in God's end of the court so he can enable us to find a job.

We believe there are three prerequisites to receiving maximum help from God:

1. Recognizing and accepting the lordship of Christ (Galatians 2:19–20; Romans 12:1–2)
2. Having a pure heart; willingness to hear anything, to be surprised (Proverbs 16:1–3)
3. Being sensitive to the Lord's timing (Romans 1:8–15; 1 Corinthians 7:20–24; 1 Thessalonians 3:1–10; 1 Peter 2:18–21; 4:1–16; 5:6–11)

By following these steps, the ball would be put on God's end of the court. Then you are ready to begin the search for a job.

In your job search, you should get up every morning, pack a lunch (if applicable), and spend eight hours a day, five days a week searching for a job. This search must be your full-time job. Your attitude should be "I will take any honest job I can find as long as I can do the work and it is not harmful to the cause of Christ." Do not have the attitude that a job is beneath you, too dirty for you, or that you are too educated for it.

When you have found a better job, or a job that is more suited for your talents, leave your present job in such a way that you could go back to it if necessary. If you find that you are still not able to meet your obligations, there are two possibilities: decrease your spending, or get additional training for a job that will pay for what you need.

PREPARATION OF THE RÉSUMÉ

A résumé is a summary of your previous work experience, education, accomplishments, and personal background. As Burkett and Ellis (1994) note, it is your personal sales brochure (p. 64). It is a professional advertisement that translates what you have done in the past into what you intend to do in the future. We agree with Burkett and Ellis (1994) that the primary purpose of a résumé is to convince someone to interview you for a job opening.

Writing a résumé is hard work. You can become discouraged and quit before you have a final product in hand. Recognizing this to be the case, the counselor should encourage the counselee and hold him or her accountable, realizing that people often do not do what we expect, but what we inspect. The counselee must make a commitment to stay with it until it is complete.

In the résumé, the job seeker must communicate the following (Burkett and Ellis 1994, p. 63):

What	How
Your objective	quickly
qualifications	clearly
experience and	and
accomplishments	accurately

Résumés should be:

- Limited to one page unless you have more than ten years of work experience — then keep it to two pages maximum.
- Well designed, informative, and internally consistent.
- Airy looking (no one wants to read through huge blocks of solid type).
- High quality — both content and appearance. Be sure it looks good. Laser printing is the standard. (Burkett and Ellis 1994, p. 64)

Before writing your résumé, you should be able to answer the following questions:

1. What are my skills?
2. What are my strengths?
3. What are my qualifications?

4. What are my accomplishments?
5. What do I know about my prospective employer and what he or she expects my qualifications to be?
6. What are the employer's criteria?
7. How can I present my skills and qualifications to sell myself to my prospective employer?

The answers to these questions will give you what you need for writing your résumé.

According to Burkett and Ellis (1994), there are two standard approaches to writing a résumé: chronological and functional. In the chronological format you present your work experience and education in reverse time sequence and list your achievements and responsibilities in previous jobs. You place emphasis on your most recent jobs and highlight achievements or promotions. In the functional format you highlight your abilities. You seek to draw attention to past accomplishments, including skills that have been developed outside of the workplace. You stress those things that will make you look good for the job you are seeking. You are trying to show the prospective employer what skills and experience you have that would make you suited for the position that is available. A sample résumé is included at the end of this chapter.

If the résumé is sent to a potential employer, a cover letter must accompany it. A cover letter introduces you and explains what job you are applying for, how you heard about it, and why you think you are qualified. A sample cover letter is found at the end of this chapter.

THE JOB INTERVIEW

A job interview is an opportunity for you, the job seeker, to sit down with a prospective employer and discuss mutual concerns. It is an opportunity to communicate through your presence, mannerisms, and verbal skills that you are the person for the job. To do this you should be neatly groomed. Males should not wear earrings, and they should have their pants pulled up, wear a belt, and use correct grammar. You will probably be nervous during the interview, but you can use your nervous energy to be alert, enthusiastic, and energetic.

There are several things you should do in preparation for a job interview:

1. As you meet your prospective employer, you should have a sound presentation about who you are and how you view yourself.

Present your strengths, weaknesses, academic performance, work experience, and other activities in an organized, convincing manner.

2. Show the prospective employer how your experience and qualifications can benefit the company.
3. The person interviewing you will ask questions designed to reveal your good and bad points. If you have done an adequate assessment of yourself before the interview, you will be able to direct the interviewer toward your strengths.
4. There will be many applicants for the position; your goal is to prove that you are the best person for the job.
5. Be positive about yourself, and do not allow a poor self-image to cause you to present yourself in a bad light.
6. Find out as much as you possibly can about the prospective employer, such as the history, affiliated companies, products or services, philosophy, reputation, organizational structure, and standing in that particular field. Much of this information can be found in the Career Services Library in your local town.
7. Make sure you have transportation to get to your interview.

As you go for the interview, you should have a copy of your résumé. If at all possible, you should know the name of the interviewer and how to pronounce it. Be alert and courteous but not overly friendly. First impressions are very important. You should act natural and be yourself. Do not "role-play" or falsify your personality. This may cause you to be in a job situation that you are unable to handle.

Be pleasant and easy to talk to. Show enthusiasm and interest. Rather than giving yes or no answers, take the opportunity to tell the interviewer about your goals and strong points. A trained interviewer may see some potential in you that you may not have considered.

Lying in an interview in an attempt to make yourself look good and to cover up the truth will come out later. It is better to deal with any problem that comes up in an interview immediately. If you do not know the answer to a question, be honest and tell the interviewer. Honesty is the best policy when interviewing for a job.

During the interview you should exhibit good posture, composure, and eye contact; you should listen to the interviewer and show confidence, friendliness, and genuineness. These factors have an important impact on the interviewer.

After the interview, the prospective employer should let you know the next step in the employment process and when you can expect to hear something. You should not leave the interview without seeking to obtain this information. If you have not heard anything by the date promised by the interviewer, it is your responsibility to follow up either by telephone or by mail asking for a status report. In your follow-up be polite; do not be pushy or make accusations.

PROFILE OF A TYPICAL UNEMPLOYED MAN

There are many problems that create or contribute to unemployment. The following information is based on our personal experiences with unemployed people.

Laziness. The Bible clearly states, "If a man will not work, he shall not eat" (2 Thessalonians 3:10). Yet many people feel they should not have to work, or they just plain don't want to work.

Immaturity. Unfortunately, many of our men have never matured to understand exactly what it means to be the "man" in terms of being the provider for the family and home. When a man comes from a broken and/or dysfunctional family, he has usually been reared by a single parent, most often the mother. In many instances, he has not witnessed a positive father's role, especially in the area of provision for his family. What he has seen as male figures in the persons of his brothers, uncles, cousins, or other men from the community has given him a false impression, to say the least, of the definition of a real man.

He does not view love for his family as a means of soliciting and maintaining stable employment. He has literally been taught that "love" is closely tied to sexual activity, and provision is giving her whatever is left of his paycheck after his habits and desires have been met. To him, anything outside of this realm is either foreign or an attempt to "control" him.

With this immaturity concerning what it means to be a man also comes the same level of immaturity in regard to being a husband and father. He begins a vicious cycle. He repeats the same things that he has been taught. This "lesson" also becomes a major factor in adding to the unemployment statistics — and as a result, oftentimes the divorce rate.

Dependency. Often a man who has these characteristics has developed a sense of dependency, usually first on his mother and then, after marriage, on his wife. He sees nothing wrong with someone else's taking care of his responsibilities. In fact, to a certain degree he feels it's their obligation (especially if he doesn't have a job or is unable to make ends meet). So much so that even near the half century in age, he feels that if he asks his mother for money, furniture, appliances, and so forth, it is her responsibility to give it to him. He has somehow defined her doing this for him as "love."

This "love" becomes a major hindrance in job seeking. It relieves the person from the pressure to find and keep a job because it gives him another option. He looks to others not only to provide for his needs but also for the needs of his family.

This works both ways. His mother has also become dependent on him — expecting him to ask for whatever he needs — and, in many instances, what he wants. She too, feeling that this is her only connection of "love" to him, acts in accordance to his wishes. It is also a method of controlling on her part. She knows that this will force him to come to see her, to visit, and to help her; otherwise she might not even see him at all.

After marriage and children, his wife assumes the role (although she is sometimes unaware of doing it). She does her best to comfortably provide for her children. In the process, he gets a free ride. She too has added to the problem of his unemployment.

Irresponsibility. The Bible also states that a man who doesn't take care of his family is "worse than an infidel" (1 Timothy 5:8 KJV). However, as a child and young adult, he has never had to face up to his mistakes and failures. His mother or someone was always there to get him out of his situations. He has not learned to suffer the consequences of his actions. As a matter of fact, oftentimes he does not even associate the consequences with his actions, whether it was repeatedly getting drunk, going to jail, wrecking cars, or job terminations. He has never learned to admit or accept responsibility for his actions. If he subsequently gets married, he unfortunately brings the same immature and dependent mindset into the marriage.

Hopelessness. Sometimes, although often as a result of his own choices, his failure to either find or maintain a job (or in his mind, the "right" job) causes hopelessness to set in. He then finds himself caught up in bewilderment and puts all his mind, heart, body, and soul into what he thinks is the best thing he has found. When it all falls apart (especially when his failure is public), he feels as though he has lost all dignity, pride, motivation, and initiative. At this point in his life, especially if in the midlife age range, disappointment is born. It then gives birth to disillusionment, followed by despair, and in the final stages hopelessness is inevitable. Thus, employment becomes unreachable to him.

To further feed these emotions, job opportunities become few. After several attempts to find work — often, for whatever reasons, to no avail — he becomes despondent and ceases to earnestly seek employment.

He feels safe and nonthreatened at home or with buddies, so that's where he hangs out. To him, accepting his status of unemployment is better than risking another rejection. Those job opportunities that do surface fit what one may call "underemployment." Because of his immaturity, irresponsibility, and dependency, he refuses to accept certain low-paying jobs with little or no benefits. These types of jobs do not afford him the privilege of providing for his family and his desires. So eventually he stops searching.

Addictions. Many people do not have, cannot find, or are not looking for employment because of past failures due to addictions. These addictions serve as crutches or enablers to handle their predicaments. Therefore, the jobless trend is to look for temporary, as opposed to permanent, employment because this provides a "quick fix" to support the addictions. The temporary status requires no dedication or commitment, which is just fine from the addict's standpoint.

Lack of education. For many, lack of education is a major contributing factor to unemployment or underemployment. This not only proves true in the actual job market but also plays an effective role in job solicitation, preparation, readiness, and maintenance.

Many people simply don't know how to properly talk to prospective employers, fill out applications correctly, prepare for interviews, and so forth. Either someone else has always been there to help them in employment-seeking situations (literally speaking up for them, pulling strings, asking a friend or someone on the "inside" to help them, or using family connections) or by the grace of God and the prayers of others, they made it through.

Blaming others. As strange and irrational as it may seem, some people blame others for their lack of employment. These "others" can range from society in general, his spouse (she's holding him back, not encouraging or supporting him enough, spending too much — as long as the spending does not benefit him directly), to the White man, who is holding him back — giving the good jobs to other Whites, and so forth. Such men believe that it is not their fault that they do not have jobs. Therefore, it's not their responsibility to seriously look for work.

Since such a person's communication skills consist mainly of slang or "smooth" talk due to his immaturity and dependency, he carries this language into the job arena. When the prospective or existing employer fails to accept his level of interaction, resulting in discipline or termination, the person's level of reasoning is limited to blaming his consequences on the employer's dislike or desire to get rid of him. Either way, it is simply not his fault. And this adds to his deductive reasoning that to continue seeking employment is futile.

CONCLUSION

The job seeker should keep in mind that his primary objective is to be offered a job. Never lose sight of this objective. If you qualify for the job and believe you can handle it if you were given the opportunity, this should be emphasized to the interviewer. Self-confidence is a plus and adds to the prospective employer's confidence in you. See the following pages for a sample résumé and cover letter.

REFERENCES

Burkett, L., and L. Ellis. 1994. *Finding the career that fits you.* Chicago: Moody Press. (Revised edition 1998.)

Ellis, L., and L. Burkett. 1998. *Your career in changing times.* Chicago: Moody Press.

SAMPLE RESUME

JAMES L. LOTT
1535 Moorehouse Avenue
Mendenhall, Mississippi 39114
(999) 894–2163

POSITION OBJECTIVE
To obtain a position in a company using my talents and experience
in manufacturing.

EDUCATION
B.A. Business Administration, May 2000
Johnson Edwards College, Maryville, IN
Grade Point Average: 3.1/3.7

RELATED EXPERIENCE
Willow Creek Manufacturing Company, fall 1997–99
- Supervised third shift
- Dealt with shipping, receiving, quality control, union problems
- Managed employee working hours
- Analyzed and recommended equipment upgrades

Orange County Manufacturing Company
- Stamping Apprentice
- Stamping Supervisor Assistant
- Supervised stamping department for eight months
- Managed sixty people with a minimum of overtime

ADDITIONAL ABILITIES
Computer: Experience in operating Windows 2000
            Environment Pentium 3
Fluent in Spanish

OTHER ACTIVITIES
Boy Scout Master
Volunteer Fireman

SAMPLE COVER LETTER

Your Street Address
City, State, Zip Code
Date of Writing

Mr. or Mrs. Prospective Employer
Title of Prospective Employer
Organization
Street Address
City, State, Zip Code

Dear Mr. or Mrs. Prospective Employer:

1st paragraph: Your opening should invite and entice the prospective employer. State why you are writing, usually to apply for a position. If you are responding to a known opening, explain how you heard about it (name the publication and date). If it was through a personal reference, tell the prospective employer about it immediately. If you are writing an unsolicited letter to an organization with no announced openings, be as specific as possible about the type of job you are seeking. Tell why you are particularly interested in working for the company.

2d paragraph: Present your strongest and most relevant qualifications for the job, in decreasing order of importance. Keep the prospective employer's perspective in mind! Expand on information presented in your résumé; do not merely repeat it. Use specific examples in demonstrating what you can do for the prospective employer instead of merely listing skills you have or relevant courses you have taken. Indicate how your skills tie into the organization. Mention briefly what you know about the company or some aspect of it.

3d paragraph (optional): If you need an additional paragraph to elaborate on your accomplishments, use this paragraph.

4th paragraph: Close by making a specific request for an interview. Keep your tone confident! State that you will follow up by phone with the prospective employer to arrange the date and time. For example, "I will call you during the week of (month, date) to discuss the possibility of an interview." Allow at least one week from the day you mail the letter. Do not forget to call! If you are unable to locate any literature on that organization, request it at this time. Remind the reader that you are willing and able to be of service to the organization. Thank the prospective employer for any consideration he/she may give to your application.

Sincerely,

(Your Handwritten Signature)
Your Typewritten Name
Enclosures (i.e., résumé)

Lee N. June and Christopher C. Mathis Jr.

Chapter 19

Incorporating Research into Clinical Practice

Lee N. June is currently Assistant Provost for Academic Student Services and Multicultural Issues, Vice President for Student Affairs and Services, and Professor of Counseling Psychology at Michigan State University. He is a former director of the counseling center at Michigan State. He earned a bachelor of science in biology from Tuskegee University, a master of education in counseling, a master of arts and doctorate of philosophy in clinical psychology from the University of Illinois, Urbana-Champaign, and a certificate in theology from the Interdenominational Theological Center in Atlanta, Georgia. He also did further studies at Haverford College in psychology and at Duke University's Divinity School.

Dr. June's research and writing have been in the areas of effective counseling service delivery, psychology of the African American church, short-term counseling, and retention of undergraduate students. He is editor or coeditor of three books, *The Black Family: Past, Present, and Future; Men to Men;* and *Evangelism and Discipleship in African American Churches*. He is a member of the New Mount Calvary Baptist Church in Lansing, Michigan, and works with the Sunday school and deacon board.

A native of Manning, South Carolina, Lee is married to Shirley Spencer June, and they are the parents of Brian and Stephen.

Christopher C. Mathis Jr. is Senior Associate Research Director of 1890 Research Program and Adjunct Professor in the School of Education at South Carolina State University. He was a resident hall director for four years at Johnson C. Smith and Humboldt State University and an assistant graduate hall director for three years at Michigan State University.

Born and reared in Newberry, South Carolina, he earned a bachelor of science degree in biology and chemistry from Johnson C. Smith University, a master of arts degree in student affairs and higher administration, and a Ph.D. in agricultural extension education from Michigan State University. Christopher spent a year abroad as an international intern with Africare under the International Foundation of Education Self-Help (IFESH) program founded by the late Leon Sullivan.

He is currently an associate minister and member of Greater Faith Baptist Church in Orangeburg, South Carolina.

T he purposes of this chapter are to explore the compatibility of research and evaluation with biblical clinical and counseling practice and to offer suggestions on how to incorporate them into everyday clinical and counseling practice.

THE WHYS AND WHEREFORES OF RESEARCH

Definition of Research

Research has been defined in several ways. Wholeben (1996) defines research as "the formal, systematic application of the scientific method to the study of problems" (p. 1). The *World Book Dictionary* (1987) defines it as "hunting for facts or truth about a subject" and "the organized scientific investigation to solve problems, test hypotheses, or develop or invent new products." Isaac and Michael (1989) define it as that which, "having its origin in science, is oriented toward the development of theories and its most familiar paradigm is the experimental method, in which hypotheses are logically derived from theory and put to a test under controlled conditions" (p. 2). Therefore, in conducting research one is doing the following:

- Attempting to find new knowledge/truth
- Looking for conclusions that can be generalized to other situations
- Seeking explanatory and predictive power
- Trying to satisfy curiosity
- Looking for causes and effects
- Testing hypotheses through various designs

Two Types of Research Methodologies

Two types of research methodologies are commonly referred to in the literature: quantitative and qualitative. *Quantitative research* is primarily geared toward the statistical analyses of the data. *Qualitative research,* on the other hand, is primarily concerned with finding meaning behind the responses of the participants.

Evaluation Methodologies

Evaluation, in contrast to research, has also been defined in various ways. Isaac and Michael (1989) define it as "that which is interested in product delivery or mission accomplishment. It aims to provide feedback leading to a successful outcome defined in practical, concrete terms" (2). The *World Book Dictionary* (1987) defines it as "the act of evaluating, that is, to find out the value or the amount of."

One typically refers to evaluation methodologies as formative and summative. In *formative evaluation* the aim is to provide information for program improvement, modification, and management. The focus is on what we are doing, what we are supposed to be doing, and how we can improve. In *summative evaluation* the aim is to determine overall success or effectiveness. Focus is on the outcomes, the costs, and so forth.

Biblical Examples of Research

To what extent are the research and evaluation methodologies compatible with the Bible? We will examine some Scripture passages where an activity similar to research and/or evaluation takes place. We will then examine the biblical meaning of that word or activity by using the *New Strong's Exhaustive Concordance of the Bible* (1996). The definition will be capitalized, italicized, and placed in brackets next to the word under consideration. (All biblical quotations are from the *Scofield Reference Bible,* 1967):

- *Genesis 1:28.* "And God said unto them, Be fruitful and multiply, and fill the earth and subdue *[TO CONQUER; BRING INTO SUBJECTION]* it; and have dominion *[TO RULE]* over the fish of the sea, and over the fowl of the air, and over every living thing that moveth upon the earth."
- *Numbers 13:1–2.* "And the LORD spoke unto Moses, saying, Send thou men, that they may search *[TO SEARCH OUT; TO SPY OUT]* the land of Canaan, which I give unto the children of Israel."

- *Joshua 6:23.* "And the young men who were spies *[SEARCHERS]* went in, and brought out Rahab, and her father, and her mother, and her brethren and all that she had.
- *Daniel 1:3–4, 6.* "And the king spoke unto Ashpenaz, the master of his eunuchs, that he should bring certain of the children of Israel, and of the king's seed, and of the princes, youths in whom was no blemish, but well favored, and skillful in all wisdom, and gifted in knowledge, and understanding science *[TO KNOW BY OBSERVATION, CARE, AND RECOGNITION]*, and such as had ability in them to stand in the king's palace, and whom they might teach the learning and the tongue of the Chaldeans.... Now among these were of the children of Judah, Daniel, Hananiah, Mishael, and Azariah."
- *Acts 7:22.* "And Moses was learned *[INSTRUCT, TEACH]* in all the wisdom of the Egyptians, and he was mighty in words and in deeds."
- *2 Timothy 2:15.* "Study *[TO MAKE EFFORT, TO BE DILIGENT, LABOUR]* to show thyself approved unto God, a workman that needeth not be ashamed, rightly dividing the word of truth."
- *John 5:39.* "Search *[MAKE INQUIRY, TO SEEK, TO INVESTIGATE]* the scriptures; for in them you think ye have eternal life; and they are they which testify of me."
- *Luke 14:28.* "For which of you, intending to build a tower, sitteth not down first, and counteth *[TO COMPUTE]* the cost, whether he has sufficient to finish it?"
- *Acts 17:10–12.* "And the brethren immediately sent away Paul and Silas by night unto Berea, who, coming there, went into the synagogue of the Jews. These were more noble than those in Thessalonica, in that they received the word with all readiness of mind, and searched *[SCRUTINIZE, INVESTAGE, INTERROGATE, ASK, EXAMINE, DISCERN]* the scriptures daily, whether these things were so. Therefore, many of them believed; also of honorable women who were Greeks, and of men, not a few."

From this review, one can clearly see that investigative activities and planning took place numerous times in the Scriptures. From this we conclude that research and evaluation is compatible with the Bible.

The Scientific Method

The hallmark of research is the scientific method. The scientific method may be defined as "that method for describing and explaining phenomena which incorporates the principles of empirical verification, operational definition, controlled observation, statistical generalization, and empirical confirmation" (Anderson 1971; quoted in Wholeben 1996, p. 6).

The Joys and Benefits of Research and Evaluation

Are there joys and benefits to conducting research and evaluation? Our answer is a definite yes!

- It satisfies our curiosity.
- It adds to our knowledge base.
- It teaches us the discipline of structured inquiry.
- It provides information for improvement or modification.
- It helps us to document the effectiveness and impact of what we are doing.
- If we publish our results, we are then authors.
- It helps us to debunk some of the existing myths and misconceptions about who we are as a people.
- When we write or present, we can quote ourselves.

Basic Methods in Research

In the *Handbook of Research and Evaluation,* Isaac and Michael (1987) presented several types of research methods:

- *Correlational.* In correlational research, one studies how variations in one or more factors relate to variations in one or more other factors. An example of this type of research is the examination of how the amount of stress relates to the use of alcohol or how the expectations of the length of counseling relate to the actual amount of time spent in counseling. [EASY TO DO]
- *Historical.* In historical research, one looks at how a practice or event may have occurred over time. For example, how has biblical counseling evolved and changed over time? Or how have my clients changed over time? [FAIRLY EASY TO DO]
- *Descriptive.* In descriptive research, one seeks to describe a situation or event accurately, factually, and systematically.

Examples are the use of surveys, questionnaires, interview studies, and literature reviews in order to be able to describe a situation and what is occurring. [FAIRLY EASY TO DO]

- *Developmental.* In developmental research, one investigates patterns and sequences of growth and/or change as a function of time. An example of this is following a group of clients over a period of time to determine the changes that may occur in certain behavior patterns. [FAIRLY EASY TO DO]
- *Case and Field.* In case and field research, one studies the factors or issues related to an individual, family, group, or institution. An example of this is studying an individual client or his/her family in order to observe a pattern or issue within the individual or family. [FAIRLY EASY TO DO]
- *Causal-Comparative or "Ex Post Facto."* In this instance, one is looking for possible cause-and-effect relationships by observing some existing consequence and searching back through the data for possible causal factors. Examples of this are trying to determine why you are experiencing a high dropout rate in your caseload by examining your files over X years, or examining your records over time to determine who profits from a treatment. [FAIRLY EASY TO DO]
- *Action.* The goal of action research is to develop new skills or approaches and to solve problems by direct applications to the setting. An example of this is the application of a new approach to the ongoing counseling of a certain group and then observing/ testing its effect in the clinical/counseling setting. [FAIRLY EASY TO DO]
- *Quasi-Experimental.* A quasi-experimental design involves trying to come close to a true experiment by approximating the conditions of a true experiment. This would involve a setting where control or manipulations of all relevant variables are not possible. [HARDER TO DO]
- *True Experimental.* In a true experiment, one is investigating possible cause-and-effect relationships by exposing one or more experimental groups to a treatment and comparing the results to control groups (random assignments to the groups are essential). [THE HIGHEST FORM — HARDEST TO DO]

Ten Basic Steps in Research

In order to conduct research, ten basic steps are usually employed. These steps, according to Isaac and Michael (1989), are:

1. Identify the problem to be studied.
2. Conduct a survey of the literature regarding the problem.
3. Clearly define the actual problem in specific terms.
4. Develop testable hypotheses and define the basic concepts and variables involved (independent, dependent, and control).
5. Indicate the underlying assumption which will govern the interpretation of results.
6. Construct the research design.
   - Select subjects
   - Control and/or manipulate relevant variables
   - Establish criteria to evaluate outcomes
   - Bring instrumentation-selection or development of the criterion measures
7. Make clear the data collection procedure.
8. Select the data analysis methodology.
9. Carry out the actual research.
10. Evaluate the results and draw conclusions.

The Ethics of Research

Principles and guidelines have been developed to protect research subjects from abuses. Professional ethical codes speak to this. Universities and colleges have specific conditions that one must meet before one can conduct a study involving human subjects. At Michigan State University, for example, the panel is called the University Committee Involving Research on Human Subjects (UCIRHS).

The essential ethics of research may be summarized as follows:

- It does no harm to the subjects.
- It does not put the subjects at risk for future harm.
- Subjects must give their consent (consent form).
- Participation is entirely voluntary.
- Confidentiality of the data and of the individual must be insured

The American Psychological Association (APA 1992) has an ethical code for psychologists that would be true for other helping professions. This code obligates psychologists to do the following in regard to research:

- Make a careful evaluation of ethical acceptability.
- Determine if the participant is at risk and if so, minimize or eliminate it. If risk remains, the participant must be informed of it.
- Ensure that ethical practices are followed as research is done.
- Remove any concealment or deception.
- Allow participants to decline and/or quit at any time.
- After collecting data, inform the participants about the nature of research and try to remove any misconceptions.
- If the research produces undesirable effects, researchers must detect, remove, and correct them.
- Information collected must be kept, unless agreed upon.

Subjects and potential participants for research should be presented with a consent form regarding participation. The form should accompany the request for participation in a study. It should be attached to the instrument(s) that one is asking potential participants to complete. A sample of such a form is provided at the end of this chapter.

THREE PRACTICAL RESEARCH DESIGNS

Since research is a systematic process, one who engages in it should have a research design. A full treatment of this topic is beyond the scope of this chapter; however, a few comments are appropriate. Below, we will present and discuss three types of research methodologies (designs) that can be easily employed in clinical practice, along with steps that are necessary to implement them.

Pre- and Post-Testing/Assessment

This methodology is appropriate for assessing the effect of an intervention, the effect of different interventions, or the effect of a treatment or different treatments. The steps are:

- Decide the area you want to study (e.g., addictions, unemployment, the children of single parents, the effects of different treatments, etc.).
- Develop a hypothesis. Be specific and clear.
- Choose a measuring tool(s), including a consent form.
- Select your sample/subjects. (Include a control group, if possible.)
- Administer the instrument(s)/test(s)/questionnaire(s).
- Do the administration before and after the intervention (before or at intake and at termination).
- Analyze your results.

Note that if one does not employ a control group (that is, a group that has similar characteristics to your treatment sample but who did not receive the treatment) conclusions about the effects are limited.

Onetime Surveying

This approach is appropriate for collecting information regarding an issue, problem, or a group. It is used when one is interested in trying to determine what is contributing to the issue at a particular point in time. The steps are:

- Decide the area you want to study (e.g., addictions, unemployment, children of single parents, effects of different treatments, etc.).
- Develop a hypothesis. Be specific and clear.
- Choose a measuring tool(s), including a consent form.
- Select your sample/subjects. (Include a control group, if possible.)
- Administer the instrument(s)/test(s)/questionnaire(s).
- Analyze the data to see how the variables are related.

Focus Groups

This method is good for determining the pattern or set of issues by using a systematic group discussion format. The steps are:

- Decide the area you want to study.
- Develop a hypothesis(es). Be specific and clear.
- Develop a series of open-ended questions, along with a consent form.
- Select a sample.
- Conduct the focus group. This format permits the participants to respond to the question(s) in an open-ended format.
- Record verbatim the responses from the participants.
- Analyze the data looking for patterns/trends in the responses.

There are a number of journals related to African American issues that typically contain research articles. These journals are good sources for observing various research methodologies.

- *Journal of Black Psychology*
- *Journal of Negro Education*
- *Journal of Multicultural Counseling and Development*
- *Journal of Social Issues*

CONCLUSION

The purpose of this chapter has been to share some of the basic principles of research in order to encourage clinicians/counselors to incorporate a research methodology in their ongoing practice. To assist in this, we have given some examples of how this might be done. The joys and benefits of doing this are numerous. Those interested in a more detailed treatment of the research and evaluation methodologies are encouraged to consult a textbook on research and evaluation that can be found in most college bookstores. Those interested in some of the unique issues in racial-ethnic research should consult Ponterotto and Casa (1991) and Dana (1993).

REFERENCES

American Psychological Association. 1992. Ethical principles of psychologists. *American Psychologist.* (December): 47, 1597–1611.

Campbell, D. T., and J. C. Stanley. 1963. *Experimental and quasi-experimental designs for research.* Chicago: Rand McNally.

Dana, R. H. 1993. *Multicultural assessment perspectives for professional psychology.* Needham Heights, Mass.: Allyn and Bacon.

Isaac, S., and W. B. Michael. 1989. *Handbook in research and evaluation,* 2d edition. San Diego, Calif.: Edits Publishers.

Ponterotto, J. G., and J. M. Casa. 1991. *Handbook of racial/ethnic minority counseling research.* Springfield, Mass.: Charles C. Thomas.

Strong, J. 1996. *The new Strong's exhaustive concordance of the Bible.* Nashville: Thomas Nelson.

Wholeben, B. E. 1996. Bridging the gap between the use of quantitative and qualitative research methodologies. Special training session, Mid-America Association of Educational Opportunity Program Personnel. The Abbey on Lake Geneva, Fontana, Wisconsin.

World Book Dictionary. 1987. Chicago: World Book, Inc.

SAMPLE CONSENT FORM

Thank you for agreeing to consider participating in this study. It is being conducted by [GIVE NAME(S) AND AFFILIATION OF RESEARCHERS].

The purpose of this study is to investigate possible factors (personal and demographic) that contribute to the attractiveness to and possible success of the [GIVE NAME OF PROJECT].

There are two instruments attached which you should complete (both are designed to gather demographic information and your personal opinion concerning experiences in relating to individuals and groups). It should take approximately 15–20 minutes to complete both instruments. You are being asked to consider completing these instruments today and again at the end of the academic school year.

On the front page of the first survey, we are asking that you indicate the last five digits of your Social Security Number. This information is requested only so that we may be able to link your response from time one to time two.

All information collected will be kept strictly confidential and you will not be identified individually. Results will be reported in a group manner. You may discontinue participating at any time.

If you have any questions or concerns, you may contact [GIVE THE NAME, ADDRESS, AND PHONE NUMBER OF THE CONTACT PERSON]. If you would like results of this study, please let me know at the same address above. If you have questions about your rights as a participant, you may contact [IF APPLICABLE, GIVE THE NAME AND PHONE NUMBER OF THIS PERSON].

You indicate your consent to participate in this study by completing this survey and signing your name below. Once collected, this consent form will be separated from the questionnaire packet and destroyed.

Name (please print)_____

Signature _____

Date _____

Appendix

The National Biblical Counselors Association

WHAT IS NBCA?

National Biblical Counselors Association (NBCA) is a Christian organization, which exists to promote excellence in biblical counseling through training, study of God's Word, educational resources, and research. The goal of the association is to advance the Word of God in counseling. NBCA promotes a holistic approach in counseling; that is, the healing of mind, body, and spirit. The association provides training for both professional and lay counselors who are interested in relying on the Word of God to promote change in the lives of those they counsel.

MISSION STATEMENT

The mission of the NBCA is to advance the use of God's Word in counseling and to mobilize lay counselors for the body of Christ, partnering with professional and pastoral counselors.

VISION STATEMENT

NBCA's vision is to bring together those who counsel African Americans for the purpose of learning, research, and networking.

WHO CAN BECOME A MEMBER OF NBCA?

NBCA is committed to equipping Christian counselors, both professional and lay, who are seeking to integrate the power of the Word of God in their counseling settings.

MEMBER BENEFITS

Seminars, Workshops, and Conferences

NBCA members will receive a newsletter focusing on news relevant to biblical counselors, informing them of recommended books to read or tapes to order; promoting future workshops, seminars, and conferences; highlighting counseling tips and techniques; spotlighting specific topical information; and offering updates on the association activities. NBCA will encourage counselors to write and publish, thus aiding practitioners and clients.

NBCA Membership Certificate

This membership certificate chronicles your affiliation with the organization and emphasizes your commitment to Christian counseling.

Membership Discounts

Members of the association will be given discounted registration fees on regional and national conferences and will be alerted when Christian counseling books have been discounted.

Referrals

Members will be listed on a national registry for biblical counselors.

Spiritual Development

Therapists/counselors will have the opportunity to be fed from the precepts and principles of the Word of God on a continual basis.

Networking

Members benefit from national partnerships with churches and counseling ministries.

Consultation

Members have access to high-caliber therapists and counseling specialists to consult and to help strengthen your knowledge and skills.

Quarterly Newsletter

Members receive ideas and information about innovative counseling techniques, research information, and biblical counseling centers.

Personal Development

Members have the opportunity to develop their gifts and talents in consulting and public speaking through opportunities provided by a Speakers Bureau.

Training

Members can attend regional and national workshops offered on cutting-edge counseling, clinical, and practice management issues.

Financial Discounts

Members save money through discounted rates on items such as:

- Books
- Tapes (audio and video tapes)
- Future conferences
- Workshops and seminars

Credibility

NBCA membership places you in a special network of Christ-centered counseling professionals from all across the country!

Resources

Members can access information on books, tapes, and videos that will be helpful in developing their counseling skills.

For more information about NBCA, write:

National Biblical Counselors Association
c/o Christian Research and Development
27 W. Township Line Road, Suite 2
Upper Darby, PA 19082
Call: 1-800-5511-CRD or 610-449-8112
Fax: 610-449-8219
Web site: *www.crdonline.org*

This book for black women by black women offers direction, affirmation, and inspiration for the issues they face.

Women to Women

Perspectives of Fifteen African-American Christian Women

Dr. Norvella Carter and Matthew Parker

Through conflict and struggle, sustained by prayer and a zeal for life, African-American women have laid an enduring foundation for the lives of generations of black Americans. In *Women to Women*, fifteen black scholars, educators, and community leaders uncover the essence of the African-American woman that has made her a pillar both in her own community and in American society at large.

Whether you are a professional, a lay leader, a mother, or simply someone who wants to probe the full potential of your culture and your womanhood, you will find fresh definition, affirmation, and support plus workable solutions for life's problems and challenges. From singlehood to sisterhood to motherhood, these writers offer practical insights into some of the thorniest issues women face. *Women to Women* provides seasoned perspectives on topics such as:

- How to Deal with "isms" — Racism, Classism, and Sexism
- The Biblical Heritage of Black Women
- Facing Singlehood as an African-American Woman
- Life as a Pastor's Wife
- Rearing Christian Children in Today's Society
- Sisterhood and Mentorship

Readable, relevant, biblical, and written from the heart, *Women to Women* helps you surmount the challenges of African-American womanhood to fulfill its rich promise in your own life.

Softcover: 0-310-20145-4

Pick up a copy today at your favorite bookstore!

Here is a comprehensive guide to the how-to's of the African-American church and many aspects of its ministry.

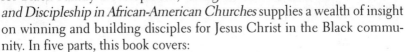

Evangelism and Discipleship in African-American Churches

Lee N. June, Ph.D. and Matthew Parker

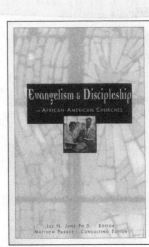

The church is the crucial center of the African-American community. Yet, while countless books have addressed individual aspects of church life, no comprehensive resource has existed that expertly explores the full scope of African-American church ministry. Until now.

Written in the proven format of the Institute for Black Family Development, *Evangelism and Discipleship in African-American Churches* supplies a wealth of insight on winning and building disciples for Jesus Christ in the Black community. In five parts, this book covers:

- History of African-American Evangelism
- Taking the Lead in Evangelism and Discipleship
- Training Laborers for Evangelism and Discipleship
- Practicing Evangelism and Discipleship at Home and at College
- Going into the Field

The contributors are all noted authorities on their topics, which range from the church's role in evangelism to Christian education to youth and college ministry to the workplace and more. Here at last is a guidebook for pastors, evangelists, teachers, and church workers who have longed for a complete, one-step resource to help their church fulfill the Great Commission.

Softcover: 0-310-22139-0

Pick up a copy today at your favorite bookstore!

This book for black men by black men offers advice, challenge, encouragement, and inspiration for issues they face.

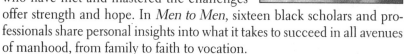

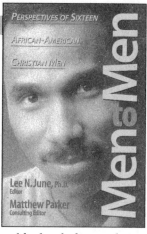

PERSPECTIVES OF SIXTEEN
AFRICAN-AMERICAN
CHRISTIAN MEN

Men to Men

Lee N. June, Ph.D.
Editor

Matthew Parker
Consulting Editor

Men to Men

Perspectives of Sixteen African-American Men

Dr. Lee N. June and Matthew Parker

In the midst of the obstacles facing today's African-American male, the voices of men who have met and mastered the challenges offer strength and hope. In *Men to Men*, sixteen black scholars and professionals share personal insights into what it takes to succeed in all avenues of manhood, from family to faith to vocation.

Whether you're a pastor, educator, counselor, lay leader, or simply someone concerned with how to apply your faith to turn life's hurdles into opportunities, *Men to Men* gives you proven perspectives that can spark success and growth in your own and others' lives. Drawing on the expertise and wisdom of their chosen fields, men such as Dr. Lloyd Blue, Dr. Hank Allen, and Dr. Lee June share practical, man-to-man advice on topics of vital interest, including:

- How African-American Males Can Build Powerful Families
- Developing and Maintaining a Commitment to Marriage
- An Action Plan for Restoring African-American Men, Families, and Communities
- Black, Biblical, and Afrocentric
- Risk and Failure as Preludes to Achievement
- Avoiding the Criminal Justice System
- The Importance of Moral Character

In-depth, biblical, encouraging, and based on the latest scholarship, *Men to Men* shows how you can bridge the pitfalls of black manhood to achieve spiritual, personal, and social prosperity.

Softcover: 0-310-20157-8

Pick up a copy today at your favorite bookstore!

ZONDERVAN®
.com

A how-to plan for evangelism and practical ministry to inner-city families.

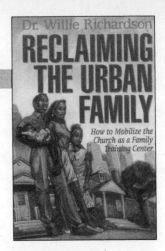

Reclaiming the Urban Family

How to Mobilize the Church as a Family Training Center

Dr. Willie Richardson

The problems urban families face — low income, drug abuse, divorce, gang involvement, domestic violence, and more — are devastating. But solutions exist in the local church that can transform troubled homes into places of love, security, hope, and growth.

In Reclaiming the Urban Family, Dr. Willie Richardson gives pastors and leaders methods that can make inner-city churches a powerful force for restoring, training, and strengthening families, single-parent homes, and individuals. Using the principles and strategies described, the family training ministry of Dr. Richardson's own Christian Stronghold Baptist Church in Philadelphia has:

- Brought about a near-zero divorce rate
- Produced strong marriages built on deep lovebonds between couples
- Helped numerous low- and moderate-income families become debt-free
- Trained men to be competent husbands and fathers
- Raised adult male membership in church to as high as 48 percent
- Lowered the number of teenage pregnancies
- Helped win to Christ those who have seen transformation in their loved ones

Reclaiming the Urban Family covers concerns as diverse as lay biblical counseling, singles and youth ministry, marriage preparation, occupational enrichment, single-parent households, evangelizing families, and more. Complete with a section of resources for African-American family ministries, it shows how local churches can become dynamic agents for building thriving homes and individuals and for evangelizing the unsaved.

Softcover: 0-310-20008-3

We want to hear from you. Please send your comments about this book to us in care of zreview@zondervan.com. Thank you.

ZONDERVAN®

ZONDERVAN.com/
AUTHORTRACKER
follow your favorite authors